Unleashing Innovation the East Asian Way

Ying Cheng · Adam Cross · Martin Hemmert ·
Agata Kapturkiewicz · Masahiro Kotosaka ·
Franz Waldenberger

Unleashing Innovation the East Asian Way

Startup Ecosystems in Japan, South Korea and China

Springer

Ying Cheng
School of Economics and Business Administration
Chongqing University
Chongqing, PR China

Martin Hemmert
School of Business
Korea University
Seoul, South Korea

Masahiro Kotosaka
Faculty of Policy Management
Keio University
Fujisawa, Kanagawa, Japan

Adam Cross
Xi'an Jiaotong-Liverpool University
Suzhou, PR China

Agata Kapturkiewicz
Sophia University
Tokyo, Japan

Franz Waldenberger
German Institute for Japanese Studies
Tokyo, Japan

ISBN 978-981-95-6512-2 ISBN 978-981-95-6513-9 (eBook)
https://doi.org/10.1007/978-981-95-6513-9

This work was supported by German Institute for Japanese Studies (DIJ).

This Springer imprint is published by the registered company Springer Nature Singapore Pte Ltd.
The registered company address is: 152 Beach Road, #21-01/04 Gateway East, Singapore 189721, Singapore

Preface

This is a book for those interested in how the East Asian economies of Japan, South Korea (henceforth Korea), and the People's Republic of China (henceforth China) both support and constrain the establishment and growth of entrepreneurial technology-intensive startup firms.

As a group of scholars, the authorship team of this book has studied startups and startup ecosystems in East Asia for more than a decade. Over this time, we have not only analysed secondary data but we have also conducted numerous interviews with startup entrepreneurs and undertaken large-scale surveys of startups across the region. Based on these data, we have published scholarly journal articles that cover a range of topics, including startup ecosystems,[1] prior research on startup ecosystems in East Asia,[2] and the role of entrepreneurial orientation[3] and of founders' human capital[4] on startup performance. We have also published a monograph on entrepreneurship in Korea.[5]

While we have already shared the findings of our studies with academic audiences, and will continue to do so, we feel strongly the need to now offer a broader, more contextual, and critical account of startup entrepreneurship in East Asia to a wider audience, including entrepreneurs, knowledge workers, investors, policymakers, and the general public with an interest in the topic. Such a broader, contextual, and critical approach could not have been adequately pursued in a journal article, and not even a special issue of a journal. It requires the format of a book to reach out to non-academic readers without compromising analytical rigour, hence our motivation to write this book.

With this book, our goal is to both increase the appreciation of cross-country differences of startup ecosystems and further the development of conceptual frameworks for studying them, with a focus on the understudied East Asian region. This book not only builds on existing research but also extends it by providing more contextualisation with regard to the national economies of East Asia, and their historical development, structural and institutional characteristics, business culture, and political economy. We do not consider startup ecosystems in isolation, but in relation to the broader cultural, institutional, economic, and political context in which they operate. For example, thinking of the evolution of digital technologies, many advances in the digitalisation of consumer electronics and the automation of production processes resulted from Japanese innovations, as demonstrated by Sony's Walkman or Toyota's production system. The same can be said for the first mobile internet service, i-mode, launched by Japan's NTT-Docomo in 1999. However, Apple's iPhone and other smartphones subsequently outcompeted Japanese mobile phones, which at the time provided more functionality. These observations suggest that East Asian companies and startup ecosystems have distinct strengths and weaknesses. But, to understand the origins and the consequences of these strengths and weaknesses, an in-depth contextualised analysis, as provided by this book, is necessary. From a geographical coverage perspective, we focus on startup ecosystems in Japan, Korea, and Mainland China. Whilst we are aware of dynamic ecosystems in other territories such as Taiwan and Hong Kong, we concentrate on the three largest economies in East Asia in a quest to limit the complexity of our analysis while covering a large majority of startup ecosystems across the region.

Overall, our aim with this book is to elevate the global understanding of startup ecosystems in East Asia in several ways. First, through a comprehensive analysis of startup ecosystems from various analytical perspectives, we offer a deep, contextualised evaluation of the origins, processes, and outcomes of startup ecosystem development that goes beyond a superficial review of some numerical indicators. Second, our contextualised analytical approach provides a nuanced understanding of how the cultural, institutional, economic, and political contexts have shaped startup ecosystems in East Asia, and how, therefore, East Asian startup ecosystems differ in important ways from their counterparts in Western countries and other parts of the world. Third, our coverage of startup ecosystems in the three largest East Asian economies uncovers the high diversity of startup ecosystems in East Asia, thereby countering shallow and stereotypical views of entrepreneurial activity across the region. Fourth, we not only offer an analysis of East Asian startup ecosystems but also spell out takeaways from our findings for a variety of ecosystem stakeholders, including entrepreneurs, knowledge workers, investors, and policymakers in a readable and understandable manner.

We are deeply grateful to the many individuals and organisations without whose support this book would not have been possible. First, we gratefully acknowledge the financial support of the Japan Society for the Promotion of Science (JSPS) which funded the research of Masahiro Kotosaka (under KAKENHI Grant Number 23K25544) and Agata Kapturkiewicz (under KAKENHI Grant Number 22K13463) into Japanese entrepreneurial systems. We also thank Korea University Business School (KUBS) and Xi'an Jiaotong-Liverpool University (XJTLU) for the financial and institutional support given to Martin Hemmert and Adam Cross, respectively, for our research on Korean and Chinese startups. Ying Cheng would also like to thank the funders of the Chongqing Social Science Planning Project (2024NDYB089), the Fundamental Research Funds for the Central Universities (2024CDJSKXYJG09), and the National Science Foundation of China Project (72572022) that supported her research on innovation and entrepreneurship. We are especially grateful to the German Institute for Japanese Studies (DIJ), Tokyo, for hosting workshops and making it possible to publish this book as open access.

On a more personal note, we would like to thank Jae-Jin Kim for his work on the Korean chapter, and Ying (Veronica) Yao and Shafeena Taylor-Cross for their various contributions to the final drafts of this book. We also extend our gratitude to those who contributed in various ways to our published research that provides the intellectual foundations for this book, including the participants of conferences where we presented our work, various journal reviewers and editors, and especially the entrepreneurial founders of Korean, Japanese, and Chinese startups who shared their valuable insights with us in interviews and surveys. We are also grateful to Springer Nature for allowing us to publish with them. Finally, to all those not named here who have contributed in ways both large and small, we offer our heartfelt thanks.

Let us now take you as our reader on an intellectual journey that explores the distinctive dynamics of startup ecosystems in East Asia.

Chongqing, China	Ying Cheng
Suzhou, China	Adam Cross
Seoul, Korea	Martin Hemmert
Tokyo, Japan	Agata Kapturkiewicz
Fujisawa, Japan	Masahiro Kotosaka
Tokyo, Japan	Franz Waldenberger
September 2025	

Notes

1. Hemmert et al. (2019), Kapturkiewicz (2022), and Kapturkiewicz (2025).
2. Hemmert et al. (2022).
3. Hemmert et al. (2023).
4. Hemmert et al. (2024).
5. Hemmert and Kim (2021).

Contents

About the Authors

Ying Cheng is Associate Professor of Management at the School of Economics and Business Administration in Chongqing University, China, with a PhD in Business Economics from Ludwig Maximilian University of Munich, Germany. Her research focuses on institutional complexity and entrepreneurship, particularly women's entrepreneurship empowerment and technology startup incubation.

Adam Cross is Professor of International Business and currently serves as Associate Vice-President for Education (AVP-E) and Academic Director of the Graduate School at Xi'an Jiaotong-Liverpool University (XJTLU), Suzhou, China.

Martin Hemmert is Professor of Global Business at Korea University. He received his doctoral degree at the University of Cologne and has held research and teaching positions at DIJ Tokyo, the University of Duisburg-Essen, the National University of Singapore, Hitotsubashi University, and Keio University. His research interests include international comparative studies of management systems, innovation systems and entrepreneurial ecosystems, organizational boundaries of firms and inter-organizational research collaborations, with a focus on East Asian countries.

Agata Kapturkiewicz is Associate Professor in the Department of Management, Faculty of Economics at Sophia University in Tokyo. She received her doctoral degree (DPhil) in Management from Saïd Business School, University of Oxford, and afterwards worked in the School of Commerce at Waseda University in Tokyo. Her research interests center on entrepreneurship, entrepreneurial ecosystems, organization theory, and comparative research.

Masahiro Kotosaka is Professor at Keio University and an Associate Fellow of Saïd Business School, University of Oxford. He is an expert in Internationalization strategy and early-stage business development, and advisor to several global start-up/multinational companies.He graduated from the University of Oxford with D.Phil. (Ph.D) in Management Studies and MSc in Management Research with Distinction.

Franz Waldenberger is Director of the German Institute for Japanese Studies (DIJ) in Tokyo. He is on leave from Munich University, where he holds a professorship for Japanese Economy. He received his PhD in economics and his habilitation from Cologne University. His research on the Japanese economy has covered many areas including industrial organization, employment, financial system, industrial policy, monetary policy and international trade. His current work focuses on corporate governance and knowledge infrastructures. At the DIJ he has, among others, implemented a research cluster on the digital transformation. He is editor in chief of the international peer reviewed journal *Contemporary Japan*.

List of Figures

List of Tables

List of Boxes

Chapter 1
Introduction: The Rise of Startup Ecosystems in East Asia

1.1 The Rise of Startup Ecosystems

Nowadays, startup ecosystems are all the buzz. While large corporations led innovation throughout much of the twentieth century, a paradigm shift has occurred, with technology startups—young, technology-based firms that are designed to grow—now playing a pivotal role in advancing cutting-edge innovation[1]. Illustrative examples in recent years include OpenAI (the developer of ChatGPT) in the USA and China's DeepSeek, both of which have achieved ground-breaking advances in artificial intelligence (AI).[1] Similarly, biotechnology startups such as BioNTech and Moderna spearheaded the development of COVID-19 vaccines, further demonstrating the transformative potential of young and agile high-growth enterprises.[2]

Technology startups could not achieve such breakthroughs on their own. Rather, they are supported by a network of interdependent actors, including risk-tolerant investors who provide them with capital amid uncertainty, capable and enthusiastic professionals who work for them, early adopter customers who are willing to embrace their unproven products, incubators and accelerators that provide them with working space and valuable advice, and specialised service providers who offer legal and operational support. Collectively, these stakeholders form a startup ecosystem—a complex network of actors that govern, coordinate, integrate, and provide the essential functions required for entrepreneurship to flourish in a particular area.[3] Consequently, the primary engines of innovation are no longer individual entrepreneurs or standalone ventures, but rather these interconnected ecosystems, which are proliferating globally and are increasingly challenging large corporations as the principal drivers of technological progress.

---

[1] We use "young, technology-based forms that are designed to grow" as the definition of startups and reserve the term specifically to newly founded firms taking advantage of the innovative potential of digital technologies as outlined in Chapter 2.

Y. Cheng et al., *Unleashing Innovation the East Asian Way*,
https://doi.org/10.1007/978-981-95-6513-9_1

This important dynamic has spurred growing interest among analysts, policymakers, and the broader public in identifying the key determinants of startup ecosystem success. The central question that emerges is what foundational conditions are necessary for startup ecosystems to thrive and, by extension, for innovation to prosper?

1.2 Startup Ecosystems: Western Dominance or East Asian Resurgence?

Unfortunately, there are no simple answers to the question of what is needed for a startup ecosystem to flourish, not least because these systems are inherently complex, multidimensional, and difficult to comprehend. Faced with this challenge, many analysts have resorted to a popular technique for gauging performance—relative benchmarking based upon expert evaluations, resulting in startup ecosystem rankings.

Generally speaking, it might be expected that Western startup ecosystems dominate global startup ecosystem rankings for various reasons. First, Western ecosystems—particularly Silicon Valley's Bay Area—have a long history of successfully scaling new ventures and fostering technological innovation. Second, the cultural mindset of disruptive entrepreneurship that challenges the status quo and established norms is aligned closely with Western, and especially North American, values and business traditions. Third, the venture capital industry, which serves as the financial backbone for high-growth startups, has reached its highest level of maturity and sophistication in Western countries.[4]

In contrast, startup ecosystems in East Asia—the world's most economically advanced non-Western region—might be expected to perform less impressively than their Western counterparts. Traditionally, technological advancement in East Asia has been spearheaded by established corporations and large industrial conglomerates rather than by entrepreneurial new ventures. Also, the cultural foundations and traditions of East Asia, which emphasise social harmony and obedience, hierarchical structures, and incremental improvements through hard work and diligence, have generally been more conducive to sustaining existing social and economic order than to disruptive innovation. Moreover, the venture capital industry in East Asia has traditionally been much smaller and less sophisticated than those in the West, not least because of more conservative investment strategies, a cultural preference for stability, and differences in how financial markets in East Asia have evolved.

However, recent global startup ecosystem rankings offer a different and more nuanced picture than the conventional wisdom described above would suggest (see Table 1.1). Annually published Global Startup Ecosystem Reports, which evaluate quantitatively hundreds of the world's ecosystems across multiple dimensions—including performance, funding, talent and experience, market reach, AI-native capabilities, and knowledge—consistently rank Silicon Valley as the world's premier startup hub, with New York City and London following closely. Notably, while East Asian ecosystems were absent from the top rankings before the 2010s, four have now firmly established themselves among the global top 15 in the 2020s: namely, Beijing, Seoul, Shanghai, and Tokyo. This remarkable ascent demonstrates that East Asia's major startup ecosystems have joined the upper echelon of global innovation centres, rivalling their Western counterparts. Particularly striking is their consistently high scoring along the 'knowledge' dimension, reflecting the accumulation of world-class entrepreneurial expertise within these globally prominent East Asian startup hubs.

The ascendency of East Asian startup ecosystems becomes even more evident when examining the global distribution of unicorns—startups with a market valuation of more than US$1bn. As of 2025, China boasts 157 unicorns, second only to the USA (704), and significantly outpacing all other nations. At the city level, Beijing (60 unicorns) and Shanghai (34) rank third and fifth globally, while Seoul (14) and Tokyo (7) also demonstrate a substantial presence in the unicorn landscape. [5]

Beyond these quantitative metrics, East Asia has produced numerous startup-to-giant transformation stories that underscore the innovative capacity of the region.

Table. 1.1 Globally Top-ranked Startup Ecosystems, 2021–2025

2021	2022	2023	2024	2025
1 Silicon Valley	1 Silicon Valley	1 Silicon Valley	1 Silicon Valley	1 Silicon Valley
2 London (tied)	2 New York City (tied)	2 New York City (tied)	2 London (tied)	2 New York City
2 New York City (tied)	2 London (tied)	2 London (tied)	2 New York City (tied)	3 London
4 Beijing	4 Boston	4 Los Angeles	4 Tel Aviv (tied)	4 Tel Aviv
5 Boston	**5 Beijing**	5 Tel Aviv	4 Los Angeles (tied)	5 Boston (tied)
6 Los Angeles	6 Los Angeles	6 Boston	6 Boston	**5 Beijing (tied)**
7 Tel Aviv	7 Tel Aviv	**7 Beijing**	7 Singapore	7 Los Angeles
8 Shanghai	8 Seattle	8 Singapore	**8 Beijing**	**8 Seoul**
9 Tokyo	**9 Seoul**	**9 Shanghai**	**9 Seoul**	9 Singapore
10 Seattle	**10 Shanghai**	10 Seattle	**10 Tokyo**	**10 Shanghai**
11 Washington, D.C.	11 Washington, D.C.	11 Washington, D.C.	**11 Shanghai**	**11 Tokyo**
12 Paris	**12 Tokyo**	**12 Seoul**	12 Washington, D.C.	12 Paris
13 Amsterdam-Delta	13 Singapore	13 Berlin	13 the Netherlands	13 Philadelphia
14 Toronto (tied)	14 Chicago	14 Amsterdam-Delta	14 Paris	14 Bengaluru
15 Chicago (tied)	15 Paris	**15 Tokyo**	15 Berlin	15 Seattle

Note East Asian startup ecosystems are highlighted in bold
Source Startup Genome (various years)

In Japan, SoftBank has evolved from a telecommunications provider into a global mobile network, internet services, and corporate investment powerhouse since its foundation in 1981, while Rakuten has emerged as a major e-commerce and online retailing player with operations in more than 30 countries after it was established in 1998. Similarly, Coupang in South Korea (hereafter: Korea), achieved nationwide e-commerce dominance within a decade of being founded (2010), while Kakao Corporation transformed quickly from an online messaging platform launched in 2010 into a diversified internet conglomerate offering instant messaging, Webtoons, digital banking and taxi-hailing services, and is now pursuing global growth. In China, Alibaba (founded in 1999) has redefined global e-commerce, and is now one of the world's largest retailer, AI company, and venture capital and investment corporation, while Xiaomi, the Beijing-based technology giant founded in 2010, is now the world's second largest manufacturer of smartphones (behind Korea's Samsung) and is rapidly diversifying its business scope into various high-tech sectors, including electric vehicles and semiconductors.

Most significantly—and as we systematically demonstrate in this book—East Asia is nurturing a new generation of cutting-edge startups poised to dominate future industries, indicating that the region's entrepreneurial ascent is likely to accelerate. This trajectory reveals a profound change: rather than being overshadowed by their Western counterparts, East Asian startups and startup ecosystems are rapidly strengthening and advancing their global standing. This development is truly noteworthy given that East Asia has primarily been renowned for large industrial companies and conglomerates rather than entrepreneurial new ventures. Indeed, the rapid emergence of world-class startups and startup ecosystems in East Asia represents a fundamental shift in the global innovation landscape—one that challenges conventional assumptions about the geography of technological leadership.

How, then, are East Asian startup ecosystems achieving this remarkable growth and enhancing their global competitiveness? A critical question emerges: are these East Asian ecosystems replicating the widely admired Silicon Valley model that has dominated global entrepreneurial discourse for decades, or have they developed from distinct institutional foundations and growth mechanisms? Surprisingly, a systematic understanding of East Asian startup ecosystems and how they work remains limited. To illustrate, our comprehensive review of scholarly literature published between 2000 and 2020 on new venture entrepreneurship in East Asia revealed a striking gap: that comparative qualitative studies on the unique structures and dynamics of East Asian startup ecosystems were virtually absent.[6] This knowledge gap highlights the need for deeper investigation into the various and distinctive pathways to global prominence being followed by startup ecosystems in East Asia.

This book addresses this critical knowledge gap through a comprehensive, in-depth, and contextually grounded analysis of East Asian startup ecosystems and their evolutionary trajectories. Our central argument is that East Asian ecosystems operate on fundamentally distinct institutional foundations and developmental mechanisms compared to Western counterparts. This may seem self-evident, as innovation and startup entrepreneurship are intrinsically linked to their cultural, institutional, economic, and political contexts—aspects often overlooked by academic studies.[7]

However, we go beyond superficial comparisons and simple statements of differences. Instead, we explain in detail why East Asian ecosystems diverge, identify the structural factors that drive these divergences, and discuss what this means for key stakeholders, from founder entrepreneurs and investors to knowledge workers and policymakers. Our analysis unfolds across four key dimensions: foundations, countries, themes, and takeaways.

1.3 Foundations

In Chapter 2, we examine how innovation processes have been fundamentally transformed over the last few decades, and what this means for startup ecosystems. Information technology has rapidly evolved, resulting in the widespread digitisation of data and information. Consequently, the marginal cost of replicating data and information has converged towards zero. This (near) zero cost of replication has opened the door to the ascent of startups and startup ecosystems, which are becoming the main drivers of innovations across economies at large, and beyond the specific realm of information technology industries such as computers or semiconductors. We explain how the peculiarities of startups and the importance of startup ecosystems are related to three features typical of innovative solutions based on digital technologies: (i) an abundance of innovative ideas, (ii) low setup costs for applying and testing innovative ideas, and (iii) an enormous scalability potential for startups that pass viability thresholds. While technological progress was once driven primarily by individual companies and their research and development (R&D) laboratories, often operating in relative isolation, it now emerges mostly through dynamic networks of startups, customers, enterprises, and investors, all deeply embedded within and empowered by thriving startup ecosystems. The chapter establishes how these structural shifts have redefined the geography and mechanisms of value creation in the digital age.

Then, in Chapter 3, we critically review the concept of startup ecosystems as dynamic engines of innovation and economic growth by tracing the intellectual origins, conceptual evolution, and inherent limitations of startup ecosystem frameworks as presented in scholarly literature. While the ecosystem metaphor has gained traction as a framework for analysing entrepreneurial environments, Western-centric assumptions frequently neglect the distinctive sociocultural, institutional, and historical factors influencing new venture formation in East Asia. Our analysis disentangles the ecosystem approach from related concepts like industrial clusters and innovation systems, emphasising its focus on interactions between actors (entrepreneurs, investors, universities, and other support institutions) and structural elements (such as cultural norms, local and international networks, physical infrastructure, and government policy). We identify gaps in current conceptualisations and call for frameworks that foreground contextual relevance. Ultimately, we argue that understanding East Asian ecosystems requires the reconciliation of global entrepreneurial trends with deeply contextualised regional particularities.

1.4 Countries

In the second part of the book, we analyse the evolution of startup ecosystems in the three largest East Asian economies: Japan, Korea, and China—in the historical order of their industrial development in the twentieth century.

Chapter 4 presents a comprehensive analysis of Japan's startup ecosystems, tracing their evolution through three distinct phases of development, and identifying structural challenges and recent transformations. Beginning with the post-war recovery and technological catch-up (1950s–1980s), it explains how pioneering firms like Sony, Honda, and Kyocera leveraged government-backed industrial policies and technological innovation to drive economic growth. The rise of consumer-driven businesses further diversified the entrepreneurial landscape, fuelled by rapid urbanisation and shifting consumption patterns. Japan's distinct corporate structures, including the main bank system and lifetime employment, created stability but constrained startup growth. However, the late 1990s and early 2000s marked a turning point, as policy reforms—financial deregulation, venture capital market development, and enhanced university-industry collaboration mechanisms—stimulated entrepreneurial activity. As a result, in the contemporary phase (2010s to present), Tokyo emerged as the nation's dominant startup hub, attracting the majority of investment and talent, while secondary ecosystems in Fukuoka and Osaka are gaining traction through targeted policy support and the leverage of regional advantages. Furthermore, while Japanese firms often struggle to expand globally, the chapter discusses how the latest wave of deep-tech and cross-tech startups in sectors such as robotics, biotech, and advanced materials are combining the nation's technical strengths with increasingly agile business models to bridge this gap.

Chapter 5 examines the evolution of startup ecosystems in Korea. While there has been a high level of entrepreneurial activity in Korea throughout the twentieth century, startup entrepreneurship took off only in the late 1990s and, following a startup winter in the 2000s, again from the 2010s onwards. The second and lasting startup boom has been driven by strong government support, shifting cultural attitudes, and growing private investment. Initially dominated by state funding, startup ecosystems in Korea now benefit from increased venture capital and private investment. Young professionals, once focused on stable careers in large conglomerates, are increasingly drawn to startups due to better work-life balance and work autonomy. Seoul, with its concentration of talent and capital, leads the startup scene, particularly in information and communication technologies (ICT), boasting numerous unicorns. Furthermore, Daejeon has emerged as a strong secondary hub, focusing on science-based industries like biotechnology and robotics. However, Korean startups face challenges, including talent retention outside Seoul, limited experienced mentors, and weak global connectivity. While international students and eased immigration policies offer potential for greater diversity, certain cultural barriers remain. The chapter concludes by assessing how Korea's unique blend of rapid digital adoption, manufacturing prowess, and creative content industries positions its startups for regional leadership, provided that systemic weaknesses in diversity, openness to foreign talent, and global connectivity are addressed.

Chapter 6 reviews the dramatic transformation of China's startup ecosystems since the late 1970s. Fuelled by economic reforms and entrepreneurial spirit, China has evolved from a state-controlled economy to a dynamic innovation hub where companies like Alibaba, Tencent, and Xiaomi thrive. The government has played a vital role, fostering innovation through policies such as Reform and Opening-Up, the establishment of Special Economic Zones (SEZs) like Shenzhen, accession to the World Trade Organisation (WTO), and the Mass Entrepreneurship and Innovation initiative, which promotes supportive regulations, tax incentives, technology development, and funding. Science parks and incubators provide crucial resources and support. Furthermore, entrepreneurs—both native and returnees with international experience—drive innovation across diverse sectors. Key innovation centres have emerged in cities like Beijing, Shenzhen, Suzhou, and Chongqing, each distinguished by unique strengths: Beijing startups excel in AI and software, Shenzhen in hardware manufacturing, Suzhou in biomedicine, and Chongqing in smart manufacturing. Each of these ecosystems benefit from strong university collaborations, venture capital investments, and a growing pool of skilled talent. The entrepreneurial landscape of China continues to transform, creating unique opportunities for businesses and driving the country's economic growth.

1.5 Themes

In the third part of the book, we turn to focal themes that shape the development and growth of startup ecosystems in East Asia. Chapter 7 synthesises key findings from the country analyses presented in the second part of this book, revealing both distinctive national characteristics and fundamental regional commonalities across East Asia's startup ecosystems. Through a comparative examination of Japan, Korea, and China, we identify three constitutive dimensions or themes that shape entrepreneurial development in the region: (i) cultural foundations, (ii) policy architectures, and (iii) internationalisation patterns. Our analysis demonstrates how these interconnected factors create unique innovation ecosystems that are distinct from Western models. While Japan exemplifies corporate-startup symbiosis, Korea demonstrates *chaebol*-led ecosystem development, and China showcases state-capital coordination, all three models reflect deeper regional attributes, such as developmental state legacies, rapid digital adoption, and a capacity to innovate by creatively combining and reconfiguring existing technologies. These shared characteristics suggest the emergence of a distinctive East Asian entrepreneurial paradigm that demands re-evaluation of conventional Western-centric ecosystem frameworks.

In Chapter 8, we examine the influence of culture on East Asian startup ecosystems. Culture—the shared norms, values, beliefs and practices in a society—matters strongly for entrepreneurship. From a Western perspective, entrepreneurial culture is associated with individualism, high tolerance of risk, and egalitarian, non-hierarchical values. Traditionally, these values could not flourish in East Asia due to Confucian traditions that emphasise hierarchy, collectivism, and long-term orientation. However, Japan, Korea, and China have all undergone profound economic and cultural transformations that have fostered a more supportive entrepreneurial environment. Japan, traditionally a collectivist nation, is gradually embracing individualism, supporting its growing startup ecosystems. Korea's *chaebol*-driven industrialisation has demonstrated how Confucian values could enable bold business strategies, while recent cultural shifts, especially new generational preferences for autonomy, have fuelled the growth of startups. China, despite periods of state-imposed restrictions on private business, has recently emerged as a global entrepreneurial powerhouse. The chapter demonstrates how cultural factors in East Asia operate as dynamic enablers rather than static constraints. East Asian startup entrepreneurship differs from Silicon Valley's model but has demonstrated remarkable success, leveraging strong leadership and long-term thinking. Moreover, whereas Silicon Valley celebrates individualism, East Asian ecosystems excel through calculated risk-taking and institutionalised trust networks. This shows how distinct cultural conditions can drive entrepreneurial excellence in unique ways.

Chapter 9 reviews the pivotal role of state-led financial and institutional support in shaping the development of East Asian startup ecosystems, demonstrating how strategic government intervention has catalysed their rapid ascent. Arguably, from a Western and, in particular, from a Silicon Valley perspective, startup ecosystems are viewed largely as an outcome of "spontaneous order", emerging from decentralised entrepreneurial activities that take advantage of new profit opportunities created by digital technologies. The role of the government is seen as limited and is mainly confined to providing a fertile business environment for startups in general, with as little regulation as possible. However, governmental policies have played a much more important role in the formation and growth of startup ecosystems in East Asia, building on legacies of highly effective industrialisation policies in previous decades. In Japan, the government has introduced increasingly proactive startup support policies to reinvigorate the country's sluggish economy, including the introduction of the J-startup platform to offer systematic support for the networking, mentoring, and internationalisation of promising startups, and the designation of major cities as "Global Startup Cities". The Korean government has applied even more proactive startup support policies from the late 2000s to diversify the economy away from large business groups. Korean startups are receiving help through the provision of funding, mentoring and consulting, and support for networking and global expansion. The financial support of the Korean government is immense, providing the majority of external startup funding throughout the 2010s. Likewise, China's government has rolled out highly proactive policies to foster the formation of startup ecosystems, including the establishment of science and technology parks, startup funding programmes, and programmes to attract global talent (including Chinese returnees) for startups. Overall, the startup support policies of East Asian governments not only deviate strongly from the non-interventionist policy mindset in Western countries, but they have proven to be highly effective in bolstering the performance of startup ecosystems and the new ventures they nurture.

Chapter 10 focuses on the internationalisation of East Asian startup ecosystems, including the outward expansion by East Asian startups and the inward investment by global firms entering East Asian markets. The chapter argues that the internationalisation of East Asian ecosystems has been shaped by three key factors: (1) historical industrial pathways, where Japan's *keiretsu*, Korea's *chaebol*, and China's state-linked "national champions" created distinct templates for global market entry; (2) geopolitical realignments, particularly USA-China tensions that are bifurcating supply chains and venture capital flows; and (3) hybrid innovation models that attract both local startups and foreign multinational enterprises. These factors reflect the specific developmental paths of East Asian countries, and the geopolitical contexts which they face. Consequently, the internationalisation patterns of East Asian startups reflect an adaptive approach, as exemplified by the combination of legacy manufacturing strengths with startup-driven open innovation in Japan, Korea's online gaming and digital content firms that leverage K-pop culture for soft power, and China's "dual circulation" strategy that simultaneously promotes domestic innovation and selective global integration.

1.6 Takeaways and Contributions

Finally, we turn to the "so what" question of our analysis in Chapter 11. Based on the discussions of previous chapters, we reflect on how East Asian startup ecosystems have developed in their specific cultural, institutional, economic, and political context, and how and why they have diverged in various key aspects from their Western counterparts. Furthermore, we spell out what this means for major domestic and international stakeholders of East Asian startup ecosystems: entrepreneurs, knowledge workers, investors, and policymakers. We also discuss how theoretical frameworks of startup ecosystems, which have been almost exclusively informed by the context of Western countries, may need to be adjusted in view of the East Asian experience.

Notes

1. Spennemann (2025).
2. Meo et al. (2021).
3. Stam and Van de Ven (2021), 811.
4. Saxenian (1994); House et al. (2004); Hofstede et al. (2010).
5. CB Insights (2025).
6. Hemmert et al. (2022).
7. Hemmert (2025).

Chapter 2
The Digital Revolution and the Rise of Startup Ecosystems

2.1 Introduction

This chapter provides historical background to the rise of startup ecosystems as drivers of innovation in the digital age. The purpose of the chapter is twofold: first, to elucidate how digital technologies have redefined the nature of innovation and entrepreneurship, and second, to explain why startup ecosystems have become such a dominant organisational model for fostering innovation and entrepreneurship in the twenty-first century.

The chapter begins by contextualising the digital revolution, from its historical roots to its current manifestations in artificial intelligence (AI) and connectivity. It then explores the interplay between digital technologies and startup ecosystems, emphasising their mutual reinforcement. Finally, it highlights the unique characteristics of digital-age innovation—such as low marginal costs and rapid scalability—that make startups and their ecosystems so potent. By the end of the chapter, readers will have a foundational understanding of why these ecosystems matter globally, setting the stage for our examination of East Asian startup ecosystems later in the book.

2.2 Background and Motivation

As discussed in the opening chapter, our motivation for writing this book derives from three insights: (i) that innovation is important, (ii) that startup ecosystems are instrumental in fostering innovation in the digital age, and (iii) that startup ecosystems in East Asia matter and need to be studied not only because of their global relevance, but also because of their distinctiveness. This final point emphasises that while digital transformation and startup ecosystems constitute global phenomena, they continue to bear important national characteristics, a fact that should be taken into account by scholars, policymakers, and international investors when looking to understand the

Y. Cheng et al., *Unleashing Innovation the East Asian Way*,
https://doi.org/10.1007/978-981-95-6513-9_2

factors that shape the success and global competitiveness of startups within a given ecosystem.[1]

Today, business leaders and policymakers are more than ever stressing the importance of innovation. In part, this reflects an increased awareness that greater and faster innovation is needed to solve pressing societal issues such as environmental pollution and climate change, or to cope with the challenges associated with an ageing population, for example. At the same time, the increasingly strong emphasis on innovation is being fuelled by the vast innovative potential created by the diffusion of digital technologies and supporting infrastructures, including in information and communication technology (ICT) and, most recently, AI. The ongoing digital transformation observed today confirms historical patterns whereby shifts in technological regimes generate waves of innovation across sectors and regions.[2]

In recent years, however, the world has witnessed not only growing demand and supply in innovation but also the emergence of novel organisational models for discovering and implementing "new combinations" of existing resources, technologies, or ideas. In his seminal work "*The Theory of Economic Development*" published in German in 1912, one of the most influential theorists of entrepreneurship and economic development, Joseph A. Schumpeter, envisaged the entrepreneur as a major driver of innovation, and a central agent of change in capitalism.[3] Forty years later, amid the rise of big business, Schumpeter conceded that systematic research and development (R&D) conducted by salaried employees within firms had become the dominant driver of innovation.[4] What he neither anticipated nor lived to witness was the resurgence of the entrepreneur in the 1970s, epitomised by the rise of newly founded startup companies that were harnessing and advancing digital technologies.[5] These early technology startups were not evenly distributed across the industrialised world. Instead, they clustered disproportionately in northern California's Santa Clara Valley—later dubbed "Silicon Valley" in a nod to the silicon-based semiconductors underpinning digital technologies.[6] This clustering phenomenon soon came to be interpreted as the outcome of specific and geographically-confined environmental conditions that functioned akin to a biological ecosystem.[7]

Startup ecosystems comprise local and partly national support infrastructures for technology-based, growth-oriented new firms. These firms typically pitch their business ideas to venture capitalists in the hope of securing sufficient external funding to quickly scale their business models. Startup founders often envisage an "exit" by selling their companies to larger and established corporations, or by listing them on the stock market. Both options allow the founding entrepreneur to quickly cash in on their success. The significance of venture funding and exit illustrate two core elements of a startup ecosystem, namely (i) an easily accessible and well-funded venture capital industry with sufficient appetite for risk, and (ii) the presence of potential corporate buyers or equity markets with an investment community accommodating the initial public offerings (IPOs) of startup firms.

A detailed explanation of startup ecosystems and their constituent features will be provided in the next chapter. Below, we take one step back and provide historical and theoretical background to the questions that have been motivating our research, namely why startup ecosystems attract so much attention, and why governments not only welcome them, but even seek to nurture and support them. One key to understanding the new quality of entrepreneurship and innovation, and the excitement surrounding startup ecosystems, is digital technologies. This is because without modern digital technologies ICT startup ecosystems would not exist, and without ICT startup ecosystems digital technologies could not have been developed and diffused at such speed over the last half-century. Together, they have become the engine of digital transformation that is driving the digitisation and digitalisation of nearly all facets of modern society.[8]

2.3 The Emergence of a Digital World

By tracing the historical evolution of information and communication technologies —from binary code to the internet and, most recently, AI—we can understand the profound role of digital technologies in shaping modern innovation and appreciate the forces that primed the rise of startup ecosystems, not only in East Asia, but globally. While the emergence of a digital world, as outlined in the sections below, has provided a strong foundation for the rapid growth of startups worldwide, societies have not merely adopted digital tools; they have adapted and advanced them within their distinct cultural and institutional contexts, creating ecosystems that blend technological advancements with local ingenuity and market needs. This is especially relevant in the case of East Asian ecosystems, as explained in later chapters.

Digital technologies have fundamentally transformed how we access, process, and exchange information. Whilst the present era is often termed the "information age", information itself has always been of critical importance. At the biological level, DNA-encoded information drives evolution, and at the level of the individual, information encoded within and by the human mind occupies an equally central position in the cultural evolution of our species.[9] Some commentators claim that we will soon achieve a level of AI that matches human intelligence, leading to a state of 'singularity' and potentially triggering a new evolutionary process that will no longer depend upon or be controlled by human intelligence.[10] Whether such a scenario is realistic or not is disputable. Nevertheless, it is undeniable that information-related "technologies", be it at the level of cells, organisms, or societies, fundamentally govern our biological and social existence.

Following this logic, a history of digital technologies would necessarily begin at humanity's origins, and would be nothing less than a retelling of the human experience from the perspective of information.[11] However, such a history would not have a linear chronology. For millennia, the pace of evolution driven by the circulation of information coded in pictures, music, human languages, mathematics or geometry was slow, which is not to deny that there were astonishing achievements in the arts, sciences, architecture, transportation, and social organisation. In Europe, the circulation of information accelerated with Johannes Gutenberg's invention in the 1450s of the movable type printing press. It did so not by lowering the cost of transmitting information between different locations, which continued to be tied to the speed of moving people, but by dramatically reducing the cost of reproducing information on the paper that the sharing of written information depended upon, leading to an information revolution and the unprecedented dissemination of literature throughout Europe.[12]

Later, the advent of the digital age was the result of progress along all dimensions of information technology: coding, processing, storing, copying, and transmitting or sharing. Binary code laid the foundation for programming which was first used to automate the operation of machines.[13] In 1804, the Lyonnais textile entrepreneur Joseph Marie Jacquard patented the Jacquard loom, which was able to weave complex patterns by following instructions encoded in punch cards. Binary coding was further used to store and process large amounts of information. A milestone application was the invention by Herman Hollerith—the German-American statistician, inventor, and businessman—of a punched card tabulating machine in 1884, which was used to input and compile the data of the 1890 US Census.

Binary code in the form of sound or optical signals had long been in use to transmit information over distances, but such telecommunication was naturally limited in terms of distance and by topographical and weather conditions. The discovery of electromagnetic waves in the early nineteenth century opened the door for modern telecommunication, which was soon and first explored by telegraphy. The telegraph system invented by Samuel Morse and Alfred Vail in the USA using Morse's binary signalling code established itself as the industry standard in the second half of the nineteenth century. Telegraphy fully decoupled the speed of communication from the speed of human movement. The underlying idea of transmitting information using electromagnetic waves—though not necessary as binary code—did not stop with telegraphy, but came to be exploited by telephone (voice) and facsimile (documents) services, as well as by radio and television. The latter two technologies did not rely on cables, but on the atmosphere as the medium of transmission.

The English mathematician and inventor, Charles Babbage, and his wife Eda explored the possibility to use binary code to perform complex calculations with the help of an electromechanical device, the "analytical machine" in 1837. By 1936, Alan Turing—the English mathematician and computer scientist—had derived the logical possibility of universal computing. However, the realisation of modern computing had to wait for binary coding to become embedded in electronic circuits that would not be punched, but simply switched on and off.

With the appearance of mainframe computers in the 1930s, programming became digitised, although punch cards remained to be used for writing and inputting code until the 1980s. To characterise what computers were doing, the term information technology (IT) was coined.[14] The adequacy of the terminology is questionable, because it ignores the fact that information technology in various forms has been driving both biological and cultural evolution since the very beginning.

Once programming and the storage of information had become embedded in electronic circuits the power of computing depended not just on the improvement of programming languages, but above all on making circuits continuously smaller and more energy-efficient. After transistors had replaced vacuum tube triodes as electronic circuit units, miniaturisation driven by innovation in material and production technology proceeded at an exponential rate, increasing processing speed and storage capacities and thereby decreasing the size of computers and their costs at an equally dramatic pace.[15] Supported by the development of numerous software applications and user-friendly interfaces, personal computers (PCs) started to conquer offices and homes from the mid-1970s onwards. At the same time, video games began to revolutionise entertainment. In factories, digital programs that steered numerically controlled machine tools and robots advanced automation in production, allowing for flexible, small-batch mass production.

Communication technologies have also benefited from computerisation, the improvement of transmission technologies, and the expansion of networks. However, the digital age in communication technology was not the outcome of the further evolution of existing telecommunication networks.[16] It was driven by the development of new digital networks dedicated to the exchange of data among computers starting in the 1960s with the ARPANET (Advanced Research Projects Agency Network) in the USA. Unlike the 'hub and spoke' structure of traditional telecommunication networks, these data networks had a distributed, fishnet-like structure. The avoidance of centralised hubs made them less vulnerable to acts of sabotage. Also, they were not reliant on dedicated lines for transmitting information, but on packet-switching, whereby content was split into small packages and routed through the network along telecommunication lines with free transmission capacity. In this way, the marginal cost of transmitting content came close to zero so long as the network had sufficient capacity. Various digital data networks emerged not only among research institutions, but also among businesses. The next challenge was to make these networks interoperable by standardising their communication protocols. In 1972, the US Defense Department launched the 'Internetting Project'—much like it had with ARPANET—to achieve this goal. The project successfully developed the 'internet' by introducing the TCP/IP (Transmission Control Protocol/Internet Protocol) technology that remains the backbone of internet communication today.

The internet was originally intended to support communication among computers, but it soon became clear that it could in principle also be used to access information. To do so required standardised formats for coding information, and tools to search for content. The solution came with the invention of the World Wide Web (WWW) in 1990, with a standardised address system for information locations (URL), a common coding language (HTML), and standards for the display and transfer of information (HTTP). Online searching became simplified through the development of web browsers and search engines.

With the rise of the internet and the world wide web, computing and telecommunications became integrated. One result was the possibility of transmitting audio and video content using packet-switching, which reduced the marginal cost of telephone and video calls to close to zero. With the integration of computing and communication networks, the term 'information and communication technology' began to be used from around 2000 onwards. This terminology reflected the fact that it was no longer possible to understand or analyse information and communication technology separately because of the synergies created by connectivity. Subsequently, connectivity continued to increase dramatically with the rise of mobile and wireless networks, the success of cell phones and later smartphones, and the development of sensor and other surveillance technologies, quick-response (QR) codes and radio-frequency identification (RFID). All of these innovations vastly extended the reach and density of networks beyond the early internet, computers, and people to include locations, machines, material flows, and products.

In the early 2000s, social media and commercial platforms were among the first to exploit the potential of connectivity, while at the same time further expanding them. They also prepared the stage for big data.[17] Although data were often only a by-product rather than the purpose of online interactions, they soon became a major revenue source in digital business applications. The development of artificial neural network technology in the 2010s dramatically enhanced the value of big data. The application of neural networks to big data gave birth to self-learning algorithms and machine learning. "Trained" to recognise patterns in huge amounts of data and to apply these to increasingly sophisticated intellectual tasks, these algorithms opened up a new page in the quest for artificial intelligence, the most recent example being the success of large language models (LLMs) like ChatGPT.[18] At the same time, continuing improvements in network capacities and computing power enabled new modes of simulation known as augmented reality (AR) and virtual reality (VR). These technologies not only offered new forms of entertainment and training, but also enhanced efficiency in R&D, testing, design, and—consequently—production and service quality.

2.4 Innovation in the Digital Age

Humanity has only just entered the digital age, but we can already gain some idea of its transformative power with regard to not only our economies, but to social life at large—such as communication, culture, education, work, politics, and crime. Terms like 'Digital Transformation' (DX), the German framework of 'Industry 4.0', or the Japanese vision 'Society 5.0' attempt to capture the comprehensiveness and fundamental nature of the impact of digital technologies on societies, and equate its relevance for the future of humanity with that of climate change.[19]

Innovation in the digital age is not limited to the further development of digital technologies, but comprises the whole range of tools and applications derived from the digitisation of data, the digitalisation of infrastructures, and the resulting potential of connectivity. Digital technologies are spurring innovation far beyond the ICT industries. They impact products and services, R&D, production, sales, and marketing, as well as organisational design and business models at large. Industry examples like e-commerce and e-publishing, and startup examples like Airbnb (the US operator of an online marketplace for short- and long-term homestays) and Uber (the US ridesharing and delivery company) show that many of these innovations can have a disruptive effect on existing industries. However, our interest here is not so much the enormous potential, scope and effect of innovations in the digital age, but how such innovation is organised and brought about.

Schumpeter saw innovation as the main driver of economic development and considered the individual entrepreneur as the key protagonist in a capitalist market economy.[20] Schumpeter's entrepreneur perceives opportunities and tries to exploit them at his or her own risk. Years later, in "*Capitalism, Socialism, and Democracy*" published in 1942, Schumpeter had become very sceptical about the future of capitalism, and consequently about the future of entrepreneurship.[21] He saw the entrepreneurial function as becoming obsolete due to the advance of large, management-controlled enterprises, which he paraphrased as a "bureaucratised giant industrial unit". Schumpeter foresaw the rise of R&D departments within large companies supported by national patent-systems, whose costs and legal-administrative procedures rewarded size and bureaucratic organisation.

The rise of mainframe computing and national telecommunication networks, and the observation that only large companies, for example in finance or media, could take advantage of the advances in ICT corroborated Schumpeter's view of large corporations replacing the entrepreneurial function. However, by the 1980s and with the emergence of startup ecosystems like Silicon Valley, his pessimistic predictions had become refuted. Today, we can see entrepreneurs once again occupying the forefront of innovation. Though we now speak of "startups" to describe those newly founded, entrepreneurial firms that explore the business potential of digital technologies in various sectors of the economy. We also no longer conceive these startups as independent firms growing organically while relying on internal sources of finance and being at the mercy of bankers.[22] Instead, we see them situated within geographically-confined clusters where they benefit from participating in an ecosystem that provides support infrastructures specifically tailored to their needs. This naming and setting suggest something fundamentally new about entrepreneurship and innovation.

The particularities of startups and the importance of startup ecosystems relate to three characteristics that are typical of innovative solutions derived from digital technologies, namely:

- an abundance of innovative ideas,
- low setup costs for applying and testing innovative ideas,
- enormous scalability potential for startups which pass viability thresholds.[23]

Digitalisation and connectivity offer an abundance of innovative ideas far beyond ICT industries. Their transformative power leaves no industry unaffected. Almost any process can be digitalised in any industry and at any stage of the value chain. It is not only the seemingly limitless possibility of Schumpeter's "new combinations", it is also the fact that the circle of those who can recognise and exploit innovations is no longer limited to a small group of technology experts. In the digital age, innovations do not have to take the long and complex route from basic through to applied research, and then to product or service development and marketable offers. Today, the most advanced technologies are presented to consumers worldwide at their fingertips. Almost anyone can come up with ideas about how digital solutions might improve her or his user experience, work environment, or business, and this has opened up a new age of user innovation.[24]

The development of new digital solutions usually affords relatively little setup costs. The most advanced technology is now available on smart devices and readily accessible through online networks. Computers, software, and digital networks have replaced expensive research laboratories and factories in which to test and implement new ideas. Nowadays, it is relatively cheap to produce prototypes and pitch business plans to potential investors and customers. Within this milieu, the most critical resource is human capital—knowledge and skills that humans acquire through studies and experience—that is embodied in the talent and drive of entrepreneurial teams. The power of vibrant startup ecosystems is generated by a positive feedback loop. Their dynamism attracts skilled individuals from around the world, which further feeds their dynamic development.

Scalability is another important characteristic of digital solutions. The main cost of a digital product is the R&D needed to create the first viable example. Further copies can be produced at almost zero marginal cost, since the cost of copying simply relates to the amount of electricity and physical storage consumed. The fact that new digital solutions are often embedded in physical products does not contradict the near-zero marginal cost argument. Such products typically already exist, and the new digital solution can often be installed with little adjustment cost. This is most apparent in, but not limited to, new smartphone applications that exploit the huge number of smartphones in use and the connectivity provided by existing digital networks. Consequently, startups typically do not need to invest in hardware and infrastructures to deploy their products. Instead, they can focus on tasks such as programming and marketing.

If new ideas promise a viable business, then near-zero marginal costs and scaling up are likely to result in fast growth and high profitability, although the latter may need time to realise. A strong belief in scale often allows companies to grow significantly without being profitable as they and their funders willingly forego early profits by investing in long-term growth. In the case of digital businesses, the prospects of scalability have replaced the solid track record of earnings as a predictor of future profitability. Scalability has revolutionised company evaluations and—as a consequence—the listing requirements of stock markets.

Of course, only a small minority of startups will be able to establish a sustainable business, and only an even tinier portion will become very successful.[25] Survival and success in the startup population follows a strongly skewed distribution, with huge numbers in the bottom left, earning little and eventually failing, and a very thin, but very high peak at the top right measuring the extremely profitable survivors. The impressive performance of the latter is well documented in global market capitalisation rankings. On February 17, 2025, seven of the world's ten largest companies in terms of market capitalisation, namely Apple (1), NVIDIA (2), Microsoft (3), Amazon (4), Alphabet (5), Meta Platforms (6), and TSMC (10) were all pioneers in the ICT industry, or were among the first to successfully exploit the potential of connectivity.[26] These companies not only excel in size, but also in speed. All of them achieved unprecedented growth under their founders and, for many of the younger companies, within a few years after their foundation. Not all startup founders monetise their success by listing on stock exchanges to sell shares in their company. Many, especially those in industries with inherent obstacles to growth (e.g., in biotechnology or healthcare), sell out to larger incumbent companies that possess the resources needed to better exploit the unrealised growth potentials of the innovative technology.

The thousands of high-tech startups which come and go constitute a huge testing laboratory for digital solutions. Like in any laboratory, a lot of effort goes wasted. However, important experience is gained by everyone involved—experience that can be applied in future experiments, such as new ventures. Research suggests that, despite high failure rates, venture capital funds succeed in extracting above-normal returns on average from investments in startups by effectively diversifying their portfolios. In contrast, for the founders, entrepreneurial team members, and employees of startups, the outcomes are mixed.[27] While they are exposed to the same risk, they are not able to diversify this risk as financial investors can. They usually participate in financial success but, since most startups fail, they can only hope to materialise the experience gained in their future career.

Startup ecosystems, which will be defined and analysed in more detail in the next chapter, can be envisaged as support infrastructures that are in many ways functionally equivalent to the organisational resources available to the R&D departments of large companies. However, the number of new ideas that can be tested in parallel in startup ecosystems exceeds by far the funding and R&D capacity of the largest firms. Another advantage of ecosystems, though possibly a more questionable one, results from the fact that startups tend to operate with much more favourable cost structures, especially with respect to personnel expenses, than do large businesses. Founders, entrepreneurial team members, and employees are typically overworked and underpaid. They accept unfavourable work conditions in return for pursuing their passion and living their shared dreams, including the dream of being successful at some point in the future.

In short, the digital age has transposed corporate R&D functions into startup ecosystems. As with outsourcing, this allows for the exploitation of scale and for further functional specialisation. On the one hand, the entrepreneurial element is back in the game and, on the other, the game has reached a new level of professionalism far beyond the limits of large bureaucratic business organisations. Another feature of the digital age is that while startup ecosystems are market-based, they appear in important ways to be orchestrated by an increasingly sophisticated venture capital industry that fulfils an essential gatekeeper function. This can be interpreted as the rational instrumentalisation and financialisation of entrepreneurship. It characterises neither the obsolescence of the entrepreneur as predicted by Schumpeter, nor the return to the old days studied in his business cycles. The digital age has heralded a new wave of entrepreneurial innovation.

2.5 Conclusion

The digital revolution, as chronicled above, underscores a universal truth: technology alone does not drive progress. Rather, it is the interplay of innovation, infrastructure, and human creativity that unlocks transformative potential. This interplay is today especially evident in startup ecosystems. They have emerged as the primary engines of technological and economic transformation in the digital age. By democratising access to tools, lowering costs, and enabling unprecedented scalability, they have revitalised entrepreneurship in ways that Schumpeter could not have foreseen. With their ability to test myriad ideas in parallel and attract both venture capital and human capital, they function as decentralised R&D powerhouses, complementing and partly superseding the role of large and established corporations.

Yet, these ecosystems are not uniform. They are defined by their distinct locations and embedded in specific institutional and cultural environments. Their effectiveness depends on these national components and conditions. This has particularly been the case in East Asia, where ecosystems have leveraged digital advancements to foster startups that are competitive in both domestic and, increasingly, international markets—while at the same time being deeply rooted in local realities and traditions. The distinct trajectories of startup ecosystem development in Japan, Korea, and China will be explored in the second part of this book.

Notes

1. Hemmert et al. (2019).
2. Schumpeter (1939).
3. Schumpeter (1934).
4. Schumpeter (1942), 131–134.
5. The OECD (2025) defines digital technologies as "different types of communication networks and systems, including information processing and compute capacity and the technologies used in them. This entails both the underlying 'physical layers' (e.g., communication infrastructures and devices, including semiconductors, network equipment, data centres, servers, smart sensors, Internet exchange points) and the 'digital layer' (e.g., cloud and edge computing, software) of technologies, goods and services that enable the digital technology ecosystem."
6. For more details, see Chapter 3 of this book.
7. Saxenian (1994).
8. There are many different definitions of these two terms; see for example Gradillas and Thomas (2023). In this book, the term digitisation refers to replacing or translating analogue signals by or into electronic binary code. Digitalisation uses digitisation to transform processes, services and business models. The term digital transformation describes the sum of digitalisation at different aggregate levels such as industries and societies or as a global trend.
9. For the role of information in biological evolution see Nurse (2020); for the extension to cultural evolution see Dennett (2017).
10. Kurzweil (2024).
11. It was done by Chris Haughton (2024) in his illustrated "The History of Information".
12. Wheeler (2024), 27–47. In China, mobile type printing had been invented by Pi Sheng in 1040, more than 400 years before Gutenberg, but it did not lead to a dramatic growth in book printing. Given the complex Chinese writing system,

the technology did not lead to a significant cost advantage compared to block printing (Angeles, 2017).
13. Heath (1972).
14. Leavitt & Whisler (1958).
15. The density of circuits packed on a single chip tended to double almost every ten years. The pattern was first observed and consequently used to extrapolate the future development of computing by Gordon Moore in 1965, then R&D director at Fairchild Semiconductor, who later co-founded Intel; see Haigh & Ceruzzi (2021), 169–170.
16. Wheeler (2024), 148–152.
17. The term "big data" already has a history of definitions; see Kitchin & McArdle (2016).
18. Wheeler (2024), 221–244.
19. Hitachi-UTokyo Laboratory (2020).
20. Schumpeter (1934).
21. Schumpeter (1942).
22. As the term "startup" is today commonly used for newly founded firms, we use it interchangeably in this book to describe entrepreneurial activity and the founding of companies in general.
23. The implications of digital technologies for business models and markets are analysed in Shapiro & Varian (1998).
24. Von Hippel (2005).
25. For example, the performance of digital content entrepreneurs on online platforms is heavily skewed due to the combined effects of zero-marginal costs, feedback loops, and network effects (Gala et al., 2024).
26. Source: https://companiesmarketcap.com, accessed 17 February, 2025. Tesla (8) and Broadcom (9) could also be counted as offsprings of the digital revolution.
27. A study of Danish startup employees revealed that even in the long-run early employees share in the risk of failing startups by earning less than their peers in larger companies or those lucky to be employed by successful startups (Sorenson et al., 2025).

Chapter 3
Startup Ecosystems: Conceptual Foundations, Key Elements, and Knowledge Gaps in the East Asian Context

3.1 Introduction

Entrepreneurship is often described as the lifeblood of innovation and economic dynamism. In recent decades, the concept of the startup ecosystem has emerged as a powerful lens through which to understand how new ventures are born, grow, and scale. No longer seen as isolated success stories, startups are increasingly understood as products of complex, interdependent environments—ecosystems—that shape their potential for innovation and impact. From Silicon Valley to Shenzhen, these ecosystems are made up of entrepreneurs, investors, universities, support organisations, and policymakers, all interacting within a shared cultural and institutional context.

This chapter lays the conceptual foundation for understanding how startup ecosystems function, with a deliberate focus on the unique conditions of East Asia. While much of the existing literature draws heavily from Western models—particularly the USA experience—this chapter challenges the assumption that these frameworks can be universally applied. The realities of entrepreneurship in Japan, Korea, and China are shaped by distinct cultural norms, institutional structures, and historical trajectories that differ markedly from those in North America and Europe. In East Asia, where social harmony, hierarchical business groups, and state-led development have long influenced economic life, the path to entrepreneurial success often follows a different logic to that of the West.

The purpose of this chapter is threefold. First, it traces the intellectual origins of the startup ecosystem concept, distinguishing it from related ideas such as industrial districts, business clusters, and innovation systems. Second, it identifies the core elements that constitute a vibrant startup ecosystem—cultural, relational, and structural—and examines how these interact to support entrepreneurial activity. Third, and most critically, it highlights the limitations of Western-centric theories and calls for a more context-sensitive approach to studying entrepreneurship in East Asia.

The chapter guides the reader from broad theoretical foundations to region-specific insights. It begins by reviewing the evolution of the ecosystem concept and

Y. Cheng et al., *Unleashing Innovation the East Asian Way*,
https://doi.org/10.1007/978-981-95-6513-9_3

its growing prominence in policy and practice. It then adopts a working definition of startup ecosystems before comparing them to earlier models of regional economic development. Next, it unpacks the key components of ecosystems, drawing on influential frameworks while underscoring their limitations when applied to non-Western settings. Finally, it turns to the East Asian context, identifying some critical gaps in current research and setting the stage for the country-specific and thematic analyses that follow in this book.

By grounding the discussion in both theory and regional specificity, this chapter serves as a bridge between global understandings of entrepreneurship and the distinctive pathways taken in Japan, Korea, and China. It prepares the reader for the in-depth explorations in the chapters ahead, which examine how these three nations have cultivated innovation in ways that reflect both global trends and deeply rooted local contexts.

3.2 Origins, Importance, and Limitations of the Startup Ecosystems Concept

The concept of startup ecosystems and the instrumental role they play in fostering economic development based on entrepreneurial innovation has recently attracted considerable attention within academic, policy, and practitioner fields. Much of this attention was catalysed by Daniel Isenberg's article, "How to Start an Entrepreneurial Revolution", which appeared in the *Harvard Business Review* in 2010, and by Brad Feld's influential mainstream business book, *Startup Communities: Building an Entrepreneurial Ecosystem in Your City*, published in 2012. These influential works highlighted to entrepreneurial leaders and government policymakers the profound impact that local context can exert on the entrepreneurship process. In particular, these and later works emphasise the importance of a diverse community—or ecosystem—of actors in offering emotional, financial, professional, and practical support to the entrepreneur, and how the educational, policy, and economic environments surrounding the entrepreneur provide essential resources and safeguards necessary for young entrepreneurial firms to thrive.

Since the pioneering contributions of Isenberg and Feld, the scholarly literature on startup ecosystems (also referred to as "entrepreneurial ecosystems" in academic literature) has expanded substantially.[1] A central argument in this research is that while new businesses can technically be established anywhere, certain *places*—from university-centred communities to districts, cities, provinces, and nations—possess unique combinations of opportunities, constraints, and resources that influence significantly the ability and capacity of entrepreneurs to launch, sustain, and scale innovative new ventures. Silicon Valley's mix of venture capital networks and technical talent exemplifies this phenomenon. Put simply, entrepreneurs located in a strong, well-functioning, and successful startup ecosystem are better positioned to spot untapped market niches and tap into local expertise and funding to grow new ventures into national and even international leaders than those in weaker, poorly functioning, and less successful ecosystems.

This kind of reasoning has motivated entrepreneurship researchers to explore and evaluate the types of policy interventions that governments at various levels can implement to cultivate robust and vibrant startup ecosystems within their jurisdiction.[2] The objective of much of the government-led effort is to enhance economic growth, innovation, competitiveness, productivity, and job creation, and to attract additional investment. Indeed, inspired by the rise of Silicon Valley and other US innovation hubs, many governments worldwide are increasingly viewing the startup ecosystem approach as a potent tool and strategic framework for understanding the complex interplay of factors that foster economic vitality, innovation, and growth in a region. At the same time, studies caution that even the most ambitious policy interventions—from tax incentives to incubator programs—face inherent limitations, underscoring how entrepreneurs, investors, and grassroots networks remain critical drivers of ecosystem success.[3]

Despite significant recent effort, research into startup ecosystems is still young and remains underdeveloped.[4] Scholars continue to grapple with fundamental questions about why certain regions thrive while others stagnate. One critical gap in current research lies in its disproportionate focus: scholars have prioritised descriptively dissecting successful ecosystems to extract best practices, creating a playbook for replication rather than advancing the field's theoretical foundations or subjecting assumptions to rigorous empirical testing in ways that would be expected of a well-developed academic field.[5] A second limitation lies in the lack of standardised methodologies to assess how ecosystems actually drive entrepreneurship, innovation, and new value creation. Studies often rely on ad hoc metrics or anecdotal case studies rather than a unified, testable framework, making it difficult to isolate cause and effect—or even to define what "success" truly means. A third limitation is the lack of consensus on the fundamental elements that constitute a startup ecosystem, or the indicators that should be employed to evaluate scientifically the performance of individual components within the ecosystem.[6] Without consensus on these "ingredients" or how to measure their performance, efforts to benchmark ecosystems—or replicate their success—risk oversimplifying the complex, often idiosyncratic factors that shape entrepreneurial outcomes in unique regional contexts. This problem is exacerbated by a paucity of suitably consistent and comparable data across regions, especially at sub-national levels. A fourth limitation—particularly salient for this book's focus—is the field's overwhelming bias toward Western models, with studies concentrated on North American and European ecosystems, often framed through Anglo-American norms. This has left critical gaps in understanding about how startup ecosystems function in various emerging and advanced economies and in non-Western contexts, such as those of East Asia, where distinct cultural, institutional, and historical forces reshape everything from risk-taking behaviours to public-private collaboration.[7] To illustrate, China's "national champions" model or Korea's *chaebol*-driven spin-offs stand in contrast to Anglo-American notions of grassroots entrepreneurship.

3.3 Towards a Definition of Startup Ecosystem

To derive an accurate and functional definition of a startup ecosystem, it is useful first to disaggregate the concept into its constituent terms. In this book, we refer to a startup as being a young firm established through a productive 'entrepreneurial' endeavour. Here, productive entrepreneurial activity is a key output of the startup ecosystem.[8] Productive entrepreneurship is "any entrepreneurial activity that contributes directly or indirectly to net output of the economy or to the capacity to produce additional output".[9] Thus, entrepreneurship can be viewed as a process by which individuals identify and pursue opportunities for innovation and new value creation through the establishment of innovative startups, high-growth firms, entrepreneurial teams, and other entrepreneurial initiatives that foster productivity in an economy.

The term "ecosystem" in the startup ecosystem concept draws upon an analogy, first proposed by Moore in 1993 and later popularised by Isenberg, that startup ecosystems can be likened to biological ecosystems.[10] This analogy highlights how, within a startup ecosystem, loosely interconnected living entities (biotic components of an ecological ecosystem) engage with one another and their surrounding physical environment (abiotic components) in ways that determine the dynamics of collaboration, cooperation, conflict, and survival in the ecosystem, thereby shaping its development and evolution.

Defining a startup ecosystem remains frustratingly elusive. The field's interdisciplinary, ever-evolving scholarship—drawing insights from economics, management, sociology, and urban planning—collides with the reality that these systems are never one-size-fits-all. Their dynamics differ across geographical regions, industries, and stages of economic development, shaped by hyper-local cultures, policies, and the ever-shifting interplay between actors such as investors, universities, and governments. For example, the startup ecosystem of Silicon Valley, characterised by a dominance of venture capital firms, strong academy-industry links, and a culture of normalised risk-taking and acceptance of failure is very different to, for example, the Bangalore (India) startup ecosystem, which is largely built upon the legacy of information technology (IT) services outsourcing, a talent pool of affordable engineering graduates, and various government initiatives such as Startup India funding that nuture product-driven and fintech startups.[11] In other words, each startup ecosystem is unique, in analogy to natural ecosystems.

What is more, the numerous elements that make up a startup ecosystem are *deeply interconnected* and influence each other in complex ways. This means that the precise spatial boundary of an individual startup ecosystem is often ambiguous.[12] Startup ecosystems are also not static in nature, again like natural ecosystems. The characteristics, components, and interconnections found within a particular startup ecosystem can and do *evolve over time* in response to a range of developments. These include technological advancements, economic shifts, changes in societal norms, and government policy initiatives implemented at a local, regional or national level, and through other effects and influences. Finally, *various stakeholder audiences* are likely to view the key features of a startup ecosystem differently: for instance, policymakers might focus on job creation and economic development, while entrepreneurs may prioritise access to finance and the presence of a well-educated workforce. In short, the complexity, dynamics, and variation of startup ecosystems resist simplistic analytical frameworks, leaving scholars and practitioners alike without a universal blueprint or universally applicable definition of what a startup ecosystem is.

Despite these challenges, we adopt in this book the following definition (after Stam and Spigel) that a startup ecosystem is "a set of interdependent actors and factors coordinated in such a way that they enable productive entrepreneurship within a particular territory".[13] In other words, we understand a startup ecosystem to be a community of loosely connected but interdependent and coevolving stakeholders (including entrepreneurs themselves), and the factors that interact to provide, both directly and indirectly, a supportive environment to an entrepreneur for the creation and growth of new ventures within a particular place.

3.4 Related Concepts

While recent scholarly interest in startup ecosystems has been largely atheoretical, the startup ecosystem concept is built upon strong and well-established intellectual traditions found within the entrepreneurship, applied economics, economic geography, and regional development literatures. Collectively, contributions to these schools of thought have a long history of asserting that factors external to an organisation but contained within a geographically defined territory contribute to firm-level competitive advantage, and that a firm situated in that territory contributes to a system larger than itself.[14] Firm-level competitive advantages derive from being a member of a high concentration of numerous firms in a particular location, a phenomenon also known as regional agglomeration. Such territorial agglomerations have been variously labelled by different schools as industrial districts, business clusters, innovation systems, and so forth. While each school differs in its perspectives, methodologies, and conceptualisations (see Table 3.1 for a summary), they consider much the same question: what is the relationship between the entrepreneurship process and the economic and social context within a concentration of firms in a particular geographic space?[15]

3.4.1 Industrial Districts

The intellectual origins of the startup ecosystem approach can be traced back more than a century to the British economist, Alfred Marshall, and his theorising on the economics of industries and firm agglomerations.[16] This has become known as the industrial district school, and it emphasises the division of labour of an industry in a specific territory. An industrial district is a geographic area characterised by a high concentration of typically small to medium-sized enterprises (SMEs) operating

Table 3.1 Summary comparison of industrial districts, business clusters, innovation systems, and startup ecosystems*

	Industrial district	Business cluster	Innovation system	Startup ecosystem
Components	Organizations; formal institutions; informal institutions (social capital, networks, culture).	Organizations; formal institutions; informal institutions (social capital, networks, culture).	Organizations; formal institutions; informal institutions (social capital, networks, culture).	Individuals; organizations; formal institutions; informal institutions (social capital, networks, culture).
Functions	Strengthening localised production in an industry.	Growing firm competitiveness.	Learning and diffusion of innovation.	Entrepreneurial exploration of market opportunities.
Measures of outcome	Regional economic growth (productivity).	Nationally/ internationally competitive firms.	Product and process innovations.	Productive startups and scale-ups.
Regional knowledge base required	Technical knowledge; market knowledge; management knowledge.	Technical knowledge; market knowledge; management knowledge.	Technical knowledge; market knowledge; management knowledge.	Technical knowledge; market knowledge; management knowledge; entrepreneurial process knowledge.
Industry boundaries	Bounded by one industry or sector.	Bounded by multiple interconnected industries.	Bounded by one industry.	Not bounded by industries.
Core firm focus	Small and medium enterprises (SMEs).	Export-based firms.	Innovative, high-tech firms.	Innovative, high-growth startups.
Role of entrepreneurs	Supporting.	Supporting.	Supporting.	Leading.
Role of incumbent firms	Leading.	Leading.	Leading.	Supporting.
Role of government	Leading.	Supporting.	Leading.	Supporting.

(continued)

Table 3.1 (continued)

	Industrial district	Business cluster	Innovation system	Startup ecosystem
Role of universities	Supporting.	Supporting.	Leading.	Supporting.
Input into startup ecosystem approach	Talent (labour market pooling), intermediate services (specialized goods and services), knowledge (spill-overs).	Talent, finance, knowledge, physical infrastructure (factor conditions); demand; support services and intermediaries (related and supporting industries).	Knowledge, finance, formal institutions, demand.	

* Adapted from Acs et al. (2023, pp. 13–14), and O'Connor et al. (2018, pp. 6–7)

within the same industry or manufacturing sector (or sharing a common technological base), and it often includes a complete supply chain. A classic example is the textile district in Prato, Italy. Industrial districts are known for their close-knit social and economic networks that facilitate collaboration, innovation, and competitiveness amongst actors. They benefit from economies of scale, specialised labour pools, and shared infrastructure, all of which contribute to competitive advantages in production and innovation within that specific industry and territory.

3.4.2 Business Clusters

The business cluster concept has been promoted by the Harvard researcher Michael Porter. A business cluster is a geographic concentration of multiple interconnected producers, specialised suppliers, service providers, and associated institutions that both compete and cooperate with each other in a particular geographic area.[17] Silicon Valley's technology sector is one of the most cited examples of a successful business cluster. Business clusters are known to enhance productivity and innovation through the knowledge sharing, business networking, and the collaboration and competitive forces that proximity promotes. Business clusters can span across various industries but are tied together by common technologies, skills, or market needs within a territory.

Being located in an industrial district or business cluster can increase the competitiveness of new ventures in two main ways. First, the concentration of numerous firms in the same sector or supply chain can attract and cultivate a substantial pool of specialised and skilled workers that smaller and resource-constrained firms nearby can access to reduce costs or increase innovativeness. Second, proximity to a large concentration of established firms can broaden access to a diverse array of knowledge spill-overs, advanced technologies, capabilities, complementary products, and other essential inputs that entrepreneurs need to create and scale up a new venture, while also enhancing their opportunities to discover new market niches to serve.[18]

3.4.3 Innovation Systems

The innovation system framework has been established by various (mostly European) innovation researchers since the 1980s. An innovation system encompasses the policies, institutions, and industries within a territory that collectively contribute to technological development, innovation and economic growth by facilitating flows of technology and information between actors. These actors include public and private sector knowledge-producing hubs such as universities and research institutions, and laboratories linked to innovative firms and government agencies by networks and institutions across a region, sector, or country to create, modify, and diffuse new technologies. Government policies aimed at increasing innovative capacity in their jurisdiction often focus on supporting "anchor" knowledge producers (such as large multinational corporations, universities, or research laboratories) and promoting knowledge-sharing and learning between firms and these anchor organisations. The concept can be applied at various levels, and categories include national innovation systems (NIS), regional innovation systems (RIS), and sectoral innovation systems.[19]

Like industrial districts and business clusters, the innovation systems school highlights the advantages for new ventures of building social networks among closely located entrepreneurs, innovators, and researchers. Again, proximity is beneficial for the dissemination of knowledge and identification of market opportunities, and it also facilitates access to capital and other necessary resources to create a new venture which can capitalise on that knowledge and opportunity. The innovation systems school also underscores the importance of universities and other anchor organisations in fostering innovation. These institutions act as reservoirs of advanced scientific knowledge and as talent developers, efficiently disseminating expertise to nearby firms. They can also play a pivotal role in attracting highly educated workers to the region, enhancing its innovative capacity and economic development, and further expanding the available pool of talent that new ventures can recruit.[20]

3.4.4 Comparisons with the Startup Ecosystem Approach

In many ways, the startup ecosystem approach can be regarded as an integrative framework that incorporates key aspects from the established industrial district, business cluster, and innovation system schools of thought to derive a unified approach for research and policymaking on the relationship between local context and entrepreneurship. Each school discussed above, along with the startup ecosystem approach, is similar in that it highlights the importance of geographic concentration and the benefits of proximity for collaboration, knowledge sharing, and innovation. Equivalent importance is placed on networks of interconnected stakeholders, including businesses, institutions, and sometimes government entities, that interact in ways that generate economic growth, productivity, and competitiveness.

Nevertheless, the startup ecosystem approach differs from the three established schools of thought in several important ways. First, the startup ecosystem approach incorporates a broader array of factors and stakeholders, including culture and policies, as well as the support systems specifically designed to encourage entrepreneurship and innovation. These factors and stakeholders are not always the central focus of the other schools of thought.

Second, and most importantly, the emphasis of the startup ecosystem approach is on individuals and their social interactions rather than on larger, more established incumbent firms or slower-growing SMEs. Expressed another way, it is the entrepreneur, rather than the firm, that is the focal point of analysis in the startup ecosystem approach.[21] The high-growth startups that form the basis of this approach are not necessarily captured by the traditional and established schools, which typically view new venture startups as smaller versions of larger, more established, or international corporations, rather than recognising them as distinct organisational entities endowed with unique capabilities and resources.[22]

Crucially, the startup ecosystem approach not only views entrepreneurship as the primary output of the system, but positions the entrepreneur as the central figure or leader in the development and evolution of a startup ecosystem, and in maintaining its vitality. Successful entrepreneurs with a long-term commitment to the startup ecosystem are often well-positioned to recognise the opportunities and restrictions that characterise the system. They are able to leverage their own experiences, social networks, access to capital, and relations with other stakeholders (such as government, customers, and local citizens) to legitimise new ventures, facilitate business transactions, and make suggestions for public interventions to address problematic issues. Through this engagement, the entrepreneur can help to improve the overall environment for further entrepreneurial endeavours. Consequently, unlike the traditional top-down policy initiatives advocated by the business cluster and innovation systems schools, the startup ecosystem approach positions entrepreneurs as co-creators and developers of the system itself. This perspective reduces emphasis on the state, institutional support, and policy frameworks as key drivers of innovation, and it places considerably more importance on the pivotal role played by individual entrepreneurs than the other approaches.

Consequently, a third distinction is that the startup ecosystem approach views the role of government not as a "leader" that directly orchestrates the creation and development of a startup ecosystem, but rather as a "feeder" that nurtures it.[23] Governments can do this in various ways. They can modify laws and regulations to eliminate or lessen barriers to entrepreneurship, and they can offer support to rectify deficiencies in areas such as the knowledge and skills base, access to investment capital, and infrastructure. Often these are challenges that only the state can address comprehensively to create a favourable economic and social environment in which entrepreneurship can flourish.[24]

As with the startup ecosystem approach, each of the established schools discussed above view market and technical knowledge as a key driver of entrepreneurial innovation within a concentration of firms. However, a fourth important distinction of the startup ecosystem approach relates to a particular type of knowledge that is necessary for startups to be established and flourish, namely knowledge about the entrepreneurial process itself.[25]

Establishing and building a new venture requires a specific set of skills and capabilities that is seldom, if ever, emphasised by research on industrial districts, business clusters, and innovation systems. Entrepreneurs require strong strategic thinking and problem-solving skills to navigate challenges, identify opportunities, and make informed decisions that are critical for the growth and sustainability of their ventures. Financial acumen, business planning, and the ability to manage resources efficiently are important, too. In addition, entrepreneurs need effective communication and leadership abilities to build relationships with stakeholders, inspire their teams, and to articulate their vision clearly and persuasively to a range of stakeholders, such as investors, customers, and partners. These capabilities, along with the ability to abide by cultural norms concerning how entrepreneurs should act and present themselves, are often crucial when building legitimacy with startup ecosystem stakeholders and when maximising the benefits of proactive engagement in a wide social network within the system.

Some of these skills and knowledge can be acquired through entrepreneurship training, formal business education, or from secondary sources such as books and websites on entrepreneurship. However, it can also be developed through prior working experience (for instance, in an established firm or an earlier startup), and through interactions with more experienced founders or business mentors (especially those working at other new ventures nearby), as well as from a general immersion in the entrepreneurial milieu of a region. In short, entrepreneurial process knowledge is essential in helping the entrepreneur to anticipate and overcome many of the challenges (that is, the "liabilities of newness") inherent to startup formation. These challenges include the need to develop new products and services, find and effectively serve initial customers, and to scale up firms that characteristically often experience severe resource and reputational constraints.[26]

A fifth and final distinction between the traditional schools of thought on firm concentrations and the startup ecosystem approach lies in the consideration of industries and sectors.[27] The industrial districts and business clusters schools primarily focus attention on existing industries and firms, emphasising manufacturing and production efficiency, and innovativeness within one or several industries. Therefore, these concepts focus on the dynamics of competition and also on the technical knowledge flows and other exchanges among firms that operate within the same market or supply chain. In contrast, the startup ecosystem approach adopts a broader focus that encompasses new venture creation and technological innovation. Crucially, it places particular importance on the exchange of entrepreneurial knowledge and skills, rather than industry-specific expertise, that transcends industry boundaries within a geographic territory. The startup ecosystem approach asserts that the strategies for establishing and scaling a business, including effective hiring and building an efficacious organisational culture, are applicable across various and unrelated sectors, thereby fostering mutual learning among entrepreneurs in proximity to each other.[28] Such benefits promote cooperative growth and learning despite competitive pressures from outside the startup ecosystem. This contrasts with Porter's view of competition as a driver of business cluster competitiveness,[29] and it highlights the unique advantage of startup ecosystems in driving market competitiveness through a trust-based, collaborative learning environment.

3.5 Constituent Elements of a Startup Ecosystem

As mentioned above, what precisely comprises a startup ecosystem has been the subject of much debate in the entrepreneurship literature. Various conceptual frameworks and models have been advanced to define the necessary economic and social conditions for a strong startup ecosystem.[30] Nevertheless, a single agreed-upon typology of startup ecosystems is missing, and there are disagreements about the exact mix of elements that constitute a well-performing one.

In the entrepreneurship practice-oriented literature, Isenberg[31] was first to propose a startup ecosystem model, consisting of six domains (policy, finance, culture, support, human capital, and markets) made up of twelve subdomains. Later, Feld[32] identified nine attributes of a successful startup community. Building upon this work, Stam[33] identified four framework conditions (formal institutions, culture, physical infrastructure, and market demand) and six systemic conditions (networks, leadership, finance, talent, knowledge, and support services) that promote entrepreneurial activity as an output and aggregate value creation as an outcome of a startup ecosystem.

Subsequently, other frameworks have also been developed. Spigel[34] suggests that a startup ecosystem consists of the interactions and relationships between three categories of elements, namely cultural, social, and material, comprising ten individual attributes. He posits that vibrant startup ecosystems are characterised by a culture of entrepreneurship and histories of successful entrepreneurship (cultural attributes), by resources that are accessed through social ties, such as worker talent, investment capital, social networks, and entrepreneurial mentors (social attributes), and by attributes grounded in a specific geographic place, particularly government policies, universities, support services, physical infrastructure, and open local markets (material attributes). Theodoraki, Messeghem and Rice[35] propose a social capital perspective, which includes three main components: i) a structural dimension (links, configuration, stability), ii) a cognitive dimension (shared objectives and language, shared narratives), and iii) a relational dimension (norms, members' obligations, trust, identification). Vedula and Kim[36] highlight five general dimensions of regional startup ecosystems that impact venture survival and are common across most studies,

Table 3.2 Overview of constituent elements of startup ecosystems*

Categorisation by types of elements	Example key elements of startup ecosystems	Representative authors
Cultural/cognitive	Supportive entrepreneurial culture.	Isenberg (2010), Stam (2015), Spigel (2017), Vedula and Kim (2019).
	Innovation capacity.	Vedula and Kim (2019).
Relational	Networks.	Stam (2015), Spigel (2017).
	Human capital.	Isenberg (2010), Spigel (2017), Vedula and Kim (2019).
	Financial capital.	Isenberg (2010), Stam (2015), Spigel (2017), Vedula and Kim (2019).
Structural	Physical infrastructure.	Stam (2015), Spigel (2017).
	Availability of support organisations and intermediaries.	Isenberg (2010), Stam (2015), Spigel (2017), Vedula and Kim (2019).
	Access to markets.	Isenberg (2010), Spigel (2017).
	Policy and governance.	Isenberg (2010), Spigel (2017), Vedula and Kim (2019).

*This overview is a synthesis of typologies proposed by Spigel (2017), Isenberg (2010), Stam (2015), Vedula and Kim (2019), and others. Since there are many overlaps and interconnections between the elements of startup ecosystems, the above categorisation should be treated as indicative rather than a definitive classification.

which are a supportive entrepreneurial culture, access to finance, access to human capital, innovation capacity, and formal support organisations for entrepreneurs.

We now synthesise these and other seminal studies to present an overview of startup ecosystem elements that are highlighted in major, albeit mainly Western-based, contributions to the literature (see Table 3.2 for a summary). We also extend our discussion by explaining which constituent elements deserve particular attention when exploring how startup ecosystems have developed and function in the three East Asian countries of Japan, Korea, and China.

3.5.1 Cultural and Cognitive Elements

It has been argued that culture shapes the attitudes towards entrepreneurship within a startup ecosystem, especially in relation to the tolerance of risk.[37] Relevant studies assume that societies and cultures that embrace risk and that view failure as a learning opportunity tend to foster more entrepreneurial activities. Such a culture is found in Silicon Valley, for example. Cultures that normalise the risks associated with entrepreneurship are also associated with the presence of histories of success stories about other entrepreneurs that legitimise and therefore encourage subsequent entrepreneurial activity. By contrast, in contexts where failure is stigmatised potential entrepreneurs may be discouraged from leaving stable employment or pursuing risky innovative ventures due to a fear of social and financial repercussions. Such cultural considerations may also determine the willingness of organisations and individuals such as financial institutions, venture capitalists, and angel investors to invest in risky new ventures.

In addition, the cultural context can influence the dynamics of a startup ecosystem through the norms, values, attitudes and behaviours of societies, communities, and individuals found within a particular geographic place in ways that can either significantly enable or hinder the entrepreneurial process.[38] Such considerations are especially relevant in emerging market contexts, and also in regions of the world that have received comparatively less attention from startup ecosystems scholars, such as those of East Asia.

Culture can shape the entrepreneurial landscape by influencing attitudes towards entrepreneurship that extend beyond the issue of risk tolerance to consider perceptions of entrepreneurship and collaborations. For example, a culture that values innovation, creativity, and life-long learning can create an environment where entrepreneurial ideas can flourish. Consequently, societies that prioritise education and research and development, and that celebrate innovative achievements, are more likely to foster a vibrant startup ecosystem. In particular, individualistic cultures that emphasise personal achievement and autonomy may encourage entrepreneurship by supporting the pursuit of individual ideas and ventures. In contrast, collectivist cultures such as those of East Asia focus more on community and familial support systems, which can also benefit entrepreneurship through strong networks of social support but may place less emphasis on individual risk-taking.

High levels of trust and social capital within a culture can facilitate business dealings, partnerships, and the flow of knowledge and information, all of which are crucial in providing the startup founder with access to the resources and networks needed to grow an entrepreneurial venture. Cultures that foster trust and strong social networks can significantly ease the process of starting and scaling a new business. Culturally-derived perceptions of wealth and success may also impact entrepreneurial motivation. In cultures where entrepreneurs are celebrated and success is admired, the motivation to pursue entrepreneurial endeavours is likely to be strong. Conversely, if success and wealth accumulation are viewed with suspicion or envy, this can dampen entrepreneurial spirit. Cultural norms surrounding gender roles and inclusivity may also influence who participates in entrepreneurship. To illustrate, cultures that promote gender equality and inclusivity are likely to see a more diverse pool of entrepreneurs, and this can enhance creativity and innovation within the startup ecosystem.

3.5.2 Relational Elements

Researchers argue that culture alone is insufficient in sustaining long-term entrepreneurial development.[39] Entrepreneurs need to draw on a variety of resources as they start and scale up new ventures. These resources can be also described as "social" because they are primarily accessed through social networks.[40] Dense social networks in a location have long been viewed as a determinant of entrepreneurship and innovation because they facilitate the flow of information and knowledge about new opportunities, new technologies, and the entrepreneurship process more generally.[41] Research has also demonstrated the importance of networks linking to other locations and ecosystems—both domestic and international—to promote access to resources, opportunities, and markets.[42]

At the level of an individual, entrepreneurs can leverage their social networks to gain access to investment and talented workers with the requisite skills and capabilities to flourish in a young high-growth company, or to work with mentors who can support and advise them to realise their entrepreneurial ambitions. Depending on the context, the availability of worker talent can differ greatly. This is especially so when we consider certain characteristics deemed important for such talent to thrive in the demanding process of building and growing entrepreneurial ventures. For example, some scholars have noted that workers "must also have a similar tolerance for risk as entrepreneurs themselves in order to thrive in the chaotic environment of a start-up".[43] However, finding such talent might be very difficult in places where risk tolerance is low. Also, some locations, including those in East Asia, might have a relatively small pool of both entrepreneurs and workers with international experience, sufficient access to global networks, and so forth. In turn, this is likely to negatively impact the ability of new ventures to not only be (potentially) "born global" from the outset but also to internationalise later on.[44]

Venture capitalists and angel investors can also draw upon their own social networks to vet and accurately evaluate high-potential investment candidates. Various studies have demonstrated that the role that venture capitalists play in a startup ecosystem is often much more comprehensive and "social" in nature than just providing investment funding itself.[45] Indeed, the frequency of funding opportunities in a given location can influence whether entrepreneurs choose to remain there or move elsewhere to launch a new venture.[46] Furthermore, well-functioning social networks within a startup ecosystem can also help to connect entrepreneurs in need of advice and support with mentors and role models (for example, other entrepreneurs who already have a track-record of success, such as achieving a meaningful exit of their own venture). All of this highlights the critical importance of social networks for a location to have a well-functioning startup ecosystem.

3.5.3 Structural Elements

Finally, researchers note that startup ecosystems also need material attributes, which are the institutions and organisations embedded in a particular place that support high-growth entrepreneurship.[47] These material attributes consist of many structural elements that are mostly tangible, starting with physical infrastructure. Physical infrastructure encompasses various essential features, including telecommunications and Internet access, availability of transportation, office space, and so forth. Also important are key facilities such as research universities and laboratories that help to nurture entrepreneurs and other talent relevant for new ventures, as well as advancing their skills and knowledge, and which can also help promote knowledge spill-overs in the region. Various support services, both general and specialised, constitute another key aspect of material attributes. Relevant service providers include law firms, patent lawyers, accountants, recruiters, as well as other types of organisations with a special focus on supporting new ventures, such as accelerators and incubators. All of these structures and actors can play an important role in enhancing entrepreneurship and the overall functioning of startup ecosystems in particular locations.[48]

Other important structural elements highlighted by researchers[49] include markets (which should ideally provide sufficient opportunities to find customers in a given location, as well as a possibility to access wider and even global markets), and policy and governance. It has been noted that while the policy and governance are perhaps slightly less "physical" in nature, they have tangible manifestations in specific regulations.[50] Public policies can support entrepreneurship through numerous tools, including direct financing (such as subsidies, grants, and other incentives), the provision of entrepreneurial training, and the enforcement of legal rights. There has been much debate about the role and effectiveness of policy and governance for building well-functioning startup ecosystems, with some scholars advocating for a less top-down and more bottom-up approach.[51] Nevertheless, there is also substantial evidence pointing to the importance of policies (even if they are insufficient by themselves without the development of at least some of the other startup ecosystem elements), for example in emerging economy or non-Western contexts.[52]

3.5.4 Distinctiveness of the East Asian Context

Our analysis of startup ecosystem components not only maps their foundational roles in entrepreneurship research but also helps us to identify where critical gaps lie in our understanding of how these systems have evolved and function across Japan, Korea, and China—the East Asian contexts that are central to this book.

First, cultural and cognitive elements (including aspects such as attitudes towards risk, collectivist versus individualistic culture, gender dynamics, the value placed on innovation, and so forth) are important startup ecosystem dimensions that in East Asia are likely to significantly differ from the more well-researched Western contexts. To illustrate, Confucian emphasis on social harmony in China, the hierarchical corporate networks underpinning Korea's *chaebol*-driven economy, and Japan's societal prioritisation of stability over disruptive innovation each cultivate distinct entrepreneurial strategies—such as incremental scaling or reliance on established industry partnerships—that diverge sharply from Western emphases on rapid disruption and founder-centric individualism. We can therefore expect that the antecedents of startup ecosystem performance and success will differ in East Asia compared to Western contexts. Second, and with respect to relational elements, the availability of a pool of entrepreneurs and workers with the skillsets and characteristics required to establish and scale-up a new venture (including risk tolerance, international experience, access to global networks, and so forth) is likely to be a key bottleneck for startup ecosystems in East Asia. This is because Japan's rigid labour markets have prioritised lifetime employment over entrepreneurial risk-taking, Korea's hyper-competitive education system has funnelled talent toward established *chaebol* conglomerates, and China offers uneven access to global networks—despite "sea turtle" returnee entrepreneurs who have previously worked or studied abroad—all of which leaves many East Asian startups navigating difficult talent shortages and market access challenges. The human capital and network aspects can also be expected to impact the opportunities for internationalisation of East Asian ventures. Third, these kinds of challenges can be addressed through the structural element of government policy and support initiatives. Still, such interventions are unlikely to be sufficient by themselves, even in regions such as East Asia where governments play a significant facilitating role in startup ecosystem development.

3.6 Evolution Trajectories and Comparative Evaluations of Startup Ecosystems

Above, we highlight several topics related to startup ecosystems that deserve particular attention in the East Asian context. They encompass certain key elements of startup ecosystems that in Japan, Korea, and China may have limitations or function differently than in the West. Understanding these aspects—for example, regarding cultural foundations, government policy and support, and inbound and outbound internationalisation networks—is necessary if we are to grasp the (evolving) dynamics of innovation and entrepreneurship in East Asia.

Our focus on the context-specific nature of the startup ecosystem elements we describe above is especially important in light of past research on new venture entrepreneurship, which shows that startup ecosystems can have a variety of evolution trajectories and different configurations of key actors and components at different moments in their development.[53] In short, there are claims that "both entrepreneurial quality and quantity can be created through the interaction between factors and the presence of multiple, equally effective pathways that lead to the same outcomes".[54] Potentially, some well-developed startup ecosystem elements could even compensate for the absence of others. However, the extent to which this happens and the consequences of such developmental trajectories require further examination. For example, in a study on US startup ecosystems, entrepreneurship experience has been found to compensate for insufficiencies in venture capital, human capital, and regional innovation capacity, but not for the gaps in "entrepreneurial culture, access to loans and grants, and resources provided by formal support organisations such as universities, accelerators, and incubators".[55]

Overall, achieving a better understanding of under-researched non-Western startup ecosystem contexts, such as those found in East Asia, greatly benefits from tracing the evolution trajectories and configurations of startup ecosystem elements over time. This can be further enriched by in-depth comparisons that have the power to illuminate meaningful similarities and differences across locations (but which remain relatively scarce), and by studies that pay attention to the potential role of cross-border linkages between ecosystems.[56] All these approaches are employed in this book to identify and explain the distinctiveness of East Asian startup ecosystems.

In the chapters that follow, we discuss the emergence and development of startup ecosystems in East Asia, first country by country (since each ecosystem is unique, in analogy to natural ecosystems), and then in relation to each other, by focusing on common issues highlighted across key startup ecosystem elements. Our in-depth perspective is important considering the currently shallow understanding of the characteristics and performance of East Asian startup ecosystems. In particular, while commonly available rankings such as the Global Startup Ecosystem Reports show the overall strengthening of startup ecosystems in the East Asian region,[57] data and interpretations available in these types of comparative evaluations are mostly useful to establish rough profiles of startup ecosystems, and an indication of how they compare especially to consistent rank leaders like the dominant Silicon Valley startup ecosystem. However, since startup ecosystems are often at different stages of development and can represent vastly contrasting startup ecosystem types, these popular rankings suffer from the "apples" versus "oranges" comparison problem, with only limited help to those who want to know more about the development and distinctiveness of specific startup ecosystems.[58] This book offers an in-depth, yet readable account of the under-researched East Asian startup ecosystems through both a longitudinal approach *and* a targeted comparative perspective regarding relevant startup ecosystem elements and the antecedents of their performance outcomes.

3.7 Conclusion

This chapter provides a conceptual roadmap for understanding startup ecosystems, with a clear emphasis on the need to move beyond one-size-fits-all models derived from Western experiences. We argue that while the ecosystem metaphor is useful for capturing the complexity of entrepreneurial environments, its application to East Asia requires careful adaptation. The dynamics of entrepreneurship in Japan, Korea, and China cannot be fully understood without accounting for cultural values such as collectivism and social harmony, institutional structures like Korea's *chaebols* or Japan's lifetime employment system, and the strategic role of state-led development policies.

Three key takeaways emerge. First, startup ecosystems are not simply clusters of firms or innovation hubs—they are living, evolving systems in which entrepreneurs, investors, institutions, and policies interact in dynamic (and often unpredictable) ways. Second, the success of these ecosystems depends not only on access to capital or talent, but also on less tangible factors such as cultural attitudes toward risk, failure, and individual initiative. Third, and perhaps most importantly, there is no single pathway to building a thriving entrepreneurial environment. In East Asia, alternative models of innovation that we discuss later in the book—characterised by incremental growth, corporate interactions, and strong state involvement—are not deviations from the norm, but valid and effective trajectories in their own right.

These insights set the stage for the remainder of the book. The following three chapters explore the historical development of startup ecosystems in Japan, Korea, and China, tracing how each country has navigated the tension between global entrepreneurial trends and local socio-economic conditions. Subsequent thematic chapters explore the critical dimensions of culture, government policy, and internationalisation, offering comparative perspectives that reveal both common challenges and distinctive strategies across the region.

Understanding East Asia's entrepreneurial landscapes requires more than adopting Silicon Valley's playbook. It demands a nuanced appreciation of context—the invisible architecture that shapes who becomes an entrepreneur, how they start, whom they collaborate with, and where they find success. This chapter has laid that foundation. What follows is a journey through the diverse, dynamic, and increasingly influential world of East Asian innovation and entrepreneurship—where tradition meets disruption, and where the future of entrepreneurship is being redefined.

Notes

1. See reviews and discussion in Acs et al. (2017), Cao and Shi (2020), Velt et al. (2020) and Wurth et al. (2022).
2. See, for example, Brown and Mason (2017).
3. See Thompson et al. (2018).
4. Root (2023).
5. See, for example, Stam (2015) and Theodoraki et al. (2022).
6. See, for, example O'Connor et al. (2018) and Feldman et al. (2022).
7. Cao and Shi (2020).
8. Stam (2015).
9. Baumol (1993) 30.
10. See Moore (1993) and Isenberg (2010).
11. See, for example, Kapturkiewicz (2022) and Kaur et al. (2024).
12. See, for example, Wurth et al. (2022).
13. Stam and Spigel (2016), 1.
14. Spigel and Harrison (2018).

15. Our focus in this book is on geographically defined startup ecosystems. However, we recognise that, increasingly, such ecosystems can be found in virtual, online spaces, as evidenced by the Bitcoin movement and the recent rapid proliferation of Artificial Intelligence (AI) startups supported by online communities such as those found on Hugging Face.
16. Marshall (1920).
17. Porter (1998), 78–79.
18. Adapted from Spigel and Harrison (2018), 154.
19. See Cooke et al. (1997) and Lundvall (1992).
20. Adapted from Spigel and Harrison (2018), 155.
21. See O'Connor et al. (2018), 8, and Spigel and Harrison (2018), 156–157.
22. Adapted from O'Connor et al. (2018), 5.
23. Feld (2012).
24. See O'Connor et al. (2018), 8, and Spigel and Harrison (2018), 156–157.
25. See Spigel and Harrison (2018), 156.
26. Adapted from Spigel and Harrison (2018), 156.
27. Adapted from Spigel and Harrison (2018), 156–157.
28. We note also that startup founders can take inspiration and lessons from entrepreneurs located in more distant places, with individuals like Elon Musk and Steve Jobs often cited in this role.
29. Porter (1998).
30. Spigel and Harrison (2018).
31. Isenberg (2010).
32. Feld (2012).
33. Stam (2015).
34. Spigel (2017).
35. Theodoraki et al., (2018).
36. Vedula and Kim (2019).
37. This section draws on the works of Spigel (2017) and Spigel and Harrison (2018).
38. Hannigan et al. (2022).
39. This section is based on Spigel (2017) and Spigel and Harrison (2018).
40. Spigel and Harrison (2018), 153.
41. Hoang and Antoncic (2003), cited in Spigel and Harrison (2018), 153.
42. Bresnahan et al. (2001) and Kapturkiewicz (2025).
43. Spigel (2017), 54.
44. Hemmert et al. (2019).
45. Such as the influential work of Ferrary and Granovetter (2009) on the role of venture capitalists in Silicon Valley.
46. Stephens et al. (2019), 279.
47. This section draws on Spigel (2017) and Spigel and Harrison (2018).
48. See, for example, the study by Goswami et al. (2018) on the instrumental role of accelerators in Bangalore, the prominent Indian startup ecosystem.
49. See, for example, Spigel (2017) and Isenberg (2010).
50. Spigel (2017), 54.
51. See, for example, Thompson et al. (2018).
52. Kantis and Federico (2012).
53. See Alves et al. (2019), Kapturkiewicz (2022), and Spigel (2017).
54. Xie et al. (2021), 499.
55. Vedula and Kim (2019), 849.
56. Alvedalen and Boschma (2017).
57. Startup Genome (2025).
58. Kapturkiewicz (2022).

Chapter 4
The Emergence of Startup Ecosystems in Japan

4.1 Introduction

This chapter is the first of three to examine the historical development of startup ecosystems in the three major economies of East Asia. It traces the evolution of Japan's startup ecosystems, from its post-war industrial resurgence to its current status as a dynamic hub for innovation. We examine how historical legacies, structural challenges, and policy shifts have shaped entrepreneurial activity in Japan, offering insights into the nation's unique path to technological and economic growth.

The chapter begins by exploring Japan's post-war recovery, highlighting pioneering firms like Sony and Honda that laid the groundwork for postwar entrepreneurship. It then analyses the rise of consumer-driven new businesses in retail and logistics, which capitalised on Japan's rapid urbanisation and growing middle class. We also consider the constraints imposed by Japan's traditional management system—such as lifetime employment and the main bank system—and how outliers like SoftBank and Nintendo navigated these barriers.

Later sections probe into pivotal reforms of the 1990s and 2000s, including financial deregulation and the rise of venture capital, which spurred Japan's first wave of internet startups. The chapter also addresses setbacks, such as the Livedoor scandal and the Global Financial Crisis, which impacted investor confidence and startup strategies. Today, Tokyo remains Japan's startup epicentre, while cities like Fukuoka and Osaka have emerged as secondary hubs through targeted policy support. The chapter concludes with an examination of Japan's growing focus on deep-tech and cross-tech ventures, as well as the persistent challenges of international expansion.

By situating Japan within East Asia's broader entrepreneurial landscape, this chapter lays the groundwork for understanding the region's divergent yet interconnected innovation trajectories. It sets the stage for subsequent chapters on Korea and China, while foreshadowing thematic discussions on culture, policy, and internationalisation in the third part of this book.

Y. Cheng et al., *Unleashing Innovation the East Asian Way*,
https://doi.org/10.1007/978-981-95-6513-9_4

4.2 Post-War Recovery and Emergence of New Japanese Firms

The significant growth of Japan in the Meiji era following its opening to the outside world towards the end of the Edo period was driven by various entrepreneurs such as Iwasaki Yataro (1835–1885), the founder of Mitsubishi (one of Japan's largest multinational corporations), and Zenjiro Yasuda (1838–1921), who founded the financial conglomerate Yasuda, and by investors such as Eiichi Shibusawa (1840–1931), an industrialist generally regarded as the father of Japanese capitalism. Later, entrepreneurial firms in Japan played a crucial role in Japan's post-war recovery following the conclusion of World War II in 1945, a period marked by numerous challenges, including resource shortages and a severely damaged industrial base. Despite these constraints, the emergence of new businesses after the war, particularly in the manufacturing sector, was a testament to the nation's unwavering resilience. Pioneers of this entrepreneurial wave, such as Sony (established in 1946) and Honda (founded in 1948), were among the first to emerge.

From 1946 to the mid-1950s, Japan faced a daunting task of economic recovery, a challenge that was met with major governmental support. The Japanese government's policies, which encompassed financial aid, technological assistance, and industrial policy reforms, played a pivotal role in rejuvenating Japan's industrial base, fostering innovation, and stimulating private sector growth.[1] Key measures included: (i) the implementation of the Dodge Plan in 1949, which was led by the USA and aimed to stabilise the Japanese economy through fiscal austerity and monetary reform; (ii) the establishment of the Ministry of International Trade and Industry (MITI) in 1949, which guided industrial policy and promoted technological advancements; and (iii) the introduction of the Priority Production System (*Keisha Seisan Hoshiki*), which focused on allocating scarce resources to critical heavy industries such as coal, steel, and chemicals. Furthermore, the government's efforts to promote export-driven growth through policies such as the Foreign Exchange Allocation Policy and various tax incentives for exporters in the 1950s also contributed to creating a fertile environment for entrepreneurs who took the risk for growth.

Among the firms that emerged at this time, Sony focused on consumer electronics, starting with tape recorders and later revolutionising the market with game-changing products like the Walkman and the Trinitron television. Honda, initially a motorcycle manufacturer, strategically tapped into the growing demand for affordable and reliable transportation, eventually diversifying into automobiles against the will of MITI—a move that made it a major global player in the automotive industry and a symbol of Japan's post-war economic resurgence. Other notable firms companies that emerged during this period included Kyocera, founded by Kazuo Inamori in 1959. Initially a ceramics company, Kyocera's success can be attributed to its distinct corporate culture, which emphasises employee involvement and continuous improvement. Later, Kyocera expanded its product line to include electronic components and telecommunications equipment, becoming a global company.

These companies were not just survivors of the post-war era but pioneers of innovation and resilience, driving Japan's 'economic miracle' from the mid-1950s to the mid-1970s. Some of them evolved into *keiretsu* conglomerates—sets of companies with interlocking business relationships and shareholdings, and financed by city banks—that harnessed advanced technologies, innovative production methods, and efficient resource allocation to become internationally competitive and rebuilt Japan's economy, laying the groundwork for the next generation of entrepreneural firms. Japan's rapid industrial growth at this time also saw the rise of other manufacturing companies established prior to World War II, such as Panasonic (founded in 1918) and Toyota (founded in 1937), which also became synonymous with manufacturing innovation and quality. These companies, along with the newly formed firms enterprises that emerged after the war, were not only players in Japan's post-war economic success but were also architects of it, each making significant contributions to their respective industries.

4.3 Innovation beyond Manufacturing

Japan's economic growth in the post-war period was not limited to the manufacturing sector; it also encompassed consumer businesses, including retail, food, media, and hospitality industries. With major improvements in living standards and increased spending power, Japan's rising middle class played a pivotal role in fuelling consumer business development, particularly in sectors such as corporate retail, restaurant chains, and hotel chains.

Between 1950 and 1973, Japan's GDP grew at an average annual rate of approximately 9.6%. Growth of around 3.8% continued from 1973 to 1987, one of the world's highest rates at that time.[2] This rapid economic growth significantly increased domestic consumption. For instance, household expenditure per capita rose from about JPY 120,000 in 1955 to over JPY 1,500,000 by 1980.[3] In the retail sector, the number of supermarkets increased dramatically. By 1970, there were over 4000 supermarkets nationwide, a significant increase from the fewer than 100 in the early 1950s. This growth reflected the broader trend towards corporate retailing, which offered consumers a more comprehensive array of goods and more convenient shopping experiences, providing a strong foundation for various new consumer businesses to emerge.

The power of consumer spending was a driving force in the growth of these industries, reflecting Japan's changing economic landscape. For example, entrepreneurial firms such as the restaurant chain Skylark (founded in 1962), the supermarket company Daiei (founded in 1957), and the department store group Seibu (which opened its doors in 1949), became significant players in these service sectors. Skylark revolutionised the restaurant industry by introducing family dining concepts, making eating out accessible and affordable for the average Japanese family. The company expanded from a single store in 1970 to over 1000 outlets by the end of the 1980s. Daiei, a supermarket chain pioneer, transformed the retail landscape by offering a wide range of products at competitive prices, enhancing consumer convenience and choice. By the early 1980s, it operated 160 stores and controlled one-fifth of Japan's food retail market. Seibu, initially a department store, expanded its operations to include hotels and supermarkets. It created a diversified business model that catered to various consumer needs, capturing diverse consumer needs around its flagship department stores.

The growth of Japan's retail and food industries also led to the emergence of new forms of consumer businesses. For example, convenience stores, most notably 7-Eleven Japan (founded in 1973), renovated the concept initially invented in the USA to develop a highly efficient and scalable retail business model that changed the way people purchase fast-moving consumer goods. This convenience-oriented business model caters to the fast-paced lifestyle of urban populations and has become a staple of Japanese consumer culture. Another significant player in Japan's evolving consumer economy was Yamato Transport Company, renowned for its innovative express delivery service that offers reliable, next-day delivery of parcels to households and businesses nationwide. By the late 1980s, Yamato's *Takkyubin*—its trademarked door-to-door delivery service—had become integral to Japan's logistics infrastructure, enabling young consumer product manufacturers to ship goods directly to customers efficiently and cost-effectively, thereby boosting their own competitiveness.

Companies such as these capitalised on the growing demand for convenient shopping and dining options, and their success marked a shift towards a consumer-driven economy in Japan, fostering further entrepreneurial activity in related industries, including logistics, food processing, media, and entertainment. The 1970s and 1980s also saw the introduction of innovative marketing strategies and customer service practices, further fuelling the growth of entrepreneurial firms in these sectors.

4.4 Emergence of the Japanese Management System and Implications for Startups

As the Japanese economy gradually recovered and developed during the 1950s, its rapid growth was accompanied by the formation of a distinctive Japanese management system, particularly in terms of finance and labour.

Concerning finance, Japan's banking system, called "Main Bank system", provided financial stability and close oversight, enabling the managers of the client companies to plan for the long term and confidently invest in large-scale projects. This system involved a primary bank (typically one of the large city banks) taking a central role in providing generous loans, financial services and governance to companies, and by formalising cross-shareholdings in diverse industries, thus ensuring steady capital flows and strategic alignment with national development priorities.[4]

The networks of companies in Japan, known as *keiretsu*, while providing stability and fostering long-term relationships among member companies, created barriers to the development of the new entrepreneurial firms. Interlocking business relationships and cross-shareholdings meant that established companies primarily conducted business within their *keiretsu* group networks, making it extremely difficult for new companies to access large corporate customers or supply chains. The procurement practices of *keiretsu*-affiliated companies favoured long-term relationships with trusted suppliers over innovative but unproven newcomers, creating a "valley of death" for new ventures seeking market entry.

With respect to labour, Japan's lifetime employment system, seniority-based pay, and corporate unions fostered employee loyalty and a stable workforce, all of which were essential for maintaining high productivity levels and low turnover rates.[5] These traditional Japanese labour practices emerged in the post-war period, encouraging employees to invest in their company specific asset through continuous self-improvement and skills development, knowing that their jobs were secure. All this facilitated cooperative labour relations, promoting harmony between management and workers, and allowing for tailored working environment processes that were aligned with each company's unique circumstances.[6] While this management system provided stability and long-term planning advantages to large, established companies, it posed significant challenges to the growth of new companies.[7] The emphasis on lifetime employment and seniority-based promotions created rigid corporate structures that were often resistant to innovation and change, limiting the ability of promising new firms to recruit capable and experienced talent. Furthermore, the banking system benefited larger companies while frequently restricting access to capital for smaller, newer enterprises, inhibiting their growth and scalability.[8]

Further, Japan's postwar economic governance has often been described as a form of corporatism, characterised by close coordination between the state and organised business interests. Rather than laissez-faire or purely pluralist competition among interest groups, Japan developed institutions that integrated large businesses into the policy design process. The corporatist approach meant that major policies—from postwar industrial plans to recent startup initiatives—were often formulated via consensus among bureaucrats and corporate stakeholders, aligning national goals with private-sector buy-in. This tight government–business partnership (sometimes dubbed "Japan Inc.") helped drive rapid recovery and growth by mobilising resources and information across the public-private divide. At the same time, it has been critiqued for marginalising independent voices and slowing the entry of outsiders, a tension that continues to shape Japan's startup ecosystem today.

Similarly, Japan's business culture has been influenced by Confucian values that emphasise hierarchy, harmony, and collective responsibility over individual entrepreneurial risk-taking. Confucian principles, deeply embedded in Japanese business culture, traditionally discouraged the kind of personal initiative and risk acceptance that characterises successful entrepreneurship. The emphasis on group consensus ('*wa*') and respect for seniority created organisational structures that favoured stability over innovation and established relationships over new venture creation. These cultural values contributed to the preference for lifetime employment and incremental innovation within established firms rather than disruptive innovation by newcomers.

Despite these challenges, some entrepreneurs managed to navigate this environment by focusing on niche markets and leveraging unique innovations. For instance, Nidec Corporation, founded by Shigenobu Nagamori in 1973, became a global leader in precision motor production. Nidec's success was driven by its aggressive expansion strategies, including numerous acquisitions that allowed the company to diversify its products and markets. Shigenobu Nagamori's leadership style, characterised by a relentless focus on growth and efficiency, enabled Nidec to thrive despite the rigid structures of the traditional Japanese management system.[9] However, later allegations concerning accounting practices drew scrutiny and raised questions about the firm's alignment with strengthening corporate governance norms in Japan. Another notable example is SoftBank Group, the Japanese multinational investment holding company founded by Masayoshi Son in 1981. It succeeded by adopting unconventional business models and capitalising on emerging technology trends. SoftBank initially focused on software distribution and publishing before expanding into telecommunications and investment. Masayoshi Son's clear vision for the future of information technology enabled the company to continually update its business model and capitalise on various new trends and growth opportunities, particularly in the fields of robotics, broadband, fixed-line telecommunications, and e-commerce.[10] A similar example is Nintendo. Although initially established as a handmade playing card manufacturer in 1889 by Fusajiro Yamauchi, it made a significant pivot into video games in the 1970s under the leadership of Hiroshi Yamauchi. By consistently focusing on creative product development—from the early Game & Watch (one of the first handheld video game systems) to the iconic Family Computer (Famicom) console—Nintendo leveraged unique gaming innovations to capture global markets.[11]

These examples demonstrate that, even within the constraints of the Japanese management system, entrepreneurial companies in Japan can find pathways to success through innovation, strategic focus, and adaptation to emerging market trends.

4.5 Emergence of Japan's First Generation of ICT Startups

In the early 1990s, the first generation of internet startups emerged in Japan. Many experts agree that the introduction of NTT's Dial-Q2 in 1989 created the first wave of digital startup growth. Dial-Q2 was a premium-rate telephone service that enabled content providers to monetise their multimedia content. Innovators like Sanada Tetsuya and Itakura Yuichiro leveraged these opportunities to develop early information services.[12] Despite these advancements, launching and scaling new ventures in Japan continued to remain challenging. For example, due to public pressure regarding the sensitive content offered on Dial-Q2, the service was ultimately terminated.

Meanwhile, around the same period, the TRON (The Real-time Operating System Nucleus) project—a computer operating system designed by Tokyo University's Ken Sakamura in the mid-1980s—continued to improve and attract interest due to its flexible, open design. Subsequently, various derivatives, such as ITRON (one of the world's most widely used operating systems in the early 2000s) for embedded systems and BTRON for personal computing, were actively explored by Japanese companies like NEC, Fujitsu, and Hitachi, fostering a homegrown software ecosystem that encouraged collaboration between academia and industry. This progress showed Japan's ability to innovate technologically, and it highlighted the role of universities in driving innovation, even though it did not fit the typical internet startup model emerging at the time.

Another noteworthy example from the 1990s of a Japanese internet startup is Internet Initiative Japan (IIJ), founded in 1992 by Koichi Suzuki. As one of the first commercial internet service providers (ISPs) in Japan, IIJ played a crucial role in building the nation's internet infrastructure, collaborating with various established companies and research institutes. The consortium's focus on robust network services and early adoption of global internet standards helped pave the way for subsequent Japanese startups, setting foundational technical and business models that would later benefit the broader online ecosystem across the country.

During the 1990s, Japan's internet startup ecosystem was still immature, primarily composed of foreign companies that struggled to adapt to the country's well-established but conservative business environment. This situation gradually changed after an economic slowdown that triggered subsequent policy adjustments. After Japan's bubble economy burst in the early 1990s, the country experienced a prolonged economic stagnation, often called the "lost decade". This slowdown coincided with the 1997 Asian Financial Crisis. Although the 1997 crisis primarily affected other East Asian tigers, Japan was indirectly impacted. The sight of neighbouring economies in freefall, combined with domestic financial failures starting in 1997 (such as the abrupt collapse of Hokkaidō Takushoku Bank and Yamaichi Securities), created a sense of urgency in Tokyo to address structural weaknesses. Policymakers and business leaders increasingly recognised that Japan could no longer rely solely on its established corporate giants and convoy-style banking system to drive growth.

As a result, policymakers were motivated to look towards Silicon Valley's vibrant startup ecosystem for inspiration. By then, Silicon Valley's success was driven by robust venture capital investment, a supportive startup incubation system, and a culture that embraced risk-taking and innovation. In response, Japan introduced several key initiatives to emulate this model. Policymakers and the government started to facilitate the policy framework and support infrastructures for 'Silicon Valley-type' venture incubation in Japan.[13] One of the fundamental policy changes included the Financial System Reform Act of 1997 (also known as the "Japanese Big Bang"). This set of reforms aimed to deregulate Japan's financial industry, encouraging greater competition and innovation within the financial services sector. It included measures to liberalise interest rates, remove barriers between banking and securities businesses, and improve transparency in financial markets. Additionally, the amendment to the "Small and Medium Enterprise Basic Law" in 1999 aimed to facilitate venture capital investment and provide a supportive framework for startups. The law was designed to reduce barriers for new businesses by offering tax incentives, easing regulatory requirements, and enhancing support structures.

At the same time, universities began to play a more active role in nurturing startups in Japan, particularly after the establishment of Technology Licensing Organisations (TLOs) following the passage of the TLO Act in 1998. This allowed universities to start actively commercialising research outputs more effectively, fostering entrepreneurship among faculty and students, and collaborating more closely with industry. The 2004 national university corporatisation, which required national universities to be more independent from the government, further enabled universities to flexibly manage resources for incubation programs and accelerator initiatives, solidifying their position as key contributors to Japan's innovation ecosystem.

Another crucial development in Japan was the establishment of new stock exchanges, such as the Tokyo Stock Exchange's Mothers (purportedly an acronym of "market of the high-growth and emerging stocks") index in 1999, where the shares of startup companies are listed and traded. Established as an alternative to the NASDAQ Japan of the Osaka Stock Exchange, Mothers provided a dedicated platform for high-growth startups to raise capital and go public, offering more flexible listing requirements than the leading exchanges. This encouraged a wave of initial public offerings (IPOs) by internet and technology startups. The expansion of JASDAQ (Japan Association of Securities Dealers Automated Quotation) also played a significant role. Initially an over-the-counter market, JASDAQ was restructured in the late 1990s to become a full-fledged stock exchange focusing on emerging companies. This provided another valuable avenue for startups to access capital and gain visibility.

As a result, Japan's first generation of internet startups utilised these new policies and incubation systems while adapting to the local market. These companies faced numerous challenges, including a conservative business culture, competition from established *keiretsu* conglomerates, and limited early-stage funding. However, they managed to carve out market niches through innovation, strategic partnerships, and persistence.[14]

For example, Voice Media Inc. was established by Masatoshi Kumagai in 1991. In 1995, it launched the world's first internet connection service that did not require customers to register an account. Under the new names of InterQ, Global Media Online then GMO Internet, the company diversified into various internet-related services, including domain registration, web hosting, payment services, and online advertising. A second example is Yahoo! Japan, which was founded in 1996 as a joint venture between the US internet provider Yahoo! and SoftBank. Yahoo! Japan quickly became Japan's leading web portal and search engine by tailoring its services to local preferences and needs. Another startup, Cybird, which was established in 1998, focused on mobile internet services, capitalising on Japan's early adoption of mobile technology. The company offered a diverse range of mobile content and services, including games and ringtones, capitalising on Japan's expanding mobile phone market. Also founded in 1998 (by Susumu Fujita) was the digital advertising company CyberAgent Inc., which expanded into blogging platforms, social networking services, and online gaming after initially focusing on Internet advertising. Another example is the technology conglomerate Rakuten, founded in 1997 by Hiroshi Mikitani, and sometimes referred to as the "Amazon of Japan".

Centred around the online retail marketplace Rakuten Ichiba, the company has rapidly expanded into various sectors, including travel, banking, securities, digital content, and communications services, as well as professional sports. Another example is DeNA, the Japanese mobile portal and e-commerce website provider, which was started in 1999 by Tomoko Namba. DeNA quickly pivoted to mobile gaming after being established as an online auction business. The launch of its mobile gaming platform in 2006 enabled users to play games, connect with friends, and make in-app purchases, capitalising on the early adoption of mobile technology in Japan.

The period from the early 1990s to the mid-2000s was transformative for Japan's startup ecosystems. By learning from Silicon Valley and implementing supportive policies, Japan created an environment that enabled internet startups to thrive. Companies like Yahoo! Japan, Cybird, GMO Internet, CyberAgent, Rakuten, and DeNA successfully navigated traditional corporate challenges and set the stage for future innovation and growth in Japan's advanced technology industries. These startups contributed to the development of a digital economy, helping to shift the country's economic focus towards technology and innovation, and paving the way for the next generation of entrepreneurs.

This wave of entrepreneurial growth did not occur in isolation. It was deeply influenced by the USA internet bubble of the late 1990s, which not only heightened global enthusiasm for internet ventures but also encouraged the establishment of new capital markets such as Mothers (1999) and JASDAQ. While this helped accelerate the rise of internet firms in Japan, it also made them more vulnerable to the volatility of shifting investor sentiment.

4.6 The Livedoor Scandal

The initial growth of the first generation of Internet startups was challenged by a public backlash against the aggressive takeover bids and assertive stance of Takafumi Horie, the founder of the ISP, Livedoor (established in 1996). Following the Livedoor scandal in 2006, which involved allegations of securities fraud and led to Horie's arrest (see Chap. 8 for more details), the Tokyo Stock Exchange (TSE) Mothers index experienced major turmoil.

The Livedoor scandal shook investor confidence and caused a sharp decline in the Mothers index, which dropped by approximately 50% in 2006 from its peak in 2005, reflecting widespread scepticism about the viability and transparency of emerging internet companies (see Fig. 4.1). This decline underscored the challenges that startups often face in maintaining investor trust and navigating Japan's regulatory environment. Indeed, at the time of writing the TSE Mothers index has yet to rebound to its record 2005 level.

For these reasons, numerous Japanese startups saw sluggish growth in their core businesses during the 2000s. To sustain growth and retain customers, numerous startups diversified their operations—a response driven in part by Japanese society's reluctance to adopt and adapt to new forms of business transactions.[15] Rakuten and

Fig. 4.1 Tokyo Stock Exchange Mothers Index performance. *Source* JPX Market Innovation & Research. Available at https://www.jpx.co.jp/english/markets/indices/line-up/files/e_fac2_5_mothers

CyberAgent exemplified this diversification strategy by expanding their business through the creation and acquisition of group companies. Rakuten grew from an online marketplace into a major player in various sectors, including the travel site Rakuten Travel, the financial services provider Rakuten Bank, the mobile carrier Rakuten Mobile, and the professional sports team Tohoku Rakuten Golden Eagles. In this way, Rakuten created a comprehensive group company structure that attracted and retained customers across a broad range of service sectors.

Similarly, CyberAgent Inc. initially focused on internet advertising. The company expanded its reach by creating and acquiring subsidiaries in various digital and entertainment sectors. Today, CyberAgent's group includes Ameba (a popular blogging platform), AbemaTV (an internet TV station), and numerous gaming companies. This diversification allowed CyberAgent to leverage synergies between its business units and to sustain growth despite challenges to its core advertising business. The strategy of both Rakuten and CyberAgent to expand through group companies helped them navigate the slow adoption of new technologies in Japan, enabling them to build resilient, multifaceted business groups that continue to influence the Japanese information and communications technology (ICT) landscape. Nevertheless, it was still difficult for Japanese startups to continue their growth and become influential in a single business area.

In 2008, Apple's iPhone was eventually launched in Japan. Customers were initially reluctant to switch from highly functional feature phones. However, Apple's introduction of subsequent models and the variety of Android phones offered by various manufacturers led to the further growth of mobile internet on smartphones, creating new opportunities for startups. This regenerated the momentum that was temporarily lost due to the capital shortages caused by the Global Financial Crisis of 2008.

4.7 Gradual Development of Japanese Startup Ecosystems

The Global Financial Crisis impacted many national economies, including Japan, in major ways. However, the aftermath of the crisis marked a turning point for Japan's startup ecosystems, especially in the ICT industry. Several vital changes gradually became evident, setting the stage for a more robust and dynamic startup environment across the nation.[16]

One of the most significant developments was the accumulation of management talent in Japan with experience in IPOs and rapid growth. As more Japanese startups achieved successful IPOs, a pool of experienced entrepreneurs and executives was created.[17] These individuals possessed valuable knowledge and skills, as well as cash from the IPOs, which they could apply to new ventures or share with other budding entrepreneurs.[18] Notable examples include former executives from companies such as Rakuten, DeNA, and Gree, who have influenced the strategy and organisation of new startups by demonstrating established methods to accelerate growth. These experienced leaders often reinvest in startup ecosystems by becoming angel investors or mentors to entrepreneurs, further enriching the talent pool available to new startups in Japan.

Between 2013 and 2023, the amount of startup investment in Japan increased at a rate of around 30% per annum (see Fig. 4.2). Various founders who provided funding at different stages of startup growth also contributed to the development of Japan's ecosystems.[19] Seasoned entrepreneurs who had previously succeeded in their ventures began reinvesting their capital and expertise into new startups. This trend helped bridge the funding gap often experienced by early-stage startups. For example, Taizo Son, the founder of GungHo Online Entertainment, established Mistletoe, an incubator and venture capital firm that supports startups from seed to growth stages. These new investors provided startup firms with financial support, strategic guidance, and access to a broader network of industry contacts. They also collaborated with several newly formed Corporate Venture Capital funds (CVCs) and financial institutions that made available significantly larger sums of capital in the later growth stages of startups. The 2023 vintage roster was dominated by CVCs or VCs affiliated with financial institutions (See Table 4.1). Along with the increasingly prominent presence of overseas investors coming to Japan, startups have started to enjoy a more favourable financing environment in recent years.

Over the past decade, larger companies in Japan have also begun to take a more active stance in collaborating with startups, providing funds, technologies, and resources that are beneficial for scaling up a business.[20] CVC funding has become increasingly common, with firms like Toyota and SoftBank investing heavily in startups to foster innovation and remain competitive. For instance, Toyota has established Toyota Ventures (formerly Toyota AI Ventures fund) to invest in early-stage companies in artificial intelligence, robotics, and autonomous mobility. To encourage collaboration between large firms and startups, established Japanese conglomerates began investing in facilities to showcase their operations and explain the challenges they aimed to address through partnerships with younger, smaller ventures,

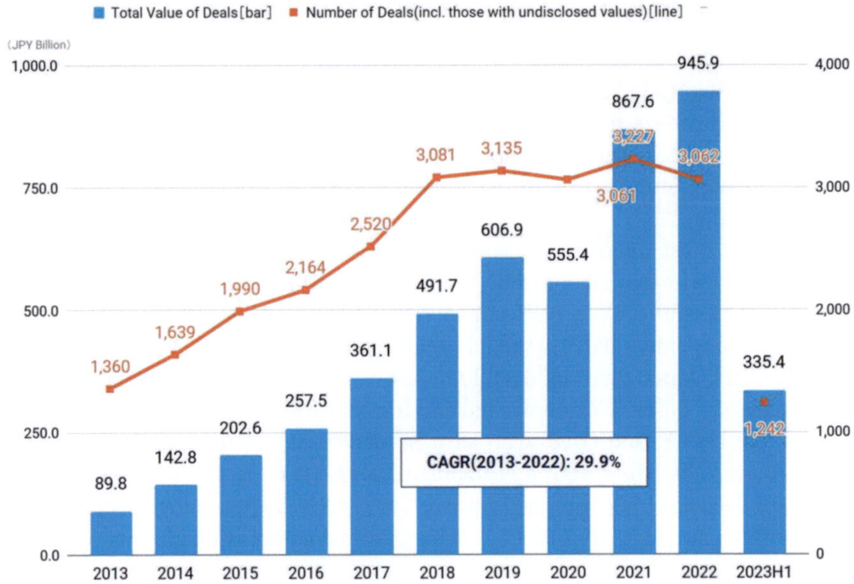

Fig. 4.2 Startup investment amount in Japan. *Source* Globis Capital Partners (2024, p. 7)

with examples including Konika Minolta's Business Innovation Center, Tokyo Gas's Tokyo Gas Accelerator, and Mitsui Real Estate's 31 Ventures.[21] These types of collaborations provided startups with the capital needed to innovate, while also giving larger companies access to cutting-edge technologies and new business models.[22]

As Japan's startup ecosystems developed further, there was a significant increase in business support services tailored to the needs of startups. Legal, accounting, and recruiting firms began to specialise in helping startups navigate the complexities of rapid growth. For instance, Deloitte Tohmatsu Venture Support offers comprehensive services ranging from business strategy to financial advisory; AZX Professionals Group assists with accounting, legal, and patent needs; Plutus Consulting specialises in startup-friendly accounting and tax services, and a company called "for Startups" offers recruiting and talent acquisition services, connecting startups with the skilled professionals they need to grow. Other examples include Novasell, which specialises in marketing and sales solutions, helping startups enhance their market presence and customer engagement, and Speeda, which incorporated the former INITIAL startup data platform, that provides data and insights on startup ecosystems, offering valuable market intelligence that young firms can leverage for strategic decision-making. These support services play a crucial role in enabling startups to focus on their core business activities while ensuring compliance and operational efficiency within Japan's ecosystems.

The role of the government and public institutions in nurturing Japan's startup ecosystems has been weak for many years. Historically, Japan's consensus-driven approach to policy design has influenced the pace and nature of startup ecosystem

Table 4.1 Top 10 new funds launched in 2022 and 2023

Top 10 Funds Launched in 2022		
Fund Name (Management company name)	Size (¥B)	Vintage Date
JIC VGF2 (JIC Venture Growth Investments Co., Ltd.)	200	2022/12
Globis Fund VII, L.P. ★ (Globis Capital Partners & Co.)	72.7	2022/4
JP Investment II (Japan Post Investment Corporation)	70	2022/7
JAFCO SV7 ★ (JAFCO Group Co., Ltd.)	56	2022/6
82 Sustainability I (82 Investment)	30	2022/1
EEI5 ★ (Energy & Environment Investment, Inc.)	30	2022/9
Eight Roads Ventures Japan III, L.P. (Eight Roads Ventures Japan)	28	2022/6
Sony Innovation Fund 3 L.P. (Sony Ventures Corporation)	26.5	2022/2
UMI3 ★ (Universal Materials Incubator Co., Ltd.)	17.1	2022/9
DNX Partners Japan IV, LP ★ (DNX Ventures)	16	2022/10
SBI Venture Fund2023/SBI Digital Space Fund (SBI Investment Co., Ltd.)	100	2023/9
JICVGI Opportunity Fund No.1 (JIC Venture Growth Investments Co., Ltd.)	40	2023/9
Mitsubishi UFJ Capital IX (Mitsubishi UFJ Capital Co., Ltd.)	30	2023/3
SMBC-GB Growth (Global Brain Corporation)	30	2023/7
SMBC Asia Rising (Incubate Fund Management Pte. Ltd.)	27	2023/4
NTT Investment Partners Fund IV (NTT Docomo Ventures, Inc.)	20	2023/4
Mitsubishi UFJ Life Science IV (Mitsubishi UFJ Capital Co., Ltd.)	20	2023/4
QR2 (QR Investment Co., Ltd.)	20	2023/7
ALL STAR SAAS FUND THREE PTE. LTD. ★ (BEENEXT Cap. Man. Pte. Ltd.)	15.7*	2023/8
Delight Ventures No. 2 (Delight Capital Co., Ltd.)	15.1	2023/4

Note Size in billion yen as of February 2024; ★VCs managed by independent manager (not affiliated with any parent organization; *USD 110M, converted at USD 1 =J PY142.7 (According to the company's press release in August). *Source* INITIAL

development. This approach requires extensive consultation and agreement-building among stakeholders before policy implementation, ensuring broad support but often slowing response times to rapidly changing technology markets. The process involves informal consensus-building (*nemawashi*) followed by formal documentation and approval circulation (*ringi*), which can take months or years for major policy decisions.

Over the past decade, however, the Japanese government has begun to increasingly recognise the importance of startups in driving economic growth. It has included them as a critical element of its new growth strategy. While the government's consensus-driven approach has limited Japan's ability to implement rapid, targeted support for specific startups or emerging technologies for many years, it has also ensured that startup policies, once implemented, enjoy broad institutional support and sustainability. For example, initiatives like the Abenomics (e.g., "Japan Revitalisation Strategy", launched in 2013), aimed to create a more favourable environment for startups through regulatory reforms, tax incentives, and funding programs. In 2018, the government established the "J-Startup" program to support selected high-potential startups by providing them with comprehensive support and access to various resources, including mentoring and networking opportunities with global investors, all of which was explicitly aimed at nurturing "unicorn" companies (startups valued at over US$1bn). Also, Japan's adoption of regulatory sandboxes represents a shift toward more flexible policy frameworks for startups. The cross-governmental regulatory sandbox program, launched in 2018, has facilitated fintech experiments, including blockchain-based services and robo-advisors. This approach marks a departure from Japan's traditionally cautious regulatory stance, reflecting the government's recognition that rigid compliance frameworks can stifle innovation. For startups, these sandboxes provide opportunities to validate business models and demonstrate regulatory feasibility to investors, addressing one of the historical barriers to entrepreneurship in Japan's risk-averse business environment.

Moreover, many startup entrepreneurs and experts have become members of government committees to advise policymakers on developing practical policy measures that support the growth of startups. This means that Japan's policy stance toward young, small, high-growth startups has undergone a drastic shift over the past decade. At the same time, the number of startups developed or associated with universities in Japan has increased steadily, reaching a record high in fiscal year 2023 (see Fig. 4.3).

Collectively, these factors accelerated the further development of startup ecosystems across Japan. The increased availability of experienced management talent, diverse funding sources, supportive corporate partnerships, specialised business services, and proactive government policies created a more conducive environment in which startups could thrive.[23] This multifaceted support system enhanced the chances of startup success and encouraged a culture of innovation and entrepreneurship, positioning Japan as a competitive player in the global emerging technology landscape. Despite these advancements, however, startup ecosystems in Japan continue to face several challenges, including cultural resistance to risk, regulatory hurdles, and limited international market penetration. Addressing these issues through continued policy reform, global collaboration, and cultural change will be crucial for sustaining the growth and dynamism of Japan's startup ecosystems.

4.8 Dominance of Tokyo's Startup Ecosystem

Tokyo is pivotal in Japan as a hub for innovation and economic activity, and the city is the home to a substantial portion of Japan's ICT business development. In fact, Tokyo has become a magnet for entrepreneurs and investors. In 2025, around 62% of the startups (16,107 in number) registered on the Japanese startup database, SPEEDA, were established in Tokyo, and over 75% of the total funding for Japanese startups

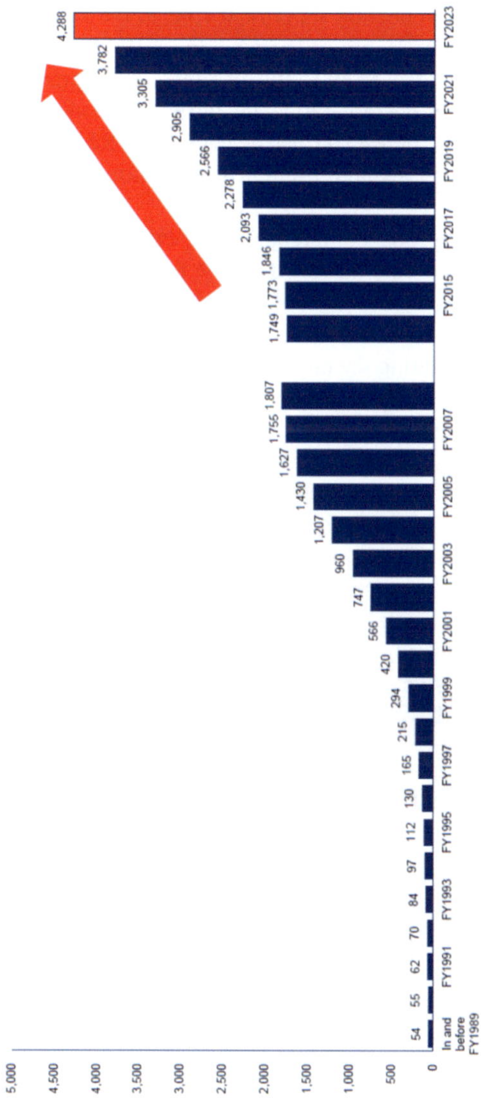

Fig. 4.3 Changes in the number of university-developed venture businesses (i.e., startups). *Source* METI (2024)

in Fiscal Year 2023, which stood at JPY 934bn, was directed towards businesses located in Tokyo.[24] This concentration of technology-intensive startups makes Tokyo the epicentre of innovation and entrepreneurship in Japan.

This concentration of startups is a result of the large economic agglomeration in the Tokyo metropolitan area. In 2023, Tokyo's metropolitan GDP was approximately JPY 106tn (USD 1.11tn), reflecting its critical role in the national economy and accounting for approximately 19.5% of Japan's total GDP. Over half of the Japanese companies with a capital of over JPY 1bn in Japan, and approximately 75% of foreign-affiliated companies operating in Japan, have their headquarters in the city.[25] Additionally, Tokyo is a hub for research and development (R&D), housing numerous research institutions, universities, and corporate R&D centres that drive technological innovation.

Tokyo also hosts numerous conferences and events that are central to the startup community. Major events include the Tech in Asia Tokyo and Slush Tokyo. These events attract global attention, providing networking opportunities, knowledge sharing, and visibility for startups. In 2024, these events collectively drew over 50,000 participants, highlighting the city's status as a global innovation hub.

Although Tokyo is often regarded as an international city, the role of foreign entrepreneurs and returnees from overseas has been somewhat limited. Notable exceptions include the early engagements by pioneering internet firms like Microsoft and Sun Microsystems, as well as several returnees, such as the entrepreneur Yoshito Hori, founder of the private business education company Globis in 1992, who studied how Silicon Valley startups are incubated and provided valuable know-how in Tokyo's formative years as a startup ecosystem. More recently, foreign entities have played less of a major role in the rise of Tokyo's startup ecosystem. Instead, domestic capital, government initiatives, and local entrepreneurship networks have predominantly driven Tokyo's ongoing growth as Japan's leading startup hub.

4.9 Fukuoka and Osaka

While Tokyo is the primary hub for entrepreneurial firms in Japan, other cities, such as Fukuoka and Osaka, have also established vibrant startup ecosystems.

The city of Fukuoka has been particularly proactive in fostering its startup environment.[26] In 2012, the city declared itself a "Startup City", marking a significant shift in its economic strategy to prioritise innovation and entrepreneurship. Since then, the Fukuoka government has launched numerous initiatives to support startups and to position the city as a key player in Japan's innovation ecosystem.

The establishment of "Fukuoka Growth Next", a public-private startup support centre housed in a repurposed former elementary school, has been a cornerstone of these efforts. This facility offers co-working spaces, mentoring programs, networking opportunities, and events that are specifically tailored to early-stage entrepreneurs. The centre has become a hub for collaboration between startups, investors, and government officials, fostering a vibrant community atmosphere. Additionally,

Fukuoka introduced the "Startup Visa" in 2015 to attract foreign entrepreneurs. This program streamlines the visa application process, enabling overseas innovators to establish their businesses in Fukuoka with fewer bureaucratic hurdles. By 2024, the initiative had successfully drawn entrepreneurs from various countries, bolstering the city's global profile and diversifying its startup ecosystem.

Historical factors and local support have also played a crucial role in shaping Fukuoka's entrepreneurial landscape. As the largest city on Kyushu Island and a gateway to Asia, Fukuoka firms can leverage their geographical proximity to key markets, such as South Korea and China, to foster international trade and collaboration. The city is also one of Japan's "National Strategic Special Zones", enabling regulatory reforms and tax incentives that create a more favourable environment for business growth. Fukuoka's universities, including Kyushu University, have strengthened ties with the local government and industry to accelerate innovation.

By 2024, these initiatives had contributed to establishing a flourishing ecosystem in Fukuoka, which is now home to an estimated 800 to 1000 startups spanning various sectors, including fintech, health tech, agrotechnology, and e-commerce. Events like the "Fukuoka Startup Conference" and participation in global networks, such as the Startup Genome Project, have drawn international attention, highlighting Fukuoka as a model for startup development in the country's secondary hubs. Despite these successes, several challenges remain, including the need for increased access to late-stage funding and the development of global-scale unicorns. To address this, the government of Fukuoka is actively exploring partnerships with international venture capital firms, expanding public funding programs, and fostering global talent through additional visa incentives and collaborative projects.

Another notable example of a city-level startup ecosystem in Japan is Osaka. Osaka is also strengthening its startup ecosystem and is becoming a key location in Japan's innovation landscape.[27] Osaka is the centre of a broader regional collaboration across Japan. The municipal government of Osaka collaborates closely with neighbouring cities, such as Kyoto and Kobe, through the Kansai Startup Ecosystem Consortium, which leverages the unique strengths of each city. This consortium supports startups through mentoring programs, funding opportunities, networking events, and global outreach activities. Notably, the consortium has been designated a "Global Startup City" under the Cabinet Office of Japan's initiative to create world-class startup ecosystems, a designation which has attracted significant government support and international attention, further positioning Osaka as a hub for innovation.

Osaka's history as a commercial powerhouse provides a strong foundation for its modern entrepreneurial efforts. The city has long been recognised as Japan's "merchant city", and its role as a trading and financial hub dates back to the Edo period and even before. Central to this legacy is the city's Dōjima area, which became the site of the world's first organised commodity futures market with the establishment of the Dōjima Rice Exchange in the seventeenth century. This innovative system facilitated rice trading and laid the groundwork for financial practices that influenced global markets, with its network of rice brokers arguably serving as forerunners to a modern banking system. Today, the spirit of commerce and innovation fostered in Dōjima continues to resonate, serving as a historical inspiration for Osaka's entrepreneurial ecosystem.

The city strategically focuses on sectors like biotechnology, healthcare, and life sciences, leveraging its proximity to major research institutions such as Osaka University, Kyoto University, and RIKEN (a Designated National Research and Development Institute). The Osaka area also benefits from its robust manufacturing base, which provides opportunities for startups to collaborate with established companies in sectors like advanced materials, robotics, and smart manufacturing. The Osaka Innovation Hub (OIH), a support centre for startups, is one of the cornerstones of Osaka's ecosystem. OIH facilitates connections between entrepreneurs, investors, and global markets by organising events such as Hack Osaka, an annual international innovation conference that attracts participants worldwide. Through these initiatives, the OIH has nurtured approximately 1400 regional startups and supported their growth and development. In recent years, Osaka has also intensified efforts to attract foreign entrepreneurs and investors. The city offers various incentives, including subsidies, office space, and streamlined visa processes, to facilitate the establishment of international startups in Osaka. These efforts have led to a growing presence of foreign-led startups and an increase in cross-border collaboration.

Notably, despite these entrepreneurial ecosystem developments across Japan, led by Osaka and Fukuoka, Tokyo remains the de facto centre of Japan's startup ecosystem. While many small-scale startups are emerging across the country, when it comes to high-growth, IPO-ready startups, Tokyo remains the dominant force in Japan. It is likely to continue doing so for the foreseeable future.

4.10 Japan's Startup Ecosystems Today and into the Future

Over the past twenty-five years, the number of listed firms on the growth market of the Tokyo Stock Exchange has increased steadily (See Fig. 4.4). This reflects healthy and growing ecosystems where companies are reaching significant milestones. Venture funding in Tokyo has also been robust. The total venture capital investment in Tokyo-based startups has exceeded JPY 300bn annually, with a noticeable increase in the number of deals year over year. For example, in 2023 alone, Tokyo startups secured approximately JPY 350bn of financing across 450 deals, indicating a thriving investment climate.

During the mid-2025s, the Tokyo Stock Exchange (TSE) announced that it would implement stricter maintenance criteria across its Prime, Standard, and Growth segments, accelerating the removal of small and underperforming public firms. Growth-segment companies listed since 2025 must reach a JPY 10bn market capitalisation within five years or be transferred to Standard; previously, they had ten years to hit JPY 4bn. While designed to promote genuine scale and encourage exits, these reforms have inadvertently reduced the number of IPOs by smaller startups,

Fig. 4.4 Number of listed companies on TSE Mothers (1999–21) and TSE growth (2022–23). *Source* Japan Exchange Group (JPX) (2024), available at https://www.jpx.co.jp/listing/co/tvdivq0000004xgb-att/tvdivq0000017jt9.pdf (in Japanese)

concentrating investor attention and capital into a handful of larger deals. Institutional investors in Japan now favour fewer, larger-scale listings rather than a diverse array of smaller startup floatings.

Most recently, Japan's startup ecosystems are increasingly embracing cross-tech (i.e., innovations that integrate knowledge and methods from multiple disciplines) and deep-tech (i.e., technologies rooted in scientific breakthroughs) sectors, where traditional industries intersect with advanced technologies. Many startups are emerging in agrotechnology, legal informatics, medical technology, and food technology. For instance, Farmnote is leveraging AI to improve livestock management, while LegalForce provides automated legal services that enhance efficiency and accessibility in the legal sector. Another example is Tabechoku, connecting farmers and consumers directly on a well-designed e-commerce platform (see Box 4.1). These are just a few examples of how traditional industries in Japan are being transformed by new technologies, creating opportunities for innovation and growth.

Until a few years ago, consumer-focused internet ventures in Japan overshadowed cross-tech and deep-tech startups. However, recent policy support, increased venture capital interest, and stronger collaboration between academia and industry have spurred a wave of new companies in areas such as robotics, AI-driven manufacturing, biotech, and advanced materials. Government-backed organisations, such as NEDO (New Energy and Industrial Technology Development Organisation), and various university-led initiatives have helped lower entry barriers, enabling startups in these capital-intensive fields to commercialise cutting-edge research more effectively. This shift is drawing attention from both domestic and international investors, highlighting the significant potential for Japan to lead in next-generation, science-based technologies.

Box 4.1 Tabechoku: Revolutionising Agri-Tech E-Commerce

Tabechoku, founded by Rina Akimoto in 2016, is a Japanese agrotechnology startup that connects agricultural producers directly with consumers through a nationwide e-commerce platform. Akimoto, who previously worked at DeNA, was motivated by her closure of her family's agricultural business to create a platform that supports local farmers and delivers high-quality, fresh food to consumers across Japan.

Akimoto applied her technology and business expertise to address the disconnect between consumers and food sources. Tabechoku partners with over 9000 producers, including farmers and fishers, to provide a wide range of fresh, high-quality food items. The platform emphasises transparency and traceability, allowing customers to understand the origin and production methods of their food. By eliminating intermediaries, Tabechoku ensures fair pricing for producers and competitive prices for consumers. The company employs advanced logistics and supply chain management to handle perishable goods efficiently.

Launching Tabechoku involved overcoming several challenges, such as convincing traditional farmers to adopt digital sales channels, and building a robust logistics network. Akimoto invested in educating producers about the benefits of e-commerce, and developed an efficient supply chain system to ensure timely and fresh deliveries.

Since its inception, Tabechoku has grown significantly, now serving over one million users and featuring products from more than 9000 producers. The company has been instrumental in supporting local agriculture, reducing food waste, and providing consumers with access to fresh, seasonal produce. Tabechoku's success has also inspired innovation in the agrotechnology sector across Japan.

Tabechoku's innovative approach and commitment to sustainability have positioned it as a leader in the agrotechnology industry. Tabechoku fosters a more transparent and equitable food system by connecting producers directly with consumers while delivering high-quality, fresh food nationwide.

Notable investments are also being made in deep-tech sectors that require substantial capital and technological expertise. For example, the Japanese biotechnology unicorn Spiber is leading the way in bioengineering with its innovative technology for producing spider silk. In the aerospace industry, ispace Inc. and Astroscale are making headlines with their ambitious plans for robotic spacecraft, lunar exploration missions, and space debris removal solutions. The deep-tech sector in Tokyo has attracted over JPY 100bn (USD 1.05bn) in venture capital in 2023 alone, highlighting the growing investor interest in these high-impact areas. Most notably, Artificial intelligence (AI) has emerged as a critical growth sector within Japan's startup ecosystem, supported by both government policy and private investment. The government's AI strategy, formalised in 2019 and updated in 2025 with comprehensive AI legislation, positions Japan as a leader in trustworthy AI development while promoting startup innovation. Japanese AI startups have attracted significant attention, with companies like Sakana AI achieving unicorn status within two years of founding. The startup, co-founded by former Google researchers, demonstrates Japan's ability to attract global AI talent and compete internationally. The government's Society 5.0 initiative has created substantial opportunities for AI startups across manufacturing, healthcare, and smart city applications, despite the challenges that remain in acquiring AI talent and competing with global tech giants.

Furthermore, many Japanese entrepreneurs have decided to rise to the challenges of globalisation. While Softbank has been considered a global startup investor, other Japanese ICT startups have not been entirely successful in international markets. Mobile gaming companies like DeNA and GREE attempted to internationalise their gaming businesses but terminated the initiatives. Rakuten's aggressive expansion also did not yield the promised results. More recently, companies such as SmartNews, Mercari, and Uzabase entered the US market but struggled to secure a foothold there (Uzabase suspended the US operation).

More recent Japanese startups, however, have been able to establish a significant presence in global markets. For example, Gojo & Company was founded in 2014 and focuses on extending financial inclusion to underserved populations in developing countries by providing microfinance services. The company has successfully expanded to several countries, including Tajikistan and India, impacting more than two million households through its financial services. Another example, Oishii Farm, established in 2017, specialises in vertical farming and the production of premium strawberries using advanced agricultural technology. With farms in Japan and the US, Oishii has gained a global customer base by blending traditional practices with modern technologies. Josys is another interesting example of a Japanese startup that has rapidly expanded into global markets by fully utilising the networks and capability of the founder, a serial entrepreneur with a track record of successful business development (see Box 4.2).

Box 4.2 Josys: Rapid Global Expansion of a Japanese Born Global Startup

Josys, founded by Yasukane Matsumoto in 2021, is a Japanese startup that quickly scaled to become a competitive global business-to-business (B2B) Software as a Service (SaaS) company. Matsumoto, a serial entrepreneur, had previously founded Raksul, Japan's largest online printing provider, which went public in 2018 with a recent peak market capitalisation in excess of US$1bn.

Matsumoto utilised his entrepreneurial experience to address the complexities of information technology (IT) operations in the hybrid work environment. Josys offers a platform that provides 360° control over SaaS applications and device inventory, helping businesses manage IT operations efficiently. Key features include cataloguing applications and devices, analysing usage, automating tasks, and managing devices, focusing on reducing IT operational costs and improving security.

Josys's rapid global expansion was driven by a strategic approach to team formation and market entry. Matsumoto and co-founder Sanjay Rajasekhar initially prioritised hiring experienced professionals from different regions. Rajasekhar, with extensive experience in multinational companies, played a crucial role in building a globally competent team. They targeted key regions like the USA, India, Singapore, Malaysia, and Vietnam, ensuring that local teams could effectively address regional needs.

The senior management team invested in building an efficient global infrastructure that supports seamless communication and collaboration across time zones and cultures . They also empower regional teams to tailor their strategies to local market conditions, ensuring that Josys was not just another SaaS provider but a partner that understood and solved local challenges.

Since its inception, Josys has grown significantly, now serving over 400 business clients with a team of more than 150 employees. The company's ability to streamline IT operations has driven efficiency and governance for businesses worldwide, making it a rapidly rising player in the global IT landscape.

Josys plans to further expand its product offerings and enter new markets. Josys's rapid ascent as a global B2B SaaS company highlights the potential for Japanese startups to scale internationally. By addressing the complexities of IT operations with innovative solutions, Josys has established itself as a market leader. Matsumoto's strategic vision and commitment to excellence continue to drive the company's success on the global stage.

These examples illustrate that while many Japanese technology companies have faced challenges in globalisation, recently emergent startups are successfully establishing themselves in global markets. Their innovative approaches and dedication to addressing global issues demonstrate the potential of Japanese startups to make a significant international impact. The internationalisation of Japanese startup ecosystems is reviewed in further detail in Chap. 10.

The gradual development of Japan's ICT startup ecosystem from the late 2000s onwards has been marked by substantial advancements in policy support, corporate collaboration, and entrepreneurial talent. Collectively, these changes have fostered a robust and dynamic startup environment, contributing to Japan's economic diversification and innovation. By continuing to build on these foundations, Japan can further strengthen its position as a global leader in technology and innovation. The ongoing evolution of startup ecosystems across Japan promises to drive future growth, create new job opportunities, and enhance the country's competitiveness on the global stage.

4.11 Conclusion

The Japanese economy, relating to new business development, has undergone a remarkable transformation, evolving from post-war industrial rebuilding to a modern innovation-driven economy.

Established post-war giants like Toshiba and Hitachi demonstrated how resilience and government support could fuel industrial reconstruction and growth, while consumer-focused firms like Daiei and Yamato Transport reshaped Japan's domestic economy. We observe how traditional management systems initially constrained entrepreneurial firms; however, firms like SoftBank and Nidec have proven that niche innovation and unconventional strategies can thrive even in conservative and inflexible business environments. Policy changes have also been important catalysts. Financial deregulation, university-industry collaboration, and the growth of venture capital in the 1990s and 2000s were pivotal in fostering Japan's first internet startups, despite setbacks such as the Livedoor scandal. We also discern various regional dynamics at play. Tokyo remains the unrivalled hub for Japan's startups, but Fukuoka and Osaka illustrate how secondary ecosystems can flourish through targeted policies, international outreach, and historical commercial legacies. Future frontiers are emerging, led by deep-tech and cross-tech startups that are addressing global challenges in biotech, agrotechnology, and space technology, though internationalisation remains a hurdle for many.

This chapter highlights Japan's ability to strike a balance between tradition and innovation. As the narrative shifts to South Korea in the next chapter, parallels and contrasts in state-led growth, corporate governance, and global ambition will emerge, further enriching our understanding of East Asia's diverse startup landscapes. The themes of culture, policy, and internationalisation—explored later in the book—will further deepen this comparative analysis, revealing how East Asian startup ecosystems have adapted to the demands of a rapidly changing global economy.

Notes

1. Flath (2022).
2. Statista (1991).
3. Koike (2019).
4. Aoki and Patrick (1994).
5. Kazuo (2005).
6. Koike (1988).
7. Nakamura (2017).
8. Aoki and Patrick (1994).
9. Nagamori (2022).
10. Inoue (2021).
11. Sheff (1993).
12. Okamoto (2000).
13. Sako and Kotosaka (2011).
14. Sako and Kotosaka (2011).
15. Sako and Kotosaka (2012).
16. Kotosaka and Sako (2017).
17. Kotosaka (2018).
18. Kotosaka (2017).
19. Kotosaka and Sako (2017).
20. Kotosaka (2019).
21. JOIC (2018).
22. The Nikkei (2018).
23. Kapturkiewicz and Kotosaka (2019).
24. Takahashi (2023), available at: https://journal.startup-db.com/articles/tokyo-overconcentration2024.
25. Tokyo Metropolitan Government (2024).

26. Fukuoka Growth Next (2024), Kapturkiewicz (2025).
27. Osaka Business Development Agency (2024), Kapturkiewicz (2025).

Chapter 5
The Emergence of Startup Ecosystems in Korea

5.1 Introduction

This chapter explores the emergence and evolution of startup ecosystems in Korea, tracing their development from the late twentieth century to the present day. While entrepreneurial activity in Korea has a long history, the modern startup ecosystem landscape took shape in the late 1990s, spurred by the Asian financial crisis and subsequent economic reforms. Since then, Korea has experienced two distinct startup booms. The first boom was driven by necessity in the wake of economic turmoil, while the second, more enduring boom was driven by deliberate government policies, cultural shifts, and growing private investment.

The chapter begins by examining the historical context of entrepreneurship in Korea prior to the 1990s, highlighting the dominance of large conglomerates (*chaebols*) and the limited opportunities for startups. Next, it analyses the transformative effect of the Asian financial crisis, which served as an inflection point for startup activity. Subsequent sections detail Korea's "startup winter", the resurgence of startups in the 2010s, and the key drivers of this second boom, including policy support and changing career preferences among young professionals. The chapter then provides an in-depth analysis of two major startup ecosystems in Korea—Seoul and Daejeon—showcasing their unique strengths, challenges, and contributions to the national economy. Finally, the chapter concludes with reflections on the current state of Korean startup ecosystems, and the obstacles they face, particularly in terms of global connectivity and talent diversity.

Y. Cheng et al., *Unleashing Innovation the East Asian Way*,
https://doi.org/10.1007/978-981-95-6513-9_5

5.2 Startup Entrepreneurship in Korea Prior to the 1990s

Since the beginning of the twentieth century, there has been a high level of entrepreneurial activity in Korea. Business entrepreneurs, many of them originating from a poor or modest background, achieved remarkable success under very difficult conditions. Korea was annexed by Japan in 1910, then divided into a communist North and a capitalist South after the end of the Second World War in 1945, and later was devastated by the Korean War between 1950 and 1953. Nonetheless, there were various highly successful entrepreneurs who identified and effectively exploited business opportunities across trade, retail and manufacturing in what was then an adverse and chaotic business environment.[1]

When the Korean economy started growing quickly from the 1960s, Korean entrepreneurs established and rapidly expanded diversified business conglomerates known as *chaebols*—large, industrial corporate groups run and controlled by an individual or family. These entrepreneurs built their success on their business acumen as well as on economic development policies by the Korean government that provided them with a wide range of preferential support measures, including low interest loans from government-controlled financial institutions, tax credits, preferential tariffs, export subsidies, and shielding of the domestic market from foreign competitors.[2] As a result of this "guided capitalism" approach, conglomerates such as Samsung, Hyundai Motor, LG, and SK became dominant forces in the Korean economy from the 1970s, especially in manufacturing, trading and heavy industry sectors. While the *chaebol* entrepreneurs themselves had emerged from humble origins, their success effectively constrained opportunities for the next generation of entrepreneurs due to the dominance of their conglomerates across many parts of the Korean economy. Furthermore, because efficient and effective resource orchestration and expansion of operations were the main success factors of Korean companies in scale-intensive manufacturing industries, the competitive opportunities available to new ventures were limited.

For these reasons, there were relatively few technology startups in Korea until the 1990s, and few policies or mechanisms were in place to support them. Gradually, the number of technology startups increased from the 1980s, as the Korean economy rapidly developed and became ever more innovation-driven. For example, in 1989 seven engineering graduates from Seoul National University founded Humax—a company that specialises in the manufacturing of set-top boxes (devices that connect TV sets with external signals) and other consumer electronics. Humax achieved success by specialising in activities that its founders were very knowledgeable about and by pursuing rapid international expansion, all of which allowed the firm to attain critical economies of scale within a niche market. Similarly, Ahn Cheol-soo, a medical doctor, founded the computer virus protection company AhnLab in 1995, capitalising on an antivirus program he had developed after his own computer was infected—an innovation that became the company's foundational product. AhnLab established a first mover advantage in a rapidly growing computer virus protection market at the dawn of the internet age, and succeeded through its strong customer orientation with frequent and reliable software updates.[3]

A defining characteristic of these and other early Korean startups was a strong reliance on the expertise of their founders, strategic targeting of niche markets overlooked by conglomerates, and minimal dependence on external support beyond consumer demand. While these ventures proved it possible to achieve startup success in Korea, they remained a fringe phenomenon until the 1990s in an economy dominated by large conglomerates, which absorbed the majority of available investment capital and attracted the highest-calibre technical and managerial talent.

5.3 The Asian Financial Crisis as an Inflection Point for Startup Entrepreneurship

The landscape for startup formation in Korea changed suddenly in 1997 when the Asian financial crisis pushed the country to the brink of national bankruptcy. To avoid default and receive an emergency loan from the International Monetary Fund (IMF), the government was forced to agree to an austerity programme and various structural reforms that resulted in a deep recession in 1998. Moreover, triggered by a severe balance-of-payment crisis, the Korean Won depreciated by roughly 50% against major global currencies, effectively doubling the debt burden of Korean firms, many of which had accumulated substantial foreign-denominated liabilities in previous years. On top of all this, foreign creditors became reluctant to extend their loans, thereby forcing Korean companies to rapidly pay down on their debt.[4]

Consequently, many Korean firms struggled to survive financially. Between 1997 and 2000, nine of the nation's 30 largest *chaebol* conglomerates either declared bankruptcy or entered bank-led debt restructuring programs. Those that avoided insolvency were compelled to undertake drastic corporate restructuring to remain viable, leading to widespread layoffs. Samsung Group, for instance, slashed its workforce from 60,000 to 40,000 during the crisis—a stark illustration of the period's economic turmoil.[5]

These events profoundly altered the perception of large conglomerates among Korean professionals and university graduates. Previously, working for these conglomerates was highly coveted—not only for the social prestige and competitive salaries, but also because jobs were considered as safe. However, this assumption was shattered as many seasoned and accomplished *chaebol* IT professionals suddenly found themselves unemployed, and young graduates from good universities no longer viewed conglomerates as guarantors of stable, long-term careers.

As a result, Korea experienced an abrupt surge in startup activity following the Asian financial crisis. Many skilled IT professionals departed conglomerates to launch their own new ventures. Among them was Kim Beom-su (also known as

Brian Kim), who left Samsung to found his first entrepreneurial endeavour—a business centred on computer gaming rooms and game development—before later establishing Kakao, Korea's dominant text messaging platform in 2010 (see Box 5.1). In 1999, Naver was spun off from a Samsung group affiliate and subsequently became Korea's foremost internet search engine and web portal under the entrepreneurial leadership of former Samsung employees, including Lee Hae-jin, now one of the richest people in South Korea. Another notable example was Kim Taek Jin, a former researcher at Hyundai Group, who left in 1997 to create NCSoft, the highly successful video game developer and distributor of massively multiplayer online role-playing games such as Lineage and Guild Wars.[6]

Box 5.1 Kim Beom-su: An Early Korean Startup Entrepreneur

Kim Beom-su was born 1966 in Seoul into a poor family, with eight people sharing one bedroom. As a result of his hard studies, he was admitted to the industrial engineering department of Seoul National University in 1986.

Kim Beom-su entered the IT service company of Samsung Group after graduation and became involved with the planning, development, and distribution of computer network communication tools. However, he left Samsung in 1997 and founded his first company, opening a computer gaming room while also developing video games. Initially, he struggled to penetrate the market with his games. He therefore changed his business model and developed an internet cafe administration software that was offered to other gaming rooms free of charge, on the condition that his company's computer games were displayed on the desktop screen of gaming room computers. This business model worked extremely well: his "Hangame" platform attracted one million subscribers within five months.

In 2000, Kim Beom-su merged Hangame with Naver, the company which developed Korea's leading internet portal and was led by his college friend and former Samsung colleague Lee Hae-jin. Kim Beom-su was the new company's joint representative and moved to Silicon Valley in 2005, receiving first-hand experience of the latest developments in IT business, including smartphone-based communication tools.

Leveraging this knowledge, Kim Beom-su returned to Korea and founded a new company in 2006 to develop mobile messaging applications. Among these applications, the KakaoTalk one-to-one mobile chatting service, introduced in 2010, was installed on more than 90% of the country's smart phones within a few years.

Subsequently, Kim Beom-su opened new revenue streams for his mobile communication platform by swiftly adding various applications, including games, taxi hailing, a mobile wallet, and other functionalities. Kakao widened its range of services in various directions, including advertising, digital comics (webtoons), fintech and artificial intelligence. Kakao's contents became popular not only in Korea, but also in Japan and other Asian countries.

Aside from leading Kakao, Kim Beom-su has also established two venture capital firms that are investing in Korean startups. Heading Kakao's startup campus, he is now mentoring young startup entrepreneurs in Seoul.

At the same time, during the late 1990s the Korean government rapidly developed and implemented startup promotion policies to support such new ventures and to help the Korean economy diversify away from a reliance on large conglomerates as drivers of economic growth. Specifically, a Special Law to Promote Venture Capital Companies was enacted in 1997. Under this Law, small- and medium-sized enterprises (SMEs) could seek official registration as venture firms if they (i) received investment by venture capital companies, (ii) were research and development (R&D) intensive, or (iii) were mainly engaged in a high technology industry. Registered venture companies became eligible for various benefits, including tax breaks.[7] These incentives were very attractive, and more than 10,000 companies had successfully applied to be classified as venture firms by 2001.

Korea's first startup boom emerged in parallel with the US dot-com bubble, both propelled by the rapid expansion of internet technologies (see Chap. 2). As in the USA, many Korean startups focused on internet-based IT solutions, including internet portal services, e-commerce, and online gaming. These ventures were predominantly clustered in Greater Seoul, encompassing the capital metropolis and its surrounding Gyeonggi-do province. This spatial concentration reflected Seoul's dominance as a hub for corporate headquarters, leading universities and, consequently, skilled talent pools. Fuelled by an influx of experienced IT professionals from conglomerates and surging customer demand for internet-related services, numerous startups achieved rapid growth and, for the first time, played a visibly important role in the Korean economy.

5.4 Korea's Startup Bust and Startup Winter

While Korea's first startup boom emerged very suddenly in the wake of the Asian financial crises, its decline proved equally rapid in the early 2000s. One major catalyst was the collapse of the US dot-com bubble between 2000 and 2002, which exposed the unsustainable nature of many internet-based business models, triggering plummeting valuations and widespread insolvencies. Given that most Korean startups had adopted similar business models to their US counterparts, scepticism about their viability spread and venture capital investment quickly dried up.

A second critical factor in Korea's startup downturn stemmed from domestic developments. Following extensive restructuring, most surviving *chaebols* emerged from the Asian financial crisis with stronger financial foundations and resumed their growth trajectories. Having now substantially reduced their debt burdens, leading conglomerates such as Samsung, Hyundai, and LG intensified their focus on industries and products where they had strong competitiveness, including semiconductors, mobile phones, home electronics and automobiles.[8] This strategic repositioning enabled them to capture greater global market share and recommence aggressive recruitment of top graduates and experienced professionals. As a result, many high-calibre individuals who had transitioned from conglomerates to startups during the Asian financial crisis reversed course in the early 2000s and returned to the revitalised *chaebols*.

Deprived of both capital and talent, many Korean startups closed their doors during the 2000s. Although some companies founded in the late 1990s survived due to the soundness of their business models and continued customer demand that enabled revenue-based financing, large conglomerates once again assumed a dominant role in many sectors of the economy, and the startup sector was relegated to the fringes of the Korean business system. The resulting "startup winter" created a paradoxical situation where Korea's economy experienced robust growth while most startups struggled to achieve viability, let alone expansion.

5.5 Korea's Second Startup Boom

The second startup boom in Korea, which began around 2010, emerged in a very different manner from the first one. Unlike the initial startup boom—which was an unanticipated consequence of sudden economic turmoil—the second boom was largely policy-driven, reflecting a deliberate governmental shift in economic strategy. While Korea's macroeconomic performance remained strong throughout the 2000s, the renewed dominance of large conglomerates in the most globally competitive sectors generated significant concerns amongst policymakers and the wider Korean society. These apprehensions stemmed from two key issues: first, the systemic risks posed by excessive economic reliance on a small number of large conglomerates, as starkly revealed during the 1997 Asian financial crisis; and second, the disproportionate focus of many *chaebols* on traditional manufacturing sectors, which contrasted with their limited presence in emerging twenty-first century growth industries—particularly technology-based or technology-enabled products and services that were often virtual and intangible. This dual concern about economic resilience and future competitiveness created widespread fear that Korea risked missing out on growth opportunities in the industries of the future.

Throughout previous decades, the Korean government had developed a wide range of support policies for SMEs to mitigate the dominance of large conglomerates. These policies included tax breaks, investment subsidies, training programmes for employees, and much more. However, the effectiveness of these measures was limited, as many manufacturing SMEs—often lower-tier suppliers of conglomerate member firms—suffered from low productivity and a lack of technical expertise amongst employees.[9] Furthermore, the majority of non-manufacturing SMEs were engaged in low value-added local services (such as small-scale retailing, restaurants, real estate agency, and hairdressing) that offered limited growth potential. As the productivity gap between large and small firms persisted and became ever more severe, Korean policymakers turned their attention to startups as a potential new growth engine.

Since the early 2010s, policy support for startups has become very strong and comprehensive in Korea. This includes a wide variety of measures, such as direct investment, matching investment, R&D support, entrepreneurship education programmes, workspace supply, mentoring and consultation programmes, and the organisation of networking events.[10] Financial support measures for startups have been particularly strong, as they encompass not only direct financing of startups through seed money grants or R&D subsidies, but also indirect financing through investment into venture capital funds. Specifically, the Korea Venture Investment Corporation (KVIC) has played a pivotal role in this regard, operating a fund-of-funds system with an accumulated investment of KRW 34.8tn (USD 41.2bn) by mid-2025.[11] As a result of such massive funding support, estimates suggest that in the early 2010s, government-backed sources accounted for at least 90% of all external startup financing in Korea.

Another critical driver of Korea's second startup boom has been an ongoing shift in career preferences among highly-skilled young professionals in knowledge-intensive industries. As mentioned above, it has been the norm for such professionals to seek employment in *chaebols* because of the relatively high salaries, as well as high perceived job security and social prestige, that these positions conferred. While perceptions of job security were battered during the Asian financial crisis, most top graduates from leading universities nonetheless sought work at large manufacturing firms like Samsung Electronics, Hyundai Motor, and LG Electronics in the post-crisis period, judging established corporations to offer superior prospects compared to unproven startups.

Such employment preferences underwent a gradual transformation in the post-2000 period, driven by growing dissatisfaction among young Korean professionals with the demanding work culture at conglomerates, such as long working hours and routine overtime work on evenings and weekends. Younger Koreans had become more mindful of a healthy work-life balance and were no longer willing to sacrifice quality time with their families and friends to the same extent as earlier generations who focused on maximising financial income when Korea was still a poor country. What is more, many younger professionals also became more sensitive to company cultures and workplace practices, which tended to be rigid and hierarchical in the large conglomerates.[12] This meant that young professionals had to strictly follow the directions and orders of their superiors and often had limited room to leverage their own skills, creativity, and ideas. Many Korean knowledge workers in their 20s and 30s became increasingly frustrated by such workplace practices and resigned from their positions in conglomerates to establish or join startups where they could enjoy more work autonomy, flexibility, and empowerment.

Driven by these transformative shifts in both government policy and the career aspirations of skilled professionals, Korea's second startup boom has proven to be far more enduring than its predecessor. This sustained growth is reflected in three key indicators: First, the number of technology startups has risen substantially, reaching approximately 53,000 by mid-2023.[13] Second, the number of unicorns—startups with a valuation of more than US$ 1bn—surged from just three in 2017 to 14 in 2025.[14] Third, and as illustrated in Fig. 5.1, venture capital investment has expanded significantly since the 2010s. Although the post-pandemic downturn mirrored global trends, venture capital funding in 2024 still exceeded 2004 levels by a factor of 5.7, underscoring the substantial maturation of Korea's startup ecosystems at that time.

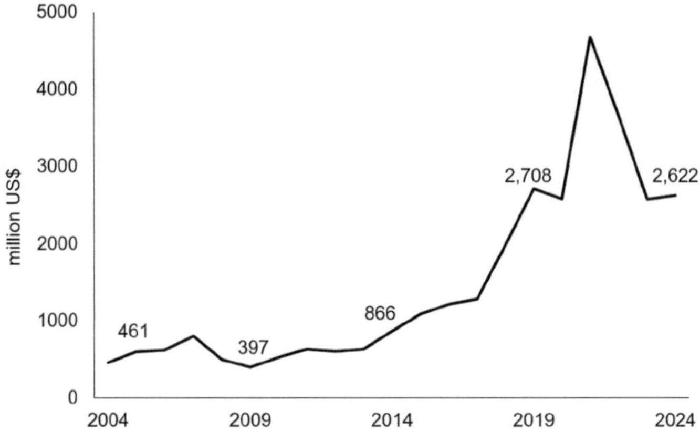

Fig. 5.1 Venture capital investment in Korea, 2004–2024

Since the 2010s, startup entrepreneurship has gained strong momentum in Korea, with technology ventures now exerting measurable influence on the national economy. This influence is not only evidenced by the rising number of startups, and the organisations that support them, but also by their impact on the job-seeking behaviour of young professionals. Indeed, the rising prominence of Korean startups has compelled large conglomerates to reform their human resource strategies to remain competitive for top graduates. In addition to improving financial remuneration, *chaebols* are now modifying traditional workplace practices, including introducing greater remote work flexibility and reducing mandatory overtime, to stem the outflow of talent to more agile startup companies.

Next, we discuss the development of two major city-level startup ecosystems in Seoul and Daejeon, showing how distinct geographic, institutional, and industrial factors have shaped divergent startup ecosystem pathways in Korea between its political-economic core (Seoul) and its premier science cluster (Daejeon).

5.6 Startup Ecosystems in Korea

5.6.1 Seoul

Seoul, officially Seoul Special Metropolitan City, is the capital and largest city of Korea, and it dominates the country's economy. In 2024, Seoul's population stood at around 9.64 million residents. In 2021, Seoul was home to 1.18 million business establishments and its gross domestic product (GDP) amounted to KRW 472bn, equivalent to 22.7% of the national GDP.[15] With approximately 50% of Korea's 52 million inhabitants concentrated in Greater Seoul—an expansive metropolitan region comprising the capital city, surrounding Gyeonggi-do province, and the adjacent port city of Incheon—this urban agglomeration now ranks as the world's sixth largest metropolitan economy.

Reflecting its broader economic dominance, Seoul has by far the largest startup ecosystem in Korea. In a major survey of startups across all regions of Korea in 2019, 53% of participating companies were located in Greater Seoul.[16] Furthermore, many Seoul-based startups are flourishing, and all of Korea's 14 unicorn companies reside in the capital region, demonstrating its overwhelming advantage in scaling new ventures. Within Greater Seoul, startups are highly concentrated in Seoul's Gangnam district and in the Pangyo district of neighbouring Seongnam City.[17] These adjacent zones (separated by just 12 km and with robust road and rail connections) function as an integrated cluster: Gangnam serves as Korea's primary business and financial centre, while Pangyo hosts most venture capital firms. Though Seoul's ecosystem supports startups across diverse sectors such as fintech and biotech, ICT startups are predominant. Several Seoul-based unicorns are now globally expanding their operations (see Box 5.2).

Box 5.2 Karrot: A Korean Peer-to-Peer Second-Hand Trading Platform

Karrot is a digital platform for second-hand peer-to-peer trading within a radius of a few kilometres of users' residential locations. The company was founded in 2015 in Seoul by Gary Kim (previously a trader at Samsung and a product manager at Naver and Kakao) and Changhun Jeon (a former software engineer at Naver).

Through the company's digital application, users can list used products and sell them to peers living nearby. Payments are made through Karrot's digital payment system. Karrot does not charge users any commission on their transactions. Instead, revenues are generated by placing companies' hyperlocal advertisements that target residents in specific geographical areas. Trust between peers is created by disclosing sellers' ratings to buyers.

Karrot's business model proved to be very successful, as it substantially facilitates the trading of second-hand goods between people living close to each other in the same neighbourhood. The company successfully addressed the previously unmet needs of many urban residents interested in selling or buying used products.

Karrot's business has grown quickly and the company achieved unicorn status in 2021. Revenues increased to KRW 189.1bn (USD 224.7 mn) in 2024 and the company posted an operating profit of KRW 37.6bn (USD 44.7 mn) in the same year.

Furthermore, Karrot has globalised its operations. As of 2025, it offers its services not only in Korea, but also in the USA, Canada, the UK, and Japan. In each of these countries, the company focuses on large urban agglomerations such as New York, London, and Tokyo. Co-founder Gary Kim moved to Canada in 2022 to facilitate Karrot's global business expansion, with experienced local experts relied upon to speed up service localisation in overseas markets.

The profiles of ICT startups in Greater Seoul are shown in Table 5.1. We can see that most ICT startups in Seoul focus on software development. Typically, these companies are founded by men with engineering backgrounds. While many startup teams include someone who has worked for a startup previously, only around 25%

have team members who have lived abroad. Foreigners are rarely part of these teams. Funding comes from a variety of sources, including financial institutions, venture capital firms, and angel investors. Although most startups begin generating revenues within their first year, relatively few earn revenues from outside Korea.

Seoul's startup ecosystem has various major strengths that contribute to its dominance in Korea. First, it is home to a large number of organisations that facilitate startup investment. For example, more than 150 venture capital firms are located in Greater Seoul,[18] and it also hosts a large number of angel investors, giving local startups far more funding options than anywhere else in the country. While government support programmes once dominated startup financing in Seoul, private funding has surged in importance. By the early 2020s, private investors accounted for roughly half of all startup funding, a dramatic jump from just 10% a decade earlier.

Second, Seoul offers an unrivalled talent pool in Korea. The city is home to 51 universities with over 840,000 students, including around 140,000 postgraduate students.[19] Seoul also hosts most of Korea's top-ranked universities, notably the prestigious "SKY" universities comprising Seoul National University, Korea University, and Yonsei University. Beyond local graduates, many students from regional universities relocate to Seoul, drawn by superior career prospects and the city's vibrant urban lifestyle.

The Seoul startup ecosystem also benefits from 'returnee' professionals—highly skilled Koreans who bring back international experience after studying or working abroad, primarily in the USA.[20] Some have leveraged this exposure to launch innovative new ventures in Korea.

For instance, after initial startup success in Korea, serial entrepreneur Kim Beom-su temporarily moved to Silicon Valley in 2005 where he gained first-hand knowledge about future business opportunities in smartphone-based communication tools. Equipped with this knowledge, he established several new companies before launching in 2010 the mobile chatting service KakaoTalk (commonly referred to as KaTalk in Korea), which later evolved into Kakao, the leading online services platform in Korea (see Box 5.1). Similarly, startup entrepreneur and Harvard-educated Kim Bom Suk applied his US consulting and entrepreneurial experience to found Coupang in 2010, which now operates Korea's leading e-commerce platform sometimes referred to as the "Amazon of South Korea".[21]

Third, Seoul offers excellent market opportunities for startups. The majority of Seoul startups that focus on business-to-consumer (B2C) mobile applications or services can rely on world-leading internet connectivity and digital infrastructure to reach out to their customers. Furthermore, Seoul's sophisticated consumers are highly familiar with online consumption patterns and thereby create strong demand for digital products and services. Seoul is also a highly attractive location for business-to-business (B2B) startups since the headquarters of most leading Korean companies and the majority of foreign multinational corporations (MNCs) with Korean operations are located here.

Fourth, Seoul provides abundant support infrastructure for startups. The capital city offers not only world-leading digital infrastructure, but also outstanding transport infrastructure. Furthermore, there is an ample supply of free education services for

Table 5.1 Profiles of ICT startups in Greater Seoul, 2021

Location	
– Seoul	67.0%
– Seongnam	11.7%
– Other locations	21.3%
Primary focus of activity (multiple categorisations allowed)	
– Software	72.2%
– Artificial Intelligence	20.4%
– Communication and security technology	9.2%
– Immersive contents	7.3%
– Digital healthcare	7.3%
– All other categories	29.6%
Founder attributes	
– Ratio of male founders	86.4%
– Average age of founders in years	39.8
– Ratio of founders with startup experience	15.0%
– Ratio of founders with a university degree	96.6%
– Ratio of founders who majored in engineering	69.8%
Startup management team attributes	
– Teams including members with startup experience	68.9%
– Teams including members international living experience	26.2%
– Average number of foreign team members	0.27
Funding sources (multiple categorisations allowed)	
– Financial institutions	46.6%
– Venture capital firms	33.5%
– Technology/credit guarantee fund	33.0%
– Angel investors/accelerators	31.1%
– Self-financed	27.7%
– Other companies	22.8%
– Central government agencies	19.9%
– City/provincial level support agencies	11.2%
Performance	
– Ratio of firms with revenues within one year of founding	77.7%
– Ratio of firms with international expansion intention	50.0%
– Ratio of firms with international revenues	18.4%

Source Extracted from Born2Global Center (2022)

starting a business, legal and accounting assistance, and subsidised workspaces, much of which is partially funded by the government. Additionally, there are numerous major startup accelerators (e.g., SparkLabs Seoul, Born2GlobalCentre, D-Camp, Samsung C-Lab, and Seoul Startup Hub) in Seoul, alongside a plethora of business incubators, co-working spaces, and faculty coaching support systems on university campuses for new ventures. Given that most new business founders primarily come from technical rather than business backgrounds, these support services are invaluable in equipping Korean entrepreneurs with essential administrative and commercial competencies. Furthermore, there are also numerous networking events in Seoul to match startup entrepreneurs with investors and other ecosystem participants.

Fifth, the Seoul ecosystem provides startups with the strongest global connectivity in the country. In terms of customers and market opportunities, numerous MNCs have established subsidiaries in Seoul, and many of these companies are potential customers for Korean startups, since they generally focus on technology-intensive business. Some foreign MNCs are proactively engaging with Korean startups. For example, the Google for Startups Campus Seoul was established in 2015 and has provided new ventures with more than US$500 mn in funding by 2025.[22] On the talent side, Seoul has the strongest pool of skilled global professionals within Korea. The country's growing international appeal and the sharp rise in global interest in Korean popular culture since the 1990s—led by K-pop, K-dramas like Squid Game, Oscar-winning films like Parasite, and referred to as the "Korean Wave" (*hallyu*) phenomenon—has seen a significant increase in foreign student enrolments at Seoul's top universities. Many of these foreign students look for professional development opportunities in Seoul after graduation, often at local technology startups. This talent base is further strengthened by Koreans who have returned home after having studied or worked abroad, mostly in Western countries.

Despite these strengths, Seoul's startup ecosystem also faces a number of challenges. First, because of the comparatively young age of the ecosystem, there are still relatively few highly experienced entrepreneurs and startup entrepreneurship experts in Seoul. Consequently, there is a scarcity of high-quality startup education and mentoring services that draw upon real-world experiences. Second, despite the influx of Korean returnee professionals and entrepreneurs, as well as the growing number of foreign students, the diversity of startup entrepreneurs in Seoul remains relatively low. Startup founders are predominantly male Koreans with an engineering background. This lack of diversity puts Seoul startups at a disadvantage when seeking innovative, "out-of-the-box" ideas and solutions, as diversity strengthens creativity.[23]

The most consequential aspect of the limited diversity of startups in Seoul is the relatively low ratio of founders and management team members with a foreign background or with international living and working experience. Consequently, Seoul-based startups are predominantly domestic-oriented and develop business models and products specifically for the Korean market. This approach differs from the "born global" strategy frequently pursued by many Western startups—the development of solutions that can be quickly rolled out across national borders from the outset. Seoul-based startups often attempt to expand internationally after having been successful within Korea. However, they typically face steep hurdles when doing so due to the lack of international expertise and international networks of their management teams, and because of the costs of adapting products for overseas customers that have been initially developed for the Korean market. Moreover, delayed international expansion frequently means competing with entrenched rival firms in foreign markets and technology sectors where first-mover advantages are critical. As a result, the global performance of Seoul startups often lags behind that of their domestic operations.

Overall, the Seoul startup ecosystem has grown impressively since the 2010s, building on its major strengths in talent supply, venture capital availability, government support initiatives, digital infrastructure, and global connectivity. It is not only the dominant startup ecosystem in Korea, but it has also joined the ranks of leading ecosystems worldwide. To illustrate, Seoul was ranked 8th in the 2025 Global Startup Ecosystem Report, which assessed 350 ecosystems around the world.[24] Seoul's global ranking has risen steadily over the years, highlighting its increasing dynamism compared to many of its international peers. However, to sustain and enhance this global competitiveness, Seoul must address a key limitation: the lack of international diversity among founders and management teams. Greater inclusion of global perspectives would enable Seoul-based startups to accelerate their international expansion—which historically has been relatively slow—and support their transition from domestic market leaders to true global contenders.

5.6.2 Daejeon

Aside from Seoul, Daejeon is home to the largest and strongest startup ecosystem in Korea.[25] Daejeon is a regional hub located 150 km south of Seoul close to Korea's geographical centre, with a population of approximately 1.5 million people. Daejeon's relevance for innovation and entrepreneurship can be traced back to the establishment of a science town in the city's Daedeok district in 1973. Inspired by Japan's Tsukuba Science City, the aim of Daedeok Science Town was to build basic research capabilities in a remote location where scientists could focus on their research without distractions. While Daedeok Science Town was initially created around newly established higher education institutions, including the prestigious Korea Advanced Institute of Science and Technology (KAIST), and various government research laboratories (such as the Electronics and Telecommunications Research Institute and the Korea Aerospace Research Institute), the number and role of companies located there, including technology startups, has increased over time. Renamed Daedeok Innopolis, the science town has now evolved into a vibrant startup ecosystem with strong networks between government research institutes, universities, and technology firms.[26] Because of the high concentration of PhD researchers in the applied sciences, and well-established long-term research programmes, the number of IT startups in both Daedeok and Daejeon as a whole has rapidly increased.

Daejeon's startup ecosystem can be characterised as a "deep science" ecosystem, where 15 leading universities with many foreign students, 46 major research institutes, 28 government agencies and thousands of startups are co-located.[27] The majority of startups are focused on biotechnology, nanotechnology, logistics and defence robotics. In particular, a strong biotechnology cluster has emerged in Daejeon that has contributed to the rapid growth of the Korean biotechnology industry as a whole,[28] and some Daejeon-based biotech companies have become very prominent in this sector (see Box 5.3).

Box 5.3 Bioneer: A Biotechnology Startup from Daejeon

Founded in 1992, Bioneer Corporation, headquartered in Daejeon, Korea, is a prominent biotechnology company. It is renowned for being the first Korean biotech company to have made significant contributions to the field of molecular biology and diagnostics. The company has been listed on KOSDAQ, Korea's stock exchange market for small and medium-sized companies, since 2005.

Park Han-Oh, the founder of Bioneer, worked as a researcher at KAIST in Daejeon after studying chemistry at Seoul National University. While working in the laboratory, he frequently used imported equipment and observed that exclusive domestic distributors of equipment imported from the USA added major markups, resulting in more than double of the price compared with US prices. Faced with this situation, he realised that it would be unfeasible to compete successfully with American researchers when starting at the same time with similar ideas. This insight motivated him to found Bioneer, with the goal of creating a genetic technology base within Korea.

Based on technologies developed in-house, Bioneer's product portfolio includes molecular diagnostics instruments and kits, oligonucleotides, and research products. The company has also developed tools for gene manipulation, such as thermostable polymerases, and it provides services in gene synthesis and protein expression.

Bioneer became well-known for its diagnostic kits and experienced dramatic growth during the COVID-19 pandemic, when it supplied COVID-19 test kits not only domestically, but also internationally. Bioneer's annual revenues skyrocketed from KRW 36bn in 2019 to KRW 224bn in 2021.

Even after the pandemic had receded, Bioneer's business performance remained strong due to its diversified product portfolio. The company has developed a range of diagnostic kits for other major diseases, including hepatitis, AIDS, and tuberculosis. Bioneer is also involved in industrial and applied sciences, offering solutions for animal and plant diseases, food safety, and nanobiotechnologies.

The Daejeon startup ecosystem has gained strength across various domains.[29] Specifically, in terms of talent supply, the ecosystem benefits from a large number of highly skilled graduates from leading universities in the city and adjacent areas, many of whom have published scientific papers and acquired patents. Approximately 40% of all startup founders in Daejeon are female, indicating a high degree of gender diversity. As regards startup funding infrastructure, 24 accelerators and three venture capital firms are located in Daejeon, and the city is seen as a regional hub of startup finance. Daejeon also offers abundant startup education facilities and coworking spaces in the public as well as the private sector. Startup networking events are frequently organised by various public and private sector organisations. Networks of startup entrepreneurs, investors and facilitators have become dense and strong, with frequent formal and informal meetings.

Nonetheless, the Daejeon startup ecosystem also faces some challenges. First and foremost, startups in the city frequently encounter difficulties in attracting and retaining highly qualified talent. Despite the high number of universities in and around Daejeon, many graduates and young professionals tend to gravitate towards the capital agglomeration of Seoul, in the belief that it will offer them superior professional development opportunities and a more vibrant personal life. Furthermore, Daejeon ecosystem participants report that it could benefit from deregulation and a reduction of administrative burdens for venture capital investment, as well as more effective information sharing across various startup support programs.[30]

Overall, while the Daejeon startup ecosystem is far smaller than its counterpart in Seoul, it has emerged as a strong regional startup cluster with a differentiated profile. Specifically, the Daejeon ecosystem has strong foundations in basic science and research, and these foundations support startups in science-based industries such as biotechnology, nanotechnology, and robotics. Arguably, the Daejeon ecosystem's growth and strong performance is very important in the Korean context, since it demonstrates that it is possible to create a competitive regional ecosystem outside of the seemingly dominant capital agglomeration of Seoul. To reinforce the competitiveness of the Daejeon startup ecosystem in the long term, it is crucial to enhance the region's attractiveness for highly skilled knowledge workers and their families as a place to work and live.

5.7 Outlook

Startup entrepreneurship has rapidly strengthened in Korea since the 2010s. While governmental funding was initially the dominant driver of the country's second startup boom, private funding now plays a bigger role for startup finance. Furthermore, attitudes towards startup entrepreneurship have clearly become more positive, not only among skilled young professionals but also among their parents, who are highly influential in determining their offspring's career choices in a country with strong Confucian cultural traditions. For all these reasons, technology startups play an increasingly important role in the Korean economy.

Inevitably, Greater Seoul has the largest and strongest startup ecosystem in Korea due to the dominance of the capital agglomeration in the national economy. Seoul's startup ecosystem is particularly impressive in the ICT industry, while there are also many startups in other industries. Numerous unicorns have emerged across a wide range of products and services, including e-commerce, cloud computing, online gaming, peer-to-peer trading, online delivery, fintech, publishing, advertising, and cosmetics. Examples of Seoul-based unicorns include Yello Mobile (founded in 2012 as a startup incubator), Viva Republica (the operator of the popular financial application Toss founded in 2014), the e-commerce companies Kurly and Wemakeprice, and the fashion company Musinsa.

Furthermore, at least one more city-level ecosystem has gained considerable momentum in recent years. Daejeon, which became the location of Korea's first major science town in the 1970s, has subsequently evolved into a strong regional startup ecosystem, with a focus on science-based industries such as biotechnology, nanotechnology and robotics. While it is challenging for startups in Daejeon to attract and retain top-notch talent due to the gravitational pull of Seoul, the success of many of these companies and the growth of the Daejeon startup ecosystem as a whole demonstrate that it is possible to establish secondary startup ecosystems in Korea that can differentiate themselves from Seoul in a sustainable manner.

While startup entrepreneurship in general, as well as startup ecosystems in locations such as Seoul and Daejeon, have demonstrated remarkable progress, significant challenges for Korean startups persist. Some barriers, such as talent acquisition difficulties (stemming from the traditional preference to work for large Korean conglomerates) and a shortage of experienced entrepreneurs to mentor the next generation of founders, are gradually easing due to cultural shifts and ongoing growth of Korea's relatively young startup ecosystems. In contrast, the relatively weak global connectivity of the country's startup ecosystems presents a more difficult and enduring challenge. Startup founders and management teams are still predominantly Korean nationals, and many lack the knowledge and perspective to launch "born globals" and expand to foreign markets from the outset. This lack of international perspective means that many Korean startups prioritise domestic markets before attempting international expansion, a sequential approach that often proves ineffective in fast-moving high-technology sectors where first-mover advantages are crucial.

In recent years, the rapidly growing number of foreign students gives Korean startups an opportunity to address their dearth of international talent. Many of these foreign students achieve high Korean language proficiency, and immigration rules have been softened to allow foreigners to apply for visas to establish technology startups. Nonetheless, foreigners still find it difficult to found or join startups in Korea due to cultural differences.[31] More openness and willingness to embrace foreign talent is needed to strengthen the diversity and global connectivity of startup ecosystems and to enable Korean startups to develop and effectively implement "born global" business strategies.

5.8 Conclusion

The development of startup ecosystems in Korea reflects a remarkable transformation from a conglomerate-centric economy to one that embraces entrepreneurial innovation. This chapter has highlighted how historical context matters for startup ecosystem development. In Korea, the dominance of *chaebols* early in the country's economic development constrained entrepreneurial activity, but crises and external shocks like the Asian financial crisis served as catalysts for new venture formation by creating the space for startups to emerge and grow. Government policy is also an important catalyst. In Korea, government support, particularly since the 2010s, has been instrumental in fostering startup growth, with initiatives ranging from financial incentives to infrastructure development.

The chapter also highlights how culture, and especially cultural shifts, can play a key role in the evolution of startup ecosystems. In Korea, changing attitudes among young professionals—who now prioritise autonomy, work-life balance, and creative freedom—fuelled to a great extent the country's second boom in startup formation, challenging the traditional allure of careers in *chaebols* and drawing attention to the significance of quality-of-life as a success factor in the performance of startup ecosystems. The chapter also draws attention to the diversity of startup ecosystems, even within countries. In the case of Korea, Seoul's dominance as a startup hub is undeniable, but secondary ecosystems like Daejeon demonstrate the potential for specialised, science-driven startup clusters to thrive outside of a nation's capital.

Finally, the chapter illustrates the important role played by internationalisation in the development of startup ecosystems, which will be discussed in Chap. 10 in further detail. On the one hand, cultural trends like the growing interest in Korean popular culture—the Korean Wave—and the advent of social media and the internet, have helped Korean companies to reach overseas audiences, and increased the attractiveness of the country as a place for foreign students to study and work. On the other hand, Korean startups often struggle to expand internationally despite their domestic success, with limited diversity in founding teams and a lack of global perspectives serving as major constraints. Addressing these shortcomings will be critical for the future competitiveness of Korean startup ecosystems, an observation that will be relevant to the development of startup ecosystems in other parts of the world.

Notes

1. Hemmert and Kim (2021).
2. Chang (2003); Hemmert (2018).
3. Hemmert (2018), 86–87.
4. Chang (2003); Hemmert (2018).
5. Rowley and Bae (2002).
6. Hemmert (2018), 88–90, 94.
7. Ko and Shin (1999).
8. Hemmert (2018), 67–79.
9. OECD (2023).
10. Hemmert and Kim (2021).
11. Korea Venture Investment Corp (2025).
12. Hemmert (2018), 193–197.
13. STEPI (2023).
14. CB Insights (2025).
15. Seoul Open Data Square (2025).
16. Hemmert and Kim (2021).
17. Born2global Centre (2022).
18. KVCA (2025).
19. Ministry of Education (2025).
20. Hemmert (2018).

21. Hemmert and Kim (2021), 57–61.
22. Google for Startups Campus (2025).
23. Talke et al. (2011).
24. Startup Genome (2025).
25. Kim and Kim (2023).
26. Hwang et al. (2018).
27. Kim and Kim (2023).
28. OECD (2023).
29. Kim and Kim (2023); KVCA (2025).
30. Kim and Kim (2023).
31. OECD (2023).

Chapter 6
The Emergence of Startup Ecosystems in China

6.1 Introduction

This third country chapter of our book reviews China's reform and opening-up since the late 1970s, and their profound impact on the evolution of startup ecosystems in the country. The focus is exclusively on the startup ecosystems of mainland China, deliberately excluding Taiwan and the special administrative regions of Hong Kong and Macau due to their significant differences in economic structures, regulatory environments, and entrepreneurial cultures. Mainland China's unique economic policies, rapid industrialisation, and vast market scale have shaped a dynamic startup landscape, warranting focused analysis. Innovation hubs such as Beijing, Suzhou, Chongqing, and Shenzhen are analysed, with comparisons made regarding their entrepreneurial environments, policy support, financing channels, and talent development, to highlight within-country similarities and differences. Our historical review and comparative analysis reveal the unique advantages and challenges each city faces in shaping its startup ecosystem, while also providing valuable insights into how various regions in mainland China adapt to entrepreneurship and innovation based on their specific economic and social contexts. Ultimately, through a comprehensive analysis of the unique entrepreneurial landscape in mainland China, the specific challenges and opportunities faced by entrepreneurs are highlighted. This exploration provides essential insights for policymakers as they seek to foster a more balanced and sustainable development of startup ecosystems in China, as well as for entrepreneurs looking to understand the distinctiveness of startup ecosystems in the country.

Y. Cheng et al., *Unleashing Innovation the East Asian Way*,
https://doi.org/10.1007/978-981-95-6513-9_6

6.2 Start-Up Entrepreneurship Prior to 2014

The emergence and evolution of startup ecosystems in China is a compelling narrative of rapid transformation and increasing globalisation. Prior to 1978, China's economy was predominantly characterised by government control, with state-owned enterprises (SOEs) central to industrial production and economic management. SOEs dominated various sectors, including manufacturing, mining, utilities, and transportation, operating under a central planning model that dictated production targets, pricing, and resource allocation. The landscape began to shift in 1978 when Deng Xiaoping initiated a wave of economic reforms known as "Reform and Opening-Up." This period marked a transition towards market mechanisms and the influx of foreign direct investment (FDI).

During the initial phase of economic reform, the focus was on revitalising agriculture. Later, these reforms gradually extended to industry and technology. The 1990s witnessed a strong commitment to market-oriented changes, leading to a reduction of the state's direct role in the economy. Decentralisation efforts resulted in significant reforms aimed at increasing efficiency. Many small and uncompetitive SOEs were privatised or closed and, by 1992, the goal of establishing a socialist market economy was set forth. The liberalisation of market access diminished direct government intervention, allowing the market to take a more important role in resource allocation. By 1997, the number of SOEs had decreased dramatically, with their share of total employment falling from over 70% in 1978 to around 30%.

The establishment of stock exchanges in Shanghai and Shenzhen during the early 1990s created opportunities for private enterprises to raise capital, aiding the transition of former SOEs into shareholding companies. By 2024, the Chinese stock markets had grown substantially, reflecting a flourishing private sector. Private companies have begun to thrive, marking a new chapter in the country's economic development.

Alongside the growth of private enterprises, various initiatives emerged to foster innovation and entrepreneurship. The inception of science parks and business incubators during the mid-1980s represented a significant milestone. In 1984, the concept of establishing such centres was introduced, leading to the creation of the first incubator in Wuhan in 1987, followed by another in Shenzhen. This trend rapidly expanded to other cities like Xi'an, Tianjin, Shanghai, Guangzhou, and Beijing, contributing to a vibrant network of startup ecosystems in the country (see Table 6.1).[1]

Notably, while these incubators have shared similarities with their Western counterparts, they are often referred to as "high-tech industrial parks" or "high-tech entrepreneurship service centres" in China. While Western incubators tend to focus on providing office space, entrepreneurial guidance, and financial support to help

Table 6.1 Total number of incubators in mainland China: 1987–1998

Year	1987	1990	1991	1992	1993	1994	1995	1996	1997	1998
Total number	2	30	36	50	60	73	73	80	90	100

young ventures progress from concept to maturity, emphasising market-driven operations, the early Chinese incubators were usually aligned with local governments and industrial policies. They were designed not only to support startups but also to drive regional economic development, industrial upgrades, and technological innovation, resembling "industrial parks".[2] Chinese incubators have benefitted from various government-led initiatives, including the provision of land, tax incentives, and financial subsidies, to attract entrepreneurs. Unlike Western incubators, which depend more on market demands with minimal government intervention, Chinese incubators are deeply linked to the country's "science and technology for national strength" strategy. This has led to the development of zones and parks that focus on technological transformation and economic revitalisation. Their dual role in advancing technology-intensive industries and economic growth distinguishes Chinese incubators from many Western counterparts, reflecting their comprehensive policy-driven mission.

As a key element of the "Torch Plan", launched by the Ministry of Science and Technology in 1988, science parks have become crucial for technology startups in China, providing essential resources such as investment funds, research facilities, and support services. They have also cultivated a vibrant entrepreneurial culture, enabling entrepreneurs to engage in resource-sharing and collaboration. Government policies have been instrumental in creating a stable framework for technology-intensive companies to thrive. By the mid-1990s, over 50 national-level high-tech zones had been established. The policy orientation, resource advantages, cluster effects, and potential opportunities represented by these regions have consequently attracted growing domestic market attention, offering startups diverse scaling opportunities.

Post-2000, as China deepened its integration into the global economy—marked by its accession to the World Trade Organisation (WTO) in 2001—greater governmental emphasis was placed on innovation and entrepreneurship. This led to a surge in startups across various sectors, including biotechnology and information technology, transforming cities like Shenzhen from manufacturing bases into recognised innovation hubs. Supported by the launch in 2010 of China's National Talent Development Plan, returnees—entrepreneurs who returned from studying or working abroad and are commonly known as "*Haigui*" which sounds like "sea turtles" in Chinese—have played a vital role in the development of Chinese startup ecosystems, bringing with them advanced knowledge and insights that drive innovation. In a way reminiscent of sea turtles returning to their natal beaches, these returnee entrepreneurs bring back advanced knowledge and global insights, enriching the domestic startup ecosystem. Their understanding of global market dynamics has been key to establishing successful technology startups like Sohu (the Internet company founded in 1996 by Charles Zhang after he had completed his PhD at Massachusetts Institute of Technology), Baidu (another Internet services and artificial intelligence company, founded in 2000 by the entrepreneurs Robin Li and Eric Xu) (see Box 6.1),[3] and HongShan Capital Group (formerly known as Sequoia Capital China), contributing significantly to job creation and economic growth in China.

Box 6.1 Robin Li and the Founding of Baidu

Dr. Robin Li (Li Yanhong) was born in 1968 in Yangquan, Shanxi Province. Both of his parents were factory workers. He is the founder, chairman, and Chief Executive Officer (CEO) of the Chinese technology MNC, Baidu Inc. In 1991, he graduated from the Information Management Department of Peking University and subsequently pursued a Master's degree and PhD in Computer Science at the State University of New York (SUNY), Buffalo, USA. During his time in the USA, Li explored search engine technology, mastering its core principles and successfully obtaining a patent for "hyperlink analysis" technology. This patent became a foundational invention that shaped the development and trajectory of modern search engines, providing crucial technical support for Baidu's future growth.

Following his graduation, Robin Li worked as a senior consultant at Dow Jones (where he designed an online real-time financial information system for The Wall Street Journal) and later as a senior engineer at Infoseek, a prominent and pioneering internet search engine company. His experience at Infoseek deepened his understanding of market demand and business models for search engines. At the same time, the Chinese internet sector was undergoing significant transformations. From 1995 onwards, Li returned to China annually for research, observing the immense growth potential for Chinese-language search engine services.

In the summer of 1998, during a technical lecture at Tsinghua University, Li inspired a group of Sohu employees who encouraged him to return to China and start his own venture. In 2000, he resigned from Infoseek and returned to Beijing's Zhongguancun to co-found Baidu with his friend Eric Xu Yong, the Chinese entrepreneur, investor and philanthropist.

Li's overseas experience had familiarised him with international capital markets, allowing him to secure US$1.2 mn in venture capital before his return to China. This initial funding was vital for Baidu's early stages, and his international background and professional reputation enhanced investor confidence in the company.

At that time, although the Chinese internet was booming, search engine technology was lagging, creating a substantial market gap. Recognising this opportunity, Li decided to introduce his patented search engine technology to China. The "hyperlink analysis" patent provided a solid foundation for the development of modern search engines, and alongside Xu Yong, they rapidly developed the world's first Chinese-language search engine, distinguished by its advanced technology and innovative approach.

In 2001, when Li proposed transforming Baidu into an independent search engine with a paid ranking system, he faced strong opposition from shareholders. They feared that shifting focus would jeopardise Baidu's existing income from providing search technology services to portal sites, especially since the new model offered no immediate revenue. Despite significant challenges to his confidence, Li remained resolute. Ultimately, his determination swayed investors, and Baidu transitioned to an end user-oriented search engine.

In October 2001, Li and Xu officially launched Baidu Search, just a year after the establishment of Google's Chinese site. In 2002, Baidu introduced the "Lightning Plan", aiming to technologically outpace Google within nine months. Although Google was the dominant global search engine, Baidu captured 80% of the Chinese market. The Lightning Plan proved successful, propelling Baidu's rapid rise in the Chinese market. By 2010, under Li's leadership, Baidu had become the world's second-largest independent search engine and the largest Chinese-language search engine.

Many returnees hold influential positions in academia, government, and industry, where they shape policies and establish supportive infrastructures for entrepreneurship. Their knowledge of global standards has driven reforms and innovations across Chinese universities, research institutions, and policy-making bodies. Initiatives like the "Thousand Talents Plan", launched in 2008, were designed to attract highly skilled scientists and entrepreneurs back to China, effectively reversing 'brain drain' into 'brain gain'. Policies influenced by returnees subsequently streamlined regulatory environments, provided new funding for startups, and established specialised incubators and accelerators to nurture entrepreneurial activities.

Returnees have also helped domestic entrepreneurs to access foreign markets and resources.[4] Their bilingual and multicultural capabilities enable them to effectively navigate both Chinese and Western business landscapes. Additionally, returnees often possess extensive international networks, connecting academia, industry leaders, venture capitalists, and entrepreneurs, which can be used to attract foreign investment and facilitate collaborations. As a result, returnees bridge the gap between China and the global business community, fostering smoother technology transfers and the exchange of ideas.

By embedding innovation into its economic framework, China has become a global powerhouse of technological entrepreneurship. By the early 2010s, its startup ecosystems had matured and diversified, with cities like Hangzhou, Chengdu, and Wuhan emerging as new innovation centres. Hangzhou, for example, has become synonymous with e-commerce entrepreneurship due to the presence of Alibaba, the e-commerce, retail, and internet multinational corporation (MNC) founded in 1999 by the businessman and philanthropist Jack Ma.

The transformation of startup ecosystems in China was marked by the growth and diversity of their support systems. A strong network of venture capital firms, angel investors, and accelerators emerged, providing essential financial and mentoring resources for startups. Government-backed funds played a crucial role in supplying seed capital for early-stage ventures, with initiatives such as the "National SME Development Fund" and various local funds aimed at supporting innovative enterprises. These funds helped mitigate risks for private investors, encouraging more private capital to flow into early-stage startups. Following China's accession to the WTO in 2001, a significant influx of foreign capital further accelerated the expansion of the venture capital landscape, with international firms like Sequoia Capital and IDG Ventures entering the market alongside flourishing domestic firms like Legend Capital and Shenzhen Capital Group. The success of Initial Public Offerings (IPOs) of technology giants such as Alibaba and Baidu legitimised venture capital as a viable investment mechanism in China.

University-led innovation also gained traction as partnerships between universities and businesses increased, facilitated by government policies that promoted public–private collaboration. Numerous Chinese universities established science and technology parks to translate academic research into commercial products. During the government's 12th Five-Year Plan (2011–2015), the "Innovation-Driven Development Strategy" emphasised the pivotal role of universities in national innovation systems, with leading institutions like Tsinghua University and Peking University becoming breeding grounds for technology-intensive startups. Efforts to attract international talent and foster partnerships enhanced the global competitiveness of these initiatives, leading to a surge in patent filings and successful commercialisation of research outcomes. By the early 2010s, universities had evolved from educational institutions into key players in China's innovation ecosystems.

This synergy between government policy, institutional support, and market dynamism created a fertile environment for startups to thrive, with major technology companies like Tencent (the Chinese technology conglomerate) and Alibaba emerging as global leaders, showcasing the effectiveness of China's startup ecosystems.[5]

6.3 Mass Entrepreneurship and Innovation After 2014

The "Mass Entrepreneurship and Innovation" (MEI) initiative, launched by former Premier Li Keqiang at the Summer Davos Forum in 2014, was a key strategy for sustaining economic growth as China navigated a new phase of slower growth in the mid-2010s. This comprehensive approach sought to create a vibrant startup ecosystem and shift China from an investment-driven to an innovation-driven economy. The MEI initiative has had a multifaceted impact on the startup landscape in China, influencing policy, funding, infrastructure, and cultural attitudes.

The government's endorsement of entrepreneurship and innovation led to a surge in supportive policies and regulatory frameworks at both provincial and municipal levels. Favourable tax policies, simplified business registration processes, and improved access to financing have significantly lowered barriers to entry for new startups, encouraging more individuals to pursue entrepreneurship. Additionally, the establishment of various grant and subsidy schemes, particularly directed towards technology-intensive and strategic emerging industries, has provided essential initial capital for operations and research and development. Consequently, the number of high-tech and knowledge-intensive startups increased markedly (see Fig. 6.1),[6] showcasing the initiative's success in fostering innovation and entrepreneurship in China.

The MEI initiative significantly strengthened the financial ecosystem for startups by attracting substantial venture capital (VC) and angel investments. Government-backed funds have been instrumental in reducing risks associated with private investments, while the presence of international VC firms like Sequoia, IDG and Hillhouse Capital has also increased. As Fig. 6.2 shows,[7] although investment amounts fluctuated, peaking in 2018 and rising again in 2021 to CNY 1,355bn (USD 197bn), the average investment size grew over time.

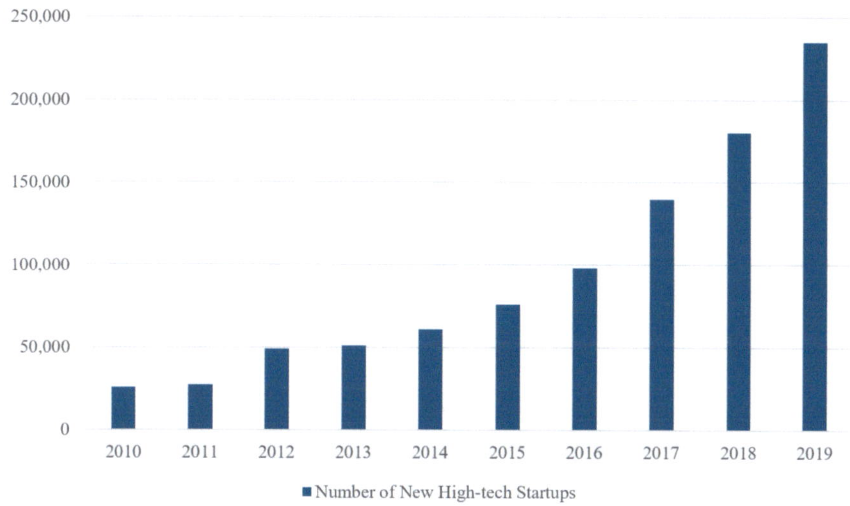

Fig. 6.1 Number of new high-tech startups in China

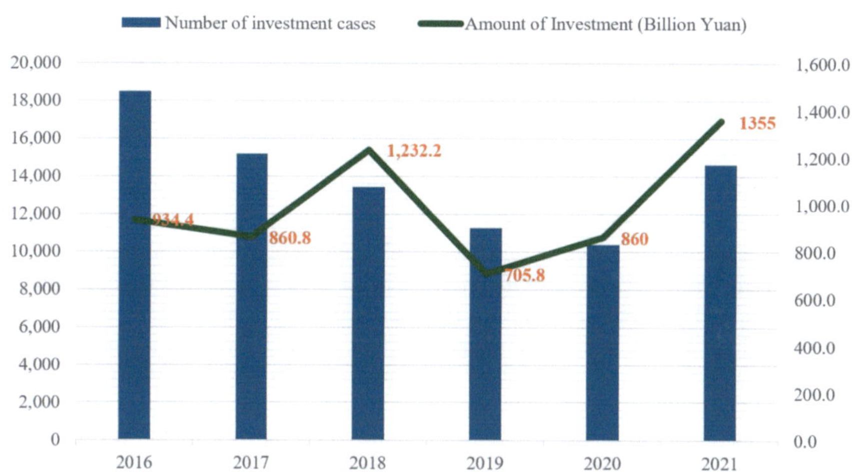

Fig. 6.2 China's total domestic VC investments vs total amount invested (in RMB)

Since the launch of the MEI initiative, the number of incubators and accelerators in China has experienced remarkable growth. By the end of 2015, there were approximately 2,900 incubators and accelerators in China, but this number surged to over 12,000 by 2024 (see Fig. 6.3).[8] These facilities have been established in both major cities and smaller regional hubs, promoting a more balanced geographic distribution of entrepreneurial activities. The Chinese government has played a vital role in this expansion, providing substantial financial support and favourable policies. National and provincial governments have allocated billions of Chinese Yuan

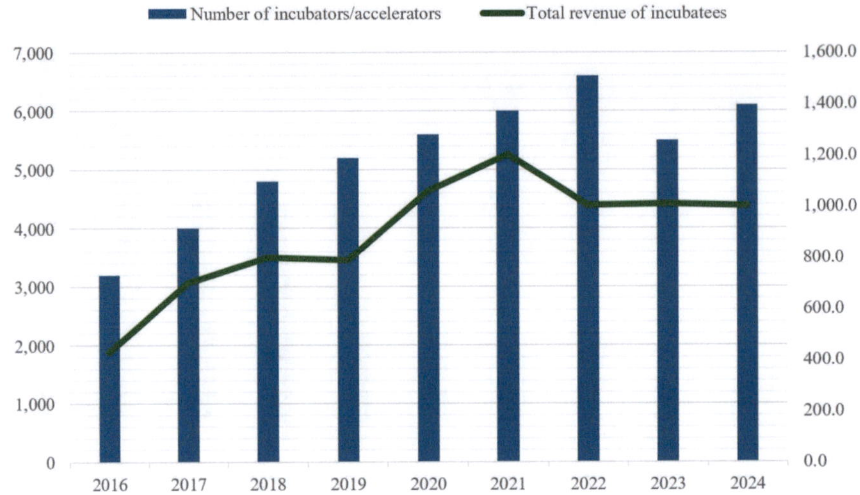

Fig. 6.3 China's number of technology-intensive incubators and the total revenue of incubatees

to develop these ecosystems. For example, the "Innovation and Entrepreneurship Development Fund", launched in 2016, allocated around CNY 40bn (USD 6bn) specifically for startups and related infrastructure.[9]

Incubators, accelerators, universities, and corporations collaborated more closely under the MEI initiative, creating more integrated startup ecosystems across the country. Institutions like the Harbin Institute of Technology and Zhejiang University have developed their own incubators and accelerators, facilitating the commercialisation of academic research. Corporate incubators, supported by industry leaders such as Haier and Legend, provide startups with access to specialised resources, mentorship, and market opportunities. Examples of startups that benefited from this support include iFlytek, a world-renowned company specialising in intelligent speech and artificial intelligence, which was incubated at Wuhan East Lake Technology Entrepreneurship Center; iROOTECH, one of China's three major industrial internet platforms incubated by Sany Group; and Cambricon, a unicorn in the AI chip field, which received multiple rounds of consecutive investments from Legend Capital and was listed on the STAR Market in 2020, with a market value exceeding CNY 290bn (USD 42.1bn) at one point.

Improvements in digital infrastructure, including enhanced internet connectivity, the widespread adoption of digital payment methods, and the rise of e-commerce platforms, have lowered operational costs and barriers for Chinese startups, particularly in technology, e-commerce, and fintech sectors. China's most notable unicorns, such as ByteDance, have successfully navigated this landscape, making a global impact alongside a robust hardware and IoT (Internet of Things) presence in Shenzhen's startup ecosystem (see Box 6.2).

Box 6.2 ByteDance: The Rise Under Improved Digital Infrastructure

ByteDance is one of the world's most successful technology unicorns, and its development history reflects the rapid advancement of China's digital infrastructure while showcasing how to secure a position on the global stage. ByteDance's success is closely linked to improvements in the internet ecosystem, including enhanced connectivity, the proliferation of digital payment systems, and the rise of e-commerce platforms. These factors collectively lowered operational costs and entry barriers for startups, particularly in the technology, e-commerce, and fintech sectors.

Founded by Zhang Yiming in 2012 and headquartered in Beijing, ByteDance emerged during a period of significant growth in the mobile internet. The widespread adoption of 4G networks and smartphones had led to a dramatic increase in mobile internet users, creating vast market opportunities. Zhang Yiming astutely recognised this trend and decided to focus on content distribution and personalised recommendation technology.

At the core of ByteDance's advantage are its powerful algorithms and artificial intelligence capabilities. The company's recommendation engine precisely delivers personalised content based on users' interests and behaviours. This technology was first leveraged in its flagship product—Toutiao, a machine-learning-based news aggregation platform. Toutiao quickly attracted a large user base, laying the foundation for ByteDance's early development.

ByteDance's globalisation strategy has been pivotal to its success. In 2017, the company launched TikTok (the international version of Douyin), rapidly introducing it to global markets. TikTok's success was enhanced by the maturity of global digital infrastructure, including efficient cloud services, strong data processing capabilities, and a comprehensive payment and logistics system. TikTok achieved remarkable success not only in the United States, Europe, and Southeast Asia, but as a cultural phenomenon among young people around the world.

While ByteDance is headquartered in Beijing, its growth has benefited from Shenzhen's strong computer hardware and Internet of Things (IoT) ecosystem. As a global centre for hardware innovation, Shenzhen has provided technological infrastructure and support to ByteDance, particularly in data centres, servers, and smart devices. This cross-regional synergy has facilitated ByteDance's rapid global expansion.

The global adoption of digital payments has also played a crucial role in ByteDance's commercialisation efforts. Utilising platforms such as Alipay, WeChat Pay, and international payment systems, ByteDance seamlessly implements user payments, advertising placements, and e-commerce transactions. This frictionless payment experience enhances user engagement and significantly contributes to the company's revenue.

Despite its remarkable success, ByteDance faces several challenges, including worldwide regulatory scrutiny, data privacy concerns, and increased market competition.

The development history of ByteDance epitomises the progress made in global digital infrastructure and the maturation of China's startup ecosystems. From Toutiao to TikTok, ByteDance has not only achieved success in the Chinese market but has also made a significant impact globally. Its story illustrates that, with the right digital infrastructure, technology companies can effectively compete with top players on the global stage, delivering innovative products and services to users around the world.

Additionally, the MEI initiative has emphasised the importance of education and skills development in building a strong startup ecosystem. By encouraging curriculum enhancements, vocational training, university-industry collaborations, and international talent acquisition, this initiative helped to equip a new generation of Chinese students and professionals with the necessary skills to thrive in an innovative economy. To illustrate, since 2015 Chinese educational institutions have increasingly integrated entrepreneurship education into their curricula. By 2017, over 200 Chinese universities had established dedicated innovation and entrepreneurship departments.[10] Courses on entrepreneurship, innovation management, and startup practices are standard offerings in China ever since, and many universities have created entrepreneurship practice platforms and incubators to provide students with practical opportunities. Some institutions have even launched Entrepreneur Colleges and Industrial-Entrepreneur Colleges to foster innovation ecosystems that connect academia, industry, and society. For example, in 2019, Xi'an Jiaotong-Liverpool University (a joint-venture university in Suzhou, founded in 2006 by a partnership between the University of Liverpool and Xi'an Jiaotong University) established its Entrepreneur College and College of Industry-Entrepreneurs to integrate industry research, solution design, talent cultivation, while obtaining support from local governments.

To complement academic education, the Chinese government has invested in programmes that equip students and young professionals with practical skills for startup creation and management. In 2016, the National Development and Reform Commission allocated approximately CNY 20bn (USD 3bn) for vocational training initiatives across various sectors.[11] Another initiative, "Internet Plus", encourages the integration of internet-based technologies with traditional industries, facilitating training programmes focused on digital skills, e-commerce, and technological innovation.

These educational and skills-development initiatives have led to measurable impacts. According to the Global Entrepreneurship Monitor (GEM) 2019 report,[12] China's early-stage entrepreneurial activity rate rose to 15%, up from 12% in 2015, indicating a growing interest and engagement in entrepreneurship.

The MEI initiative has also fostered a cultural shift in China toward greater acceptance of entrepreneurship as a viable and prestigious career path. Government campaigns and endorsements from officials, including Premier Li Keqiang, have enhanced support for entrepreneurial endeavours. This has created a positive narrative around entrepreneurship, emphasising its importance for China's innovation and economic revitalisation.

Entrepreneurship in China has been normalised as a career option through various educational initiatives, including competitions and workshops that celebrate entrepreneurial achievements. Previously, traditional careers in government or established industries were seen as the safest options; however, success stories from figures like Lei Jun (founder of the electronics company Xiaomi), Zhang Yiming (Founder of ByteDance), Wang Xingxing (founder of Unitree Robotics), Liang Wenfeng (founder of DeepSeek) have inspired many to consider entrepreneurship. According to a 2023 survey of the Central Committee of the Communist Young League,[13] nearly 60% of university students expressed interest in starting their own businesses, reflecting a significant shift in attitudes over the past decade.

Inclusivity has been a central focus of the MEI initiative, with policies aimed at supporting diverse groups, including women, rural entrepreneurs, and under-represented minorities. The Chinese government has implemented various programmes to foster entrepreneurship among these groups. For instance, the "Rural Innovation and Entrepreneurship Action Plan" offers training, financial support, and mentorship, leading to the creation of over 50,000 rural startups and generating employment for more than 1 million people by 2020.[14] The initiative also emphasised women's entrepreneurship. By the end of 2024, the total number of female-invested private firms in China exceeded 23 million, accounting for 41.6% of all private legal-person enterprises, with an average annual growth rate of 9.8% since 2012.[15]

The MEI initiative has laid a broad foundation for China's startup ecosystem. In the face of the highly challenging external environment engendered by the Sino-US high-tech decoupling, China's entrepreneurship and innovation policies have undergone profound adjustments, with the focus shifting to technological self-reliance and control, industrial chain security, and high-quality development (discussed more in Chap. 9). During this strategic transformation, cities, as the core carriers for the convergence of innovation elements and the implementation of policies, have become increasingly crucial. City-level agglomerations such as Beijing, Chongqing, Suzhou, and Shenzhen are interpreting the evolution direction and response strategies of China's startup ecosystem under pressure through their differentiated paths and practices, serving as the most direct windows to observe China's innovation resilience.

6.4 Start-Up Ecosystems in Chinese Agglomerations

Viewed collectively, China's startup ecosystems represent a rich tapestry of innovation hubs and agglomerations, each contributing uniquely to the broader entrepreneurial landscape of the country. These hubs foster vibrant environments where startups can thrive and scale. Taking Beijing as an example, its tech hub Zhongguancun has attracted over 40,000 high-tech startups, underscoring Beijing's pivotal role in hard technology and innovation. Meanwhile, Shenzhen's resilient industrial value chains, Suzhou's localisation of foreign R&D, and Chongqing's emergence as a new hub for smart manufacturing are collectively shaping the evolution and response strategies of China's startup ecosystems to a changing geopolitical environment. We now provide an overview of each of these startup ecosystems.

6.4.1 *Beijing*

Beijing, China's capital and a major economic centre, covers 16 districts over an area of 16,411 km^2. It consistently attracts a large influx of talent, with a permanent population of approximately 22 million residents in 2024, reflecting a growth trend since 2010. The city is home to around 1 million university students, comprising a diverse population, including many returnees who have made notable contributions to Beijing's entrepreneurial and economic development. The last decade has witnessed a surge in startups across various sectors such as e-commerce, biotech, and finance, positioning Beijing as a hotspot for innovation. According to the "Global Entrepreneurship Ecosystem Report 2024", Beijing ranks 8th worldwide, showcasing its competitiveness and influence on a global stage.[16]

At the heart of this thriving ecosystem is Zhongguancun, often referred to as "China's Silicon Valley", a major technology hub in the Haidian District of northwest Beijing. Established in 1953, its identity as Zhongguancun solidified when the editorial team of "China Geography" magazine adopted the name during their relocation. The area later became a hub for China's leading universities, including Peking University and Tsinghua University, as well as Beijing Normal University and the Chinese Academy of Sciences, which are nearby. Since the 1978 National Science Congress, Zhongguancun has fostered numerous private startups, leading to the emergence of a robust information and communication technology (ICT) cluster by 1987, characterised by 148 high-tech enterprises predominantly specialising in IT, now known as "Zhongguancun Electronics Street".

Since 1990s, Zhongguancun attracted more innovation resources and talent, nurturing high-tech enterprises such as Lenovo (the Chinese computer hardware and electronics MNC), Baidu (the internet services and artificial intelligence MNC, founded in 2000), and Xiaomi (the consumer electronics and computer hardware MNC, founded in 2010).[17] Today, Zhongguancun is recognised both domestically and internationally for its scientific and technological advancements. As Lei Jun, the founder of Xiaomi, remarked, Zhongguancun is a high-density information hub that gives enterprises a competitive edge in sourcing partners and talent. This area not only provides abundant human resources for entrepreneurs but also attracts international capital to support startups. In 2024, Beijing-based startups secured USD 4.8bn in VC funding, positioning the city as a top destination for VC funding in Asia, with Zhongguancun hosting over 40,000 high-technology startups, including 115 unicorns (with a combined value of around USD 594.9bn). (see Box 6.3).[18]

Box 6.3 Lei Jun and Xiaomi: An Innovation Legend from Zhongguancun to the World

In April 2010, in Beijing's Zhongguancun, often referred to as "China's Silicon Valley", Lei Jun and his founding team, including Bin Lin and Wanqiang Li, gathered in a modest office at the YinGu Building. They shared a bowl of millet porridge, a symbolic gesture marking the birth of Xiaomi Corporation. This humble yet poignant moment would later become an iconic image, embodying the spirit of innovation and entrepreneurship that defines Zhongguancun.

Lei Jun's journey is one of courage and determination. Before founding Xiaomi, he was already a successful Chief Executive Officer (CEO) at Kingsoft, a prominent Chinese software company. Yet, at the age of 40, he chose to start over, driven by an unyielding passion for innovation. His decision to step away from a comfortable position and venture into the unknown has inspired countless aspiring entrepreneurs, proving that age is no barrier to pursuing one's dreams.

Xiaomi's rise to prominence is nothing short of extraordinary. Starting with the development of the MIUI operating system, Xiaomi quickly expanded into smartphones, revolutionising the industry with its high-quality, affordable devices. Lei Jun's philosophy of "focus, extreme, word-of-mouth, and speed" became a guiding principle for the company and a model for others in the tech world.

In 2011, Xiaomi launched its first smartphone, the Xiaomi Mi 1, priced at just RMB 1,999. This disruptive pricing, combined with an innovative online sales model, allowed Xiaomi to deliver cutting-edge technology to the masses. Lei Jun's vision of "making quality technology accessible to everyone" resonated deeply, propelling Xiaomi to rapid success and reshaping the smartphone market.

But Xiaomi's story is not just about business model innovation; it is also a testament to the relentless pursuit of quality. From the meticulous craftsmanship behind the "artistic journey of a steel plate" to breakthroughs in bezel-less display technology, Xiaomi has consistently demonstrated its commitment to excellence. As Lei Jun often says, "Innovation determines how high we fly, but quality determines how far we go".

Lei Jun's "Flying Pig Theory"—the notion that even a pig can fly when positioned at the forefront of a trend—has sparked considerable discussion. Yet, Xiaomi's success extends well beyond simply capitalising on the smartphone boom. The company has expanded from smartphones to smart home devices and now into the automotive sector, continuously pushing boundaries and showcasing an unwavering spirit of innovation—an essential trait for entrepreneurs.

Xiaomi's ecosystem model has pioneered a new business paradigm. By combining investment and incubation, the company has nurtured hundreds of ecosystem partners, creating a dynamic and expansive innovation ecosystem. This philosophy of open collaboration emphasises that innovation is not a zero-sum game, but a journey of collective growth.

Today, Xiaomi has grown from a small startup in Zhongguancun to a global powerhouse, ranking among the Fortune Global 500. Lei Jun and Xiaomi's tale of ambition and resilience will surely continue to inspire generations of entrepreneurs worldwide, encouraging them to chase their dreams and redefine what is achievable.

Since the 2000s, Zhongguancun has further strengthened its ties to international innovation resources, drawing in talent and capital and enhancing the overall landscape for scientific and technological advancement. Now officially named "Zhongguancun Science and Technology Zone", the area has made significant strides in fields like artificial intelligence, big data, and cloud computing, nurturing numerous unicorns and publicly listed companies. Zhongguancun is also now home to the Chinese headquarters and research centres of numerous world-renowned technology companies, including Microsoft, Google, Intel, AMD, Oracle Corporation, IBM, and Sony.

Another vital element of Beijing's startup ecosystem is its extensive network of incubators, accelerators, and coworking spaces. Chen Chunxian—a member of the Chinese Academy of Sciences and known as "the first entrepreneur of Zhongguancun"—envisioned the area as a startup ecosystem following a government-sponsored visit to Boston and Silicon Valley, and he played a pivotal role in establishing these services in the 1980s. Today, Zhongguancun is home to about 150 incubators and accelerators, alongside over 200 coworking spaces that support various technology and service startups, making it one of the densest startup ecosystems in China. These facilities provide vital resources, mentorship, and support for startups at different stages of their growth.

Beijing's startup ecosystem is further enriched by a large pool of skilled professionals, including engineers, researchers, and entrepreneurs. The top Chinese universities and research institutions, such as Tsinghua University, Peking University, Renmin University and the Chinese Academy of Sciences, contribute world-class research facilities, funding opportunities, and vibrant academic communities, ensuring a steady influx of talent and innovation. By the end of 2023, Zhongguancun had attracted over 8,700 returnees, with the highest number of returnee startups among national science and technology zones, showcasing its role as a leading intellectual resource centre in China.

Beijing is now reshaping the core coordinates of China's hard-tech entrepreneurship map. Relying on the national key universities and research institutions, Beijing has gathered 17% of the country's "Highly Cited Scientists",[19] forming a core engine for original innovation in basic research. In addition, the pioneering policies of Zhongguancun have been continuously upgraded. After the establishment of the Science and Technology Innovation Zone of the Free Trade Zone in 2020, it was the first to pilot the "challenge and response" mechanism,[20] promoting breakthroughs in key areas. For example, Cambricon (incubated by the Chinese Academy of Sciences) launched the cloud AI chip Siyuan 370 (in 2022) based on its independent instruction set architecture, breaking through the 7 nm process barrier. Beigene (founded by a team of returnees) has established China's first global-level biopharmaceutical production base. Its self-developed anti-cancer drug Zanubrutinib achieved overseas sales of over US$1bn in 2023, marking a breakthrough in the "going global" of high-end pharmaceutical companies (see Box 6.4).

6.4.2 *Suzhou*

Suzhou is located in the heart of the Yangtze River Delta in southeast Jiangsu Province, covering an area of 8,657 km^2 and housing a population of 12.96 million residents. Known for its historic gardens and canals, Suzhou has recently emerged as a dynamic hub for innovation and entrepreneurship in China.

A key driver of this growth is the presence of industrial parks and innovation zones, which provide startups with essential resources, funding, and networking opportunities. The Suzhou Industrial Park (SIP), established in 1994 through a collaboration with Singapore, has become one of China's most successful development zones,[21] spanning 278 km^2 and hosting over 5,000 enterprises, including many MNCs and advanced technology companies. Since 2006, the park has focused on emerging industries such as biomedicine, nanotechnology, and artificial intelligence (see Box 6.4).

The biomedical sector in SIP, for instance, has attracted world-class companies like Eli Lilly and Pfizer, forming a complete industrial chain. By 2024, the annual output of the biomedical industry in Suzhou has surpassed CNY 100bn (USD 14.29bn).

Box 6.4 BeiGene: A Biotech Pioneer Rooted in Suzhou, Reaching Out to the World
BeiGene was co-founded in 2010 by John V. Oyler, aiming to transform global cancer treatment by developing innovative and affordable therapies. Originating as a small startup in Changping, Beijing, BeiGene has risen to become one of the world's leading biotechnology firms.

BeiGene's journey has been filled with challenges typical of the biotechnology industry, which requires high investment, lengthy timelines, and is characterised by substantial risks, particularly in new drug development that can take over a decade and hundreds of millions of dollars to launch. The company faced obstacles such as funding shortages, a lack of skilled talent, and intense international competition.

Support from Suzhou, especially the Suzhou Industrial Park government, was crucial during BeiGene's early development. The park provided advanced laboratory facilities and office space, while favourable government policies and tax incentives alleviated financial pressures on startups. The Suzhou government actively fostered a biotechnology ecosystem, attracting various companies and research institutions, resulting in a robust industrial cluster that offered BeiGene valuable resources and collaboration opportunities.

Additionally, Suzhou's strategic location facilitated international expansion. Its proximity to Shanghai, a global financial and logistics centre, enabled BeiGene to connect efficiently with worldwide markets, attracting international capital and talent.

A significant breakthrough for BeiGene was the development of Zanubrutinib, a next-generation BTK inhibitor for hematologic cancers. The journey from early research to clinical trials and approval took nearly ten years. BeiGene's R&D centre in Suzhou played a crucial role, as the favourable research environment and supportive talent policies attracted top scientists from around the globe.

The road to developing new drugs is fraught with uncertainty. High failure rates in clinical trials, complex regulatory processes, and intense competition posed substantial challenges. For instance, during the clinical trial phase for Zanubrutinib, BeiGene needed to comply with regulatory requirements across China, the USA, and other nations, which demanded exceptional expertise and resource management from the team.

Suzhou's international vision and government support were invaluable in navigating these challenges. Collaborating with local universities and research institutions allowed BeiGene to accelerate technology transfer, while the international service platform in the Suzhou Industrial Park helped the company effectively access global resources, bolstering its international expansion efforts.

In 2019, Zanubrutinib received Food and Drug Administration (FDA) approval, making it the first anti-cancer drug independently developed by a Chinese company to gain approval in the USA. Today, BeiGene's Suzhou facility serves as a key hub for its global R&D and manufacturing operations. The establishment of cutting-edge production facilities supports large-scale manufacturing of innovative drugs, while the ongoing industrial cluster effect in Suzhou ensures critical support, creating a comprehensive biopharmaceutical supply chain from raw material sourcing to market promotion.

In nanotechnology, the park has established a technology hub recognised as a "National Advanced Manufacturing Cluster", producing high-performance nanomaterials for global markets. A diverse array of enterprises, exemplified by Nona-Micro Technology, have flourished in this fertile environment for innovation and entrepreneurship, establishing themselves as frontrunners in the nanotechnology industry. Nona-Micro Technology is among the few global companies proficient in large-scale production technologies for both inorganic and organic nanobeads. Its global market share in biomedical chromatographic packing has grown significantly from 0.8% in 2020 to 1.5% in 2024, earning it the distinction of being the fastest-growing domestic supplier.[22] In addition, Suzhou Nano City is the largest R&D and industrial base for nanotechnology in China, attracting more than 200 related enterprises, with total investments exceeding CNY 30bn (USD 4.2bn) as of 2024.[23]

The municipal government of Suzhou has established an innovation consortium, where leading enterprises collaborate with universities and research institutes to promote technological innovation and industrial upgrading. This consortium leverages the strengths of prominent firms, driving the development of entire industrial chains. For instance, Hengtong Group, one of the world's largest manufacturers of optical fibre and cable, holds over 15% of the global optical fibre market. The company collaborates on projects with institutions like Tsinghua University and Zhejiang University, and it has co-founded the "Future Information and Artificial Intelligence Research Institute" with Soochow University, further enriching the region's innovation landscape.[24]

Xi'an Jiaotong Liverpool University (XJTLU) is located within Suzhou Industrial Park, facilitating seamless integration between academic and industrial environments. This proximity fosters regular interactions among students, faculty, and industry professionals. XJTLU tailors its curriculum to meet SIP's industrial needs, focusing on disciplines like advanced technology, engineering, business, pharmacy, biotechnology and, more recently, artificial intelligence (AI). The university collaborates with local enterprises on various R&D projects, utilising its expertise in cutting-edge technologies. Many graduates secure positions in top companies within SIP, including MNCs like Samsung and Siemens. The synergy between SIP and XJTLU illustrates how strategic collaborations between universities and private enterprise can drive innovation, economic growth, and talent development.[25]

Suzhou's startup ecosystem also benefits from the presence of established companies and MNCs that create opportunities for collaboration, mentorship, and investment. As of 2023, Suzhou is home to 171 provincial-level and 227 municipal-level regional headquarters of MNCs, along with around 18,000 foreign-invested enterprises. By fostering a culture of innovation and knowledge-sharing, these companies are instrumental in driving startup growth. For example, Johnson & Johnson established an Innovation Center in SIP, investing over US$200 mn in local biotechnology startups, and contributing to more than 15 collaborative projects by 2020. IBM's innovation centre in SIP runs incubation programmes for local startups in AI and big data, supporting over 50 local startups by 2020.[26] The German MNC, Bosch has also set up an innovation hub in Suzhou, focusing on smart manufacturing and the Internet of Things (IoT), funding over 20 local startups and driving advancements in smart factory technologies.[27]

After the US-China technological decoupling in 2020, Suzhou Industrial Park was the first to introduce the "R&D Headquarters" policy.[28] This policy requires MNCs to establish key R&D functions in China in exchange for market access, achieving a dynamic balance between security and openness. Typical examples include Johnson & Johnson Suzhou Innovation Center, constructing the largest medical device R&D base in the Asia–Pacific region. In the critical areas of semiconductor materials, high-end medical devices, and industrial software, foreign R&D localisation has transformed Suzhou into a model city balancing supply chain security management and global innovation collaboration.

6.4.3 Chongqing

Chongqing is located in southwestern China, bordered by Sichuan Province to the east, Yunnan Province to the west, Guizhou Province to the south, and Gansu and Shaanxi Provinces to the north. By 2023, the population of Chongqing's main urban area reached 16.4 million residents, making it the most populous city in Southwest China.

Chongqing's strategic geographic location positions it as a key logistical hub in China's "Belt and Road Initiative" and the Yangtze River Economic Belt, attracting substantial investments and fostering a dynamic business environment. By 2024, the city's GDP was approximately CNY 3.2tn (approximately USD 480bn), reinforcing its role as a major economic centre in China.

Historically dubbed the "Motor City of China", Chongqing has a strong foundation in heavy industries like automotive manufacturing, steel production, and machinery. Vehicle manufacturers such as Chang'an Automobile and Loncin have driven the region's economic growth. However, through strategic government policies, Chongqing is transforming from a traditional manufacturing hub to an innovation-driven economy.

Designated as a core area for the "Made in China 2025" initiative, the city has focused on upgrading its manufacturing sector with smart technologies and fostering innovation in fields such as robotics, AI, and new energy vehicles. Many of the 500 or more startups established between 2018 and 2020 specialised in innovative applications of AI and big data. By 2022, the annual revenue of the big data industry surpassed CNY 50bn (USD 7.3bn).[29] Notably, Chang'an Automobile has invested heavily in smart manufacturing, becoming a leader in autonomous driving. In 2023, it launched its first fully autonomous electric vehicle (EV), leveraging AI and IoT technologies developed in collaboration with local startups.

Chongqing's startup ecosystem is strengthened by a robust infrastructure of more than 200 incubators and accelerators, and by two major innovation hubs: the Western (Chongqing) Science City (WSC) and the Liangjiang New Area. WSC, established as a national-level innovation hub, facilitates R&D activities and houses over 500 high-tech enterprises, including the R&D centres of MNCs such as Hewlett-Packard and China Resources Microelectronics, as well as the leading EV producer SERES. The Jinfeng Laboratory, launched in 2022, has developed first-class research platforms in China, including the Intelligent Pathology Laboratory and the Space–time Genomics Center, advancing original research and breakthroughs in intelligent pathological diagnosis and immunopathology.[30]

Established in 2016, the Liangjiang New Area of Chongqing has become a focal point for innovation in IT, biomedicine, and advanced manufacturing. By 2023, the Liangjiang Collaborative Innovation Zone had developed a 3,000-acre Mingyue Lake Science and Technology Innovation Ecological Park, featuring over 700,000 m^2 of innovative space, and hosting over 50 universities and institutes, along with numerous research teams and incubators for startups. Chang'an Automobile's Global R&D Center, located here, coordinates with international teams across five countries and nine regions. It submitted 11,257 patent applications and developed 49 groundbreaking technologies by 2023.

A crucial aspect in the development of Chongqing's startup ecosystem has been talent acquisition. While the city has a strong industrial base, it needed to diversify into advanced technology and innovative sectors to sustain economic growth and competitiveness. However, Chongqing faced a shortage of talent essential for developing these new industries, particularly in technology and innovation. To address this challenge, the municipal government implemented the Chongqing Talent Plan (CTP), establishing specific goals and mechanisms for attracting and developing talent. Initiatives like the "Chongqing Elite Project" and the "Young Talent 1000 Program" have focused on recruiting top professionals from both domestic and international sources. By 2023, over 10,000 high-tech experts and young entrepreneurs had been drawn to emerging fields such as AI, biotechnology, and smart manufacturing, resulting in a notable increase in the number of PhD holders and postdoctoral researchers in the city.[31] This influx of talent has significantly boosted the growth of startups and innovative enterprises in Chongqing.

Chongqing is home to 72 universities, including two national key institutions: Chongqing University and Southwest University. These universities are intensifying their focus on innovation and entrepreneurship, further enriching the entrepreneurial environment. In 2020, Chongqing University, in collaboration with the Chongqing Liangjiang New Area and Mingyue Lake International Industrial Innovation Park, launched the Mingyue Lake Base Class. This programme draws from the training model of Olin College of Engineering in the USA, adapting it to meet the industrial needs of both China and Chongqing. The course aims to develop a unique training model that cultivates future industrial innovators to thrive in China's new economy. It features a redesigned curriculum that integrates multiple disciplines, combining mathematics, science, engineering, and design. The project-driven teaching approach offers a 1:3 in-class to out-of-class time ratio, granting students greater autonomy while involving them in thematic laboratories and practical project research aligned with social needs. By 2024, students in this programme had developed over 100 graduation design topics in collaboration with prominent companies such as China Automotive Engineering Research Institute, Chang'an Automobile, Horizon Robotics, Googoltech, and Quotient Kinematics Machine Automation. The first cohort graduated in June 2024, and two startups founded by graduates secured CNY 3 mn (USD 0.4 mn) in angel funding, with company valuations reaching CNY 20 mn (USD 2.8 mn) and CNY 30 mn (USD 4.2 mn), respectively.[32] This success highlights the effectiveness of this new engineering training model in nurturing talent for Chongqing's startup ecosystem.

In recent years, Chongqing has reorganised its industrial chain security system through an intelligent integration of complete vehicle and component collaboration models. After being approved in 2021 as one of the first national "Intelligent Connected Vehicle Access Pilot" projects (announced by the Ministry of Industry and Information Technology), Chongqing has made breakthroughs in key areas such as automotive electronics and industrial motherboards by implementing policies like "whole vehicle manufacturers + localised substitution".[33] For example, Chang'an Automobile's Global R&D Center partnered with Horizon Robotics, a leading Chinese autonomous driving technology company to develop automotive-grade MCU chips; in 2023, over 180,000 units were installed, thereby mitigating risks associated with chip supply shortages. In 2023, the added value of strategic emerging industries in Chongqing accounted for 32.2%.[34] Additionally, logistics costs declined by approximately 50% (in particular, to South Asia) through the new land-sea corridor,[35]establishing Chongqing as a model for inland regions looking to balance autonomous and controlled industrial value chains with intelligent upgrading.[36]

6.4.4 Shenzhen

Shenzhen, located at the southern tip of the Chinese mainland, is a first-tier city positioned close to Hong Kong. Its unique geographic location facilitated its establishment as one of the first three Special Economic Zones (SEZs) following China's reform and opening up, marking the beginning of its rapid economic development. The SEZs served as testing grounds for market-oriented reforms, and Shenzhen's GDP soared from US$1.42bn in 1980 to approximately US$430bn in 2024, positioning it as a model for industrialisation and technological innovation.

Renowned for its computer hardware manufacturing capabilities, Shenzhen is home to the world's largest electronics market, Huaqiangbei.[37] This district is famous for its vibrant entrepreneurial atmosphere, initially focusing on the sale and maintenance of electronic products, which attracted numerous aspiring entrepreneurs. Many of these individuals, despite lacking substantial financial backing, leveraged keen market insights and relentless effort to build successful enterprises, evolving from simple vendors into integrated R&D, production, and sales companies, and ultimately becoming industry leaders.

Huaqiangbei created a massive electronics industry cluster, reducing transaction costs and enhancing market efficiency while promoting the flow of information, technology, and capital. The area closely tracks trends in the electronic information industry, with merchants quickly launching products that meet changing consumer demands. For instance, a new pair of screen headphones developed in Huaqiangbei resembles AirPods Pro but features an additional touch screen to display the battery level, control music playback, activate noise cancellation, adjust brightness, and even takes photos remotely.

The most notable contribution of Huaqiangbei to Shenzhen's economy is its ability to capture market hotspots, fostering innovation through technological, design, and business model advancements. This spirit of risk-taking and innovation has energised the entire city, with many entrepreneurs beginning at the grassroots level, growing from humble retailers to industry leaders. This entrepreneurial drive embodies the essence of Shenzhen's spirit.[38]

Fuelled by this vibrant culture, Shenzhen's venture capital ecosystem has expanded rapidly. By 2024, the city boasted over 2,500 registered VC firms managing an estimated CNY 2tn (USD 290bn) in assets.[39] Shenzhen is also a hub for significant investments in the high-tech sector. For instance, UBTech Robotics, a leading humanoid robotics company, attracted substantial VC funding from Tencent and other investors, allowing it to push technological boundaries and achieve unicorn status with a valuation exceeding USD 5bn.[40]

The Shenzhen Stock Exchange (SZSE), established on December 1st 1990, is a vital component of China's startup ecosystem, evolving to meet the needs of high-tech companies and startups. It hosts the SME Board for small and medium-sized enterprises (launched in 2004) and the ChiNext Board for innovative startups (launched in 2009), providing access to essential capital through public listings. By the end of 2024, the ChiNext Board had listed over 1,200 companies, raising more than CNY 800bn (USD 120bn) in external funding.[41]

Public listings offer liquidity for early investors and clear market valuations for startups, attracting both domestic and international investment. This synergy between venture capital and the SZSE positions Shenzhen as a global competitor in high-tech industries. For example, BYD Auto (established in 2003), now one of the world's leading electric vehicle manufacturers and a key competitor to Tesla, leveraged significant venture capital investment before eventually listing on the SZSE. This dual access to private and public capital enabled BYD to accelerate its global expansion, with its electric buses now operating in major urban centres across Asia, Europe, and the Americas.

VCs often guide startups towards an eventual public listing. They mitigate early-stage risks by investing in promising startups, while SZSE listings provide the liquidity and capital needed for further growth and development. This balanced distribution of risk and reward supports a sustainable startup ecosystem, making Shenzhen a more attractive place for high-tech and innovative startups. According to the Shenzhen Venture Capital Association, approximately 30% of ChiNext-listed companies were initially funded by VCs, highlighting the critical role of venture capital in nurturing startups towards successful public offerings.[42]

Shenzhen's startup ecosystem also thrives on the collaboration between global technology giants and local innovators. Home to established corporations like Huawei, Tencent, and DJI (the Chinese drone manufacturer, established in 2006), Shenzhen also boasts a vibrant community of startups. Partnerships between these large companies and startups often focus on co-developing technologies that leverage their respective strengths. For instance, DJI has partnered with local startup PowerVision to advance drone automation and AI-powered navigation systems, leading to significant innovations in this high-growth sector. These corporate industry leaders provide inspiration, mentorship, and valuable resources to startup entrepreneurs, enhancing knowledge transfer and skill development. To illustrate, Huawei's "Seeds for the Future" programme trains young professionals in cutting-edge ICT technologies and encourages collaboration with startups, cultivating a skilled workforce that brings innovative insights back to their ventures. OnePlus, a smartphone brand founded by former Oppo employees, exemplifies this dynamic: early support from Shenzhen's technology ecosystem and collaborations with companies such as BBK Electronics (a leading company in China's electronic industry, founded in 2004) helped OnePlus to expand into over 40 countries, boosting Shenzhen's reputation as a global technology hub.

Government support has also been crucial in accelerating Shenzhen's startup growth. Initiatives like the Qianhai Special Economic Zone and Guangming Science City offer tax incentives, funding, and regulatory assistance, creating a favourable environment for business. The Peacock Plan, launched in 2011, was designed to attract top-tier international talent with competitive salaries, research funding, and housing subsidies. By 2020, it had attracted over 15,000 high-level professionals to Shenzhen.

The municipal government of Shenzhen emphasises the cultivation of talent, adapting its educational system to meet the demands of its innovation ecosystem.[43] The city houses high-level research-oriented institutions, including Shenzhen University and the Southern University of Science and Technology, which attract top scholars and provide essential resources for students. These universities focus on nurturing research-oriented talent with innovative and practical skills.

Additionally, Shenzhen places great importance on vocational training, with institutions like Shenzhen Vocational and Technical College committed to developing specialised personnel with practical skills. The college offers programmes that are closely aligned with local industries, such as electronic information engineering and mechanical design. Through partnerships with businesses, students gain hands-on experience and job opportunities, ensuring that many graduates become integral contributors to Shenzhen's economic development.

More recently, in response to the US Entity List sanctions and semiconductor supply disruptions, Shenzhen has restructured a secure and controllable industrial system through a "leading enterprise + ecosystem empowerment" model. For example, Huawei's wholly-owned subsidiary, Shenzhen Hubble Technology Investment (founded in 2019), had invested in more than 60 semiconductor equipment and material companies by 2025, pushing Microchip's etching machines into SMIC's 14 nm production line, raising Huawei's smartphone localisation rate from 25% before the sanctions to 75% in 2024.[44] DJI built its fully autonomous controllable drone production line through a vertical reconstruction of its supply chain. In 2023, Shenzhen's added value of strategic emerging industries accounted for 41.9% of GDP.[45] With 25,000 national high-tech enterprises,[46] Shenzhen has formed an innovation ecosystem, validating a resilience approach to industrial value chain restructuring driven primarily by market mechanisms under the pressures of security concerns, "chip neck" blockages, and high-quality development.

6.5 Similarities and Differences Among China's Startup Ecosystems

The startup ecosystems in Beijing, Chongqing, Shenzhen, and Suzhou each exhibit distinct characteristics while sharing certain commonalities. The similarities can be summarised as follows.

- *Government support and policies:* All four cities benefit from strong government support and policies that aim to promote entrepreneurship, innovation, and economic growth. Initiatives such as tax incentives, funding programmes, and regulatory reforms are common across the four cities, creating favourable environments for startups to thrive.
- *Access to funding:* Venture capital investment plays a crucial role in fuelling the growth of startups in these cities. Each of the four agglomerations has seen significant inflows of venture capital funding, providing startups with the financial resources needed for expansion and development.
- *Talent pool and education:* Each city boasts a talented workforce with expertise in various fields, including technology, engineering, and business. Proximity to top-tier universities and research institutions ensures a steady supply of skilled professionals into the startup ecosystem, supporting innovation and growth.

- *Industry diversity:* Startup ecosystems in these cities are characterised by a diverse range of industries and sectors. While technology and innovation are prominent themes, startups in the four cities span multiple areas such as advanced manufacturing, biotechnology, e-commerce, and artificial intelligence, reflecting a broad spectrum of entrepreneurial endeavours and opportunities.

At the same time, these cities have developed distinct startup ecosystems shaped by varying policy priorities, industrial specialisations, degrees of internationalisation, and levels of market-driven development. More specifically:

- *Geographical Advantages*: The geographical locations of these cities offer unique advantages to startups. Beijing's status as the capital provides proximity to government institutions, policy influencers, a high concentration of talent, and state-of-the-art innovation. Suzhou benefits from its strategic location near Shanghai, a major financial centre, enabling ready access to global markets. Chongqing's strong automotive industry foundation, combined with its strategic location in western China, presents opportunities for startups looking to tap into the region's emerging markets. Shenzhen's proximity to Hong Kong and established supply chains offers advantages for computer hardware startups and technology-related innovation.
- *Focus industries*: As a centre of scientific and technological innovation, Beijing's startup ecosystem is guided by scientific and technological innovation. The city has strengths in software and digital services, with a particular emphasis on artificial intelligence, big data and other fields. Suzhou, on the other hand, has gained recognition for its expertise in hardware manufacturing and biotechnology. Chongqing has been developing its startup ecosystem in automotives, intelligent manufacturing, advanced manufacturing and robotics, leveraging its strong industrial base. Shenzhen stands out as a computer hardware innovation hub, with a strong emphasis on electronics, computer hardware production, and related technologies.
- *Startup Infrastructure*: Each city has developed its distinct ecosystem of incubators, accelerators, coworking spaces, and innovation zones to support startups at different stages of growth. Beijing's Zhongguancun area is a well-established technology hub with a concentration of technology companies and research institutions. Suzhou's SIP is renowned for its advanced manufacturing and biopharmaceutical clusters, offering state-of-the-art facilities, robust funding resources, and an internationally collaborative environment that supports high-tech startups. Chongqing has been expanding its startup infrastructure to nurture entrepreneurship and innovation, while Shenzhen is home to Huaqiangbei, the world's largest electronics market, which serves as a resource hub for computer hardware startups.
- *Industry leaders and collaboration*: The presence of established companies and technology giants differ across these cities, influencing collaboration opportunities for startups. Beijing's ecosystem, for example, benefits from a mix of MNCs and domestic technology players like Baidu and Xiaomi, that incubate, invest

in, and collaborate with startups, driving innovation across various sectors. Startups in Suzhou SIP thrive through partnerships with advanced global manufacturing and biopharmaceutical leaders, driving significant advancements in manufacturing devices and equipment, drug development, and medical technologies. Chongqing's transition towards an innovation-driven economy is supported by industrial giants such as Chang'an Automobile, which has integrated advanced manufacturing technologies and collaborates with local startups on developing autonomous driving and smart vehicle solutions, and by emerging technology firms such as Series, which specialises in pushing the boundaries of AI applications and advanced robotics in manufacturing and smart city projects. Shenzhen hosts global technology leaders like Huawei, Tencent and BYD, which collaborate with local startups on various initiatives, particularly in 5G, AI, and IoT technologies, fostering partnerships and knowledge exchange.

6.6 Challenges and Future Development

In terms of challenges and future development, one primary concern is ensuring the sustainability and quality of startups in China. With increased funding and support, there is a risk of prioritising quantity over quality. Future policies should focus on nurturing genuinely innovative and sustainable ventures rather than merely increasing the number of startups.

Another challenge in China is the regulatory environment. As startups expand, they continue to encounter complex regulatory hurdles. Streamlining regulations and keeping pace with the rapid evolution of technology and business models is crucial for sustained success. However, the regulatory landscape in China can be unpredictable, especially following crackdowns on technology giants like Alibaba and Meituan (the Chinese online shopping platform provider), which has created uncertainties for startups aiming to scale.

A comparison of the startup ecosystems in Beijing, Suzhou, Chongqing, and Shenzhen also reveals distinct challenges for each city. With its high concentration of advanced technology firms, many Beijing startups often face fierce competition for top talent. Despite a large number of STEM graduates, the city struggles to meet the demand for skilled professionals from both startups and established companies. Additionally, the high cost of living presents challenges for employee retention and operational expenses.

In contrast, Suzhou has a less developed venture capital ecosystem. Competing with nearby Shanghai for high-end talent poses retention difficulties, despite Suzhou's complete industrial value chain in sectors such as biomedicine. Navigating the complex regulatory environment, especially in biopharmaceuticals, also remains challenging for Suzhou's startups.

Chongqing's startup scene is still in its formative stages, lagging behind in terms of both the number of startups and venture capital investments. The city's infrastructure requires further significant upgrades to support the growth of its startup ecosystem. Attracting and retaining top-tier talent is another major concern, as many professionals prefer to work in established hubs like Beijing and Shanghai.

Shenzhen, known for its high startup activity, also faces intense competition. The presence of numerous startups and established technology giants makes it tough for newcomers to secure a foothold. Additionally, rising regulatory scrutiny and costs associated with living and operations can hinder new ventures. Recent crackdowns on data privacy and cybersecurity have already impacted several technology firms in Shenzhen.

6.7 Conclusion

As with our previous chapters on Japan and Korea, this chapter once again highlights how historical context matters for startup ecosystem development. In the case of China, the evolution of startup ecosystems is a remarkable story of state-guided transformation, shifting from a centrally planned economy dominated by state-owned enterprises to one of the world's most dynamic hubs of technological innovation and entrepreneurship. This chapter has traced this journey, beginning with the market-oriented reforms of the late 1970s that created the initial space for private enterprise. We show how early government initiatives, such as the Torch Plan and the establishment of science parks, laid a critical foundation upon which China's startup ecosystems could flourish, albeit with characteristics distinct from Western counterparts.

A key takeaway from this chapter is the pivotal and ever-present role of government policy as a catalyst for the development of startup ecosystems in China. The launch of the "Mass Entrepreneurship and Innovation" initiative in 2014 marked a deliberate strategic pivot, aiming to embed innovation and entrepreneurship as core drivers of China's economic future. This top-down push demonstrably lowered barriers to entry for startups, and expanded their options for securing external financing. It also cultivated an entrepreneurial culture in which founding a new venture or working for a startup are increasingly viewed as a viable and prestigious career paths. The influence of 'returnees', who bring back global expertise and networks, and the deepening integration of universities into the innovation ecosystem, have further accelerated this development.

Our comparative analysis of Beijing, Suzhou, Chongqing, and Shenzhen demonstrates that China's startup landscape is not monolithic, highlighting once again the within-country diversity of East Asian startup ecosystems. Each Chinese city has leveraged unique geographical advantages and historical industrial strengths to cultivate distinct ecosystems. Beijing thrives as a centre for R&D and digital services, benefiting from its concentration of elite universities, the influx of foreign MNCs, and proximity to policymakers. Shenzhen has cemented its status as a global computer hardware capital, driven by the rapid innovation cycles of its vast electronics markets and a synergistic relationship between venture capital and its stock exchange. Meanwhile, cities like Suzhou and Chongqing showcase alternative paths to innovation; Suzhou excels in advanced manufacturing and biotechnology through a highly successful and government-backed industrial park, while Chongqing is leveraging its traditional industrial base and inland location to pivot towards emergent technologies such as smart manufacturing and robotics.

Despite these successes, significant challenges remain for startup ecosystem development in China, including ensuring the quality and sustainability of new ventures, navigating an often-unpredictable regulatory environment, and overcoming intense competition for talent and resources, both within and across the major ecosystem hubs.

In summary, our analysis in this chapter highlights how startup ecosystem performance is shaped by a multifaceted set of interdependent factors, and these factors exhibit substantial variation across regions—even within a single national economic context. All this points to the complexities of managing and promoting the growth of startups and startup ecosystems for policy-makers at national, provincial, and municipal levels.

In the next major part of this book, we move beyond our country-specific narratives to provide a cross-cutting analysis of three critical themes that have emerged from our review of startup ecosystem development in Japan, Korea, and China: namely the profound influence of 'culture', the multi-dimensional role of 'government policy', and the complex dynamics of 'internationalisation' in the East Asian context. This thematic focus will allow for a richer understanding of the unique characteristics of innovation and entrepreneurship the East Asian way.

Notes

1. Ou (2000).
2. Ghalayini (2023).
3. Source: https://mp.weixin.qq.com/s?__biz=MzI1NjkzNzY0NQ==&mid=2247486907&idx=1&sn=c2c8aa99d15041cd3bce44b5dfe63c05&chksm=ea1e5679dd69df6f36301b25a9427f7b6fee282ecc0dd0f7214a0796c17c269ace1e0a8e2a90&scene=27.
4. Zweig et al. (2004).
5. Yang (2007).
6. Pan et al. (2023).
7. CKGSB Knowledge (2022).
8. Source: https://www.stdaily.com/web/gdxw/2025-05/15/content_340042.html.
9. Source: https://cpc.people.com.cn/n/2015/0116/c83083-26396732.html.
10. Ministry of Education of the People's Republic of China (2017). Report on university entrepreneurship departments.
11. National Development and Reform Commission (2016). Support for vocational training initiatives.
12. Global Entrepreneurship Monitor (2019).
13. Source: https://www.toutiao.com/article/7277387785030418980/?upstream_biz=doubao&source=m_redirect&wid=1752981153939.
14. Source: http://english.moe.go.kr/sub/info.do?m=050101&page=050101&num=1&s=english.
15. Source: https://m.cqn.com.cn/zj/content/2025-03/08/content_9095682.htm.
16. Source: https://www.startupblink.com/startupecosystemreport.

17. Filatotchev et al. (2011).
18. Source: https://kw.beijing.gov.cn/ztzl/gdzt/smnchcx/202501/t20250127_4001396.html.
19. Source: https://clarivate.com.cn/highly-cited-researchers/analysis.
20. Zhongguancun (2020).
21. Inkpen and Pien (2006).
22. NanoMicro (2024).
23. Suzhou Industrial Park Administration Commission (2022).
24. Li et al. (2023).
25. Suzhou Industrial Park Administration Commission (2020–2022).
26. IBM company website (2024).
27. Bosch company website (2024).
28. Suzhou Municipal Government (2021).
29. Chongqing Intellectual Property Office (2023).
30. Source https://baijiahao.baidu.com/s?id=1772098741804802508&wfr=spider&for=pc.
31. Chongqing Government Reports on Talent Initiatives (2023).
32. Source https://baijiahao.baidu.com/s?id=1772098741804802508&wfr=spider&for=pc.
33. Chongqing Municipal Government (2021).
34. Chongqing Municipal Bureau of Statistics (2024).
35. Chongqing Investment Promotion Association (2024).
36. Source: https://www.gov.cn/xinwen/2019-01/10/content_5356464.htm
37. Zhang and Qian (2024).
38. Keane and Zhao (2012).
39. Shenzhen Venture Capital Association (2024).
40. Hurun Research Institute (2023).
41. Shenzhen Stock Exchange (2017–2023).
42. Shenzhen Venture Capital Association (2022).
43. Song (2024).
44. Source: https://baijiahao.baidu.com/s?id=1819981964238038244&wfr=spider&for=pc.
45. Department of Science and Technology of Guangdong Province (2024).
46. Source: https://www.sz.gov.cn/cn/xxgk/zfxxgj/zwdt/content/post_12312809.html.

Chapter 7
Synthesising East Asia's Startup Ecosystem Development for Thematic Exploration

7.1 Introduction

In the preceding three chapters, we provide a comprehensive overview of the evolution and dynamics of startup ecosystems in Japan, Korea, and China. We trace the historical development of entrepreneurial activity in each nation, from post-war recovery and state-led growth to the emergence of modern innovation hubs. Our discussions highlight the influence of government policies, cultural shifts, and economic crises in shaping startup landscapes, revealing how each country has cultivated distinct environments for new venture formation and scale-up. We also provide detailed comparisons of major city-level ecosystems, such as Tokyo, Seoul, and Beijing, and their smaller secondary counterparts in each country, exploring their unique strengths, challenges, and industrial specialisations. Collectively, these chapters underscore the complex interplay of a variety of factors in fostering competitive and sustainable startup growth in East Asia.

The purpose of this chapter is to serve as a bridge that transitions from our country-specific descriptions of the historical development and key features of startup ecosystems in Japan, Korea, and China to the next part of the book where we examine separately three key themes that distinguish startup ecosystem development in East Asia, especially compared to Western country contexts. We label these themes as "culture", "government policy", and "internationalisation". In this chapter, we synthesise information from the previous three chapters to highlight commonalities and differences in the development of startup ecosystems in Japan, Korea, and China, providing a foundation for our deeper exploration of each of the three themes in the chapters that follow. In short, we seek answers to the following question: what have we learned about each East Asian country that sets the stage for analysing the cross-cutting themes of "culture", "government policy", and "internationalisation" in the development of East Asian startup ecosystems?[1]

Y. Cheng et al., *Unleashing Innovation the East Asian Way*,
https://doi.org/10.1007/978-981-95-6513-9_7

7.2 Historical Trajectories and the Development of East Asian Startup Ecosystems

The first key observation to emerge from our country-specific descriptions is how the characteristics, growth, and performance of startup ecosystems in East Asia are heavily dependent upon the specific histories of each country and their regions. This reliance is evident in how past economic structures, pivotal crises, governmental policies, and local legacies have profoundly shaped the emergence and evolution of East Asian startup ecosystems at a national and sub-national level.

At a national level, we note how Japan's post-war recovery saw established companies such as NEC and Toshiba thrive under government-backed industrial policies, which fostered strategic sectors to catch up with the then more advanced Western economies. Their growth, combined with corporation-led innovation, supported economic development amidst rapid urbanisation, a growing middle class, and rising consumer spending. Industrial policy at the time did not foster new market entries, nor did it specifically address entrepreneurship. In Korea, we see how the dominance of large conglomerates (*chaebols*) has historically constrained the technology startup landscape by absorbing capital and talent. The 1997 Asian financial crisis was a pivotal juncture for Korea, abruptly undermining the perception of stable conglomerate careers and catalysing a surge in new ventures founded by skilled professionals. In China, the transformation of the startup landscape began with Deng Xiaoping's "Reform and Opening-Up" in 1978, which marked a shift from a state-controlled economy to a market-oriented one, gradually creating space for private enterprises and entrepreneurship. Early Chinese incubators, unlike their Western counterparts, were deeply aligned with local government and industrial policies aimed at regional economic development and technological innovation, reflecting a "science and technology for national strength" strategy. These distinct historical trajectories have determined to a considerable extent the nature and features of the startup ecosystems observed in each country today.

Similarly, our individual country descriptions demonstrate how the histories and specific characteristics of regions within each country have helped to establish distinctive startup ecosystems there. For example, we observe how Tokyo's dominance as Japan's primary startup hub is a direct result of its large economic agglomeration, concentration of talent, and central role as a research and development (R&D) hub, attracting the majority of investment and talent. In contrast, Osaka leverages its historical legacy as Japan's "merchant city", providing a strong foundation for contemporary entrepreneurship in sectors such as biotechnology and healthcare. At the same time, Fukuoka's initiatives as a "Startup City" build on its historical role as a gateway to Asia, with young Japanese firms leveraging the city's geographical proximity to overseas markets such as Korea and China.

Likewise, key differences between a country's capital city and regional cities for startup ecosystem development can also be observed for Korea and China. To illustrate, Seoul's overwhelming advantage in Korea's startup landscape reflects its broader economic dominance, serving as the national capital and a hub for corporate headquarters, leading universities, and skilled talent pools. Meanwhile, Daejeon, a regional hub, has developed a "deep science" ecosystem that traces back to the establishment of its science town in 1973. This historical foundation, inspired by Japan's Tsukuba Science City, focuses on science-based industries like biotechnology and robotics, leveraging its concentration of PhD researchers and research institutes. In China, we see that Beijing's Zhongguancun, often called China's "Silicon Valley", emerged from its agglomeration of leading universities and research institutions, fostering a robust information and communication technology (ICT) cluster. Shenzhen's rapid rise as a technology hub was facilitated by its establishment as one of the first Special Economic Zones (SEZs) and its Huaqiangbei electronics market, which fostered grassroots innovation in computer hardware and electronics. Suzhou's Industrial Park (SIP), established in collaboration with Singapore, became a successful development zone focused on emerging industries like biomedicine and nanotechnology, leveraging its particular collaborative history. At the same time, Chongqing transformed from a "Motor City" with a strong foundation in heavy industries by strategically pivoting towards smart manufacturing and robotics, leveraging government policies and talent plans to upgrade its industrial base.

In short, our analyses in the previous three chapters illustrate collectively that the development and performance of startup ecosystems in East Asia is intricately linked to a multifaceted set of interdependent historical factors, which vary substantially across different national and subnational contexts. Recognition of this is crucial to our analyses—and to those of researchers in general—because it counters deterministic or universalist approaches to understanding ecosystem development in East Asia. We assert that East Asian ecosystems cannot be understood through models and perspectives imported from Silicon Valley or other Western contexts, as their unique trajectories are products of distinct historical path dependencies.

Factors such as Japan's post-war industrial policy, Korea's *chaebol* structures, and the 1997 financial crisis are not merely background features or events; rather, they are active forces that have shaped East Asian startup ecosystems decisively. Consequently, a nuanced analysis that accounts for this complex historical contingency is essential if researchers, policymakers, and other stakeholders are to accurately diagnose ecosystem strengths, weaknesses, and potential future pathways in East Asia, and if lessons learned in one startup ecosystem context are to be accurately and effectively transferred to another.

7.3 Culture and the Development of East Asian Startup Ecosystems

A second key observation from our three-country chapters is how national culture—and particularly the enduring influence of Confucianism—has played a significant, albeit often complex and sometimes constraining, role in shaping the development and distinctiveness of startup ecosystems in Japan, Korea, and China. While the impact of culture manifests differently in each nation, a common thread of valuing hierarchy, group harmony, and stability has historically posed challenges to the inherently disruptive and individualistic nature of startup entrepreneurship, setting East Asia apart from Western contexts. Across East Asia, traditional values rooted in Confucianism have historically prioritised stability, collective responsibility, hierarchical organisational and social structures, respect for seniority, and group consensus. While contributing to social cohesion and long-term planning in established institutions, these values have often created an environment that is less conducive to the individual risk-taking, disruptive innovation, and rapid change that are characteristic of startup cultures in general and of the more individualistic and risk-tolerant cultural foundations often associated with Western entrepreneurship. Expressed another way, traditional East Asian cultures have tended to discourage the kind of personal initiative and disruptive risk-taking that characterises successful entrepreneurship in Western contexts. However, recent decades have seen significant cultural shifts, often spurred by economic imperatives and government policies, leading to a greater acceptance and even the embrace of entrepreneurship across East Asia.

Historically, career paths in large, established corporations (like *keiretsu* in Japan or *chaebols* in Korea) or state-owned enterprises in China were preferred over the uncertainties of newly founded companies. However, in all three countries, recognising the importance of startups in the digital age, government policy has actively sought to (and succeeded in) shifting career preferences towards entrepreneurship. In this way the government has, at least in part, contributed to the social acceptance of startups, a measure not necessary and therefore not typically seen in the evolution of Western startup hubs.

In Japan, entrepreneurship has been constrained by Confucian values that emphasise hierarchy, harmony, and collective responsibility over individual entrepreneurial risk-taking. Despite these challenges, Japanese companies like SoftBank, Nidec, and Nintendo succeeded by successfully navigating rigid business norms and adopting unconventional business models, demonstrating that entrepreneurial success was possible, albeit adapted to general cultural norms and therefore less confrontational. Yet, cultural resistance to risk remains a challenge for Japan's startup ecosystems, impacting the level of entrepreneurial activity, while emphasis on harmony continues to require balancing innovation with conformity.

For Korea, *chaebol* dominance and the culturally ingrained pursuit of traditional careers also negatively impacted startup entrepreneurship. For decades, working for large *chaebols* was highly coveted due to social prestige, competitive salaries, and perceived job security. This preference meant that *chaebols* absorbed the majority of available investment capital and attracted the highest-calibre talent, limiting opportunities for startups and constraining their access to key resources. At the same time, workplace practices in large Korean conglomerates tended to be rigid and hierarchical, often stifling individual creativity and autonomy. However, these culturally-driven conditions shifted during Korea's second startup boom since 2010. A crucial driver in recent decades has been an ongoing change in career preferences among highly-skilled young professionals. Growing dissatisfaction with demanding work cultures, long hours, and rigid hierarchies in conglomerates has led younger Koreans to prioritise a healthier work-life balance, work autonomy, flexibility, and empowerment. This marks a significant departure from earlier generations, who focused on maximising financial income. This cultural shift, coupled with government support, has led many Koreans to establish or join startups. Despite this, cultural differences still make it difficult for foreigners to found or join startups in Korea. The diversity of startup entrepreneurs in Seoul remains relatively low, with founders being predominantly male Koreans with engineering backgrounds, which can limit 'out-of-the-box' ideas and the creation of innovative business solutions. Addressing this lack of international diversity and global perspective will be critical if more Korean startups are to become 'born globals' and expand abroad effectively.

China, too, has witnessed shifting attitudes towards entrepreneurship in recent times. The "Mass Entrepreneurship and Innovation" (MEI) initiative in China fostered a general shift towards greater acceptance of entrepreneurship as a viable and prestigious career path. Government campaigns and endorsements from high-ranking officials also helped create a positive narrative around entrepreneurship, emphasising its importance for China's economic revitalisation and transformation. Entrepreneurship has now become normalised as a career option through educational initiatives, competitions, and workshops. Moreover, while traditional careers in government or established industries were once seen as the safest options, the success stories of major entrepreneurs like Lei Jun (Xiaomi) and Zhang Yiming (ByteDance) have inspired the younger generations. Nowadays, an increasing proportion of university students are expressing interest in starting their own businesses, reflecting a major change in attitudes over the past decade. The MEI initiative also focused on inclusivity, with policies aimed at supporting diverse groups, including women and rural entrepreneurs, further embedding entrepreneurship into the societal fabric of China.

In short, East Asian cultural traditions provide evidence of the distinctiveness of startup ecosystem development across the region. While Western startup cultures often celebrate the "maverick" individual entrepreneur and disruptive innovation, East Asian cultures have traditionally favoured group consensus and established hierarchical relationships. These cultural conditions enabled leaders of major companies and groups to apply entrepreneurial growth strategies effectively, as their followers implemented their directions quickly and enthusiastically, but also made it hard for new, unproven startups to gain traction without government or corporate backing. However, this is now changing, and the role of government in contributing to the social acceptance of entrepreneurship is another aspect to the distinctiveness of startup ecosystem development in the region. In particular, the explicit and large-scale government-led initiatives to promote a "culture of entrepreneurship" in East Asia, as seen with China's MEI or Korea's deliberate policy shifts post-2010, represent a more orchestrated approach to supporting startup entrepreneurs than is typically observed in Western contexts such as the USA or Silicon Valley. In the West, a culture of entrepreneurship is often seen as having emerged more organically from market forces, academic innovation, and a long-standing emphasis on individual liberty and economic freedom, rather than as an outcome of direct and indirect government intervention. At the same time, and beyond the influence of government, the cultures of East Asia are changing due to societal pressures and influence, not least in the tension found between seeking a healthier work-life balance versus the 'hustle culture' that is prevalent in many startup ecosystems globally. As discussed above, Korea, in particular, has seen a cultural shift among young professionals prioritising work-life balance and autonomy over the demanding work environment of large conglomerates. This offers a nuanced difference compared to some Western startup ecosystems where extreme working hours have long been glorified, or at least they were prior to the COVID-19 pandemic.

To sum up this discussion, while all three East Asian countries have seen their startup ecosystems flourish, they have done so by blending traditional cultural norms (especially Confucian values) that were initially restrictive to entrepreneurship with modern, less hierarchical values. This has resulted in hybrid entrepreneurial cultures where deeply ingrained traditional cultural values co-exist with recently changing attitudes of younger generations. This distinguishes East Asian startup ecosystems from the more individualistic startup environments commonly found in the West.

7.4 Government and the Development of East Asian Startup Ecosystems

A third key observation we can draw from our three-country studies is how government policy, regulations, and associated support structures in Japan, Korea, and China have impacted the development of startup ecosystems, both nationally and at a subnational level. In some respects, this governmental role differs across the countries. In China, we see a proactive, state-led approach to economic development and innovation leading up to the creation of startup ecosystems. In Korea, government involvement was less comprehensive, but public funding was essential for kick-starting the domestic venture capital industry. In Japan, government policies were more responsive. They supported already existing ecosystems through regulatory reform, by granting them public acknowledgement and social acceptance, and by strengthening international linkages. The motives behind such policies also differed. Often, this proactive stance has arisen from national strategic imperatives, such as economic revitalisation (Japan), industrial diversification (Korea), or the desire to catch up technologically (China). Nevertheless, the role of government in startup ecosystem development distinctly differentiates East Asian startup ecosystems from more market-driven Western contexts like the USA and Silicon Valley. All of this can be observed in a number of ways from the accounts of the three previous chapters.

First, governments of all three countries have demonstrated a strong inclination for direct and deliberate intervention to foster startup ecosystems. In Japan, the government has launched initiatives like the "Japan Revitalisation Strategy" (2013) and "J-Startup" (2018) to create a more favourable environment for high-potential startups and unicorn companies. Similarly, Korea's second startup boom which began in 2010 was largely policy-driven, reflecting a deliberate governmental shift to diversify its economy away from an over-reliance on large *chaebol* conglomerates. The

Korean government also rapidly developed and implemented startup promotion policies following the Asian Financial Crisis in 1997, enacting laws like the "Special Law to Promote Venture Capital Companies", and further strengthened its pro-startup policies from the 2010s. Likewise, China's economic transformation has been largely state-guided. From the "Reform and Opening-Up" era, the launch of the "Torch Plan" (1988) to establish science parks, through to the "Mass Entrepreneurship and Innovation" initiative (2014), government endorsement has been pivotal in creating supportive policies and regulatory frameworks within which entrepreneurship in China can flourish.

Second, governments have also provided substantial financial backing and various incentives to support startups. For example, Japan amended laws to facilitate venture capital investment, provide tax incentives, and ease regulatory requirements. In Korea, financial support has been particularly strong, encompassing direct financing—such as seed money, and R&D subsidies—and indirect financing through investment into venture capital funds via entities like the Korea Venture Investment Corporation (KVIC). Indeed, this government-backed funding was the predominant source of external startup financing for many years. Similarly, China has utilised government-backed funds to reduce risks for private investors, along with grant and subsidy schemes, particularly for technology-intensive industries. Initiatives like the "Innovation and Entrepreneurship Development Fund" have allocated substantial funding to startups and associated infrastructure in China.

Third, governments in Japan, Korea, and China have also contributed significantly to developing and supporting the physical and institutional infrastructure required to encourage the formation and scale-up of startups. For example, Japan established Technology Licensing Organisations (TLOs) in 1998 to commercialise university research. In Korea, science towns like Daedeok Innopolis (from 1973) were supported by various government initiatives and later evolved into important innovation clusters. Seoul also benefits from numerous government-funded education services, legal and accounting assistance, and subsidised workspaces for startups. In China, governments at various levels began to establish science parks and business incubators in the mid-1980s, which were aligned with local government and industrial policies, serving as high-tech industrial parks to drive regional economic development and technological innovation. In particular, the number of incubators and accelerators surged under China's MEI initiative.

Finally, East Asian governments have also placed particular emphasis on fostering university-industry collaboration and promoting talent development. For example, Japan saw increased university-industry collaboration after the Technology Licensing Organisation Act in 1998 and national university corporatisation in 2004, enabling universities to manage resources for incubation programs. Subsequently, the number of university-associated startups has steadily increased in Japan. At the same time, Korea's Daejeon ecosystem benefits from a high concentration of PhD researchers and strong networks between government research institutes, universities, and technology firms. Similarly, China's government policies have promoted public-private collaboration, with numerous universities establishing science and technology parks and integrating entrepreneurship education into curricula, supported by plans like the "National Talent Development Plan". In terms of talent development, China, in particular, has aggressively pursued brain gain strategies through programs like the "Thousand Talents Plan" to attract highly skilled returnees (entrepreneurs who previously studied or worked abroad) back to the country, many of whom have leveraged their global knowledge and networks to establish new ventures and support the advancement of startup ecosystems in various ways. China's approach is a more explicit, systematic, and large-scale government-led effort to reverse the brain drain phenomenon compared to those found elsewhere around the world.

In short, East Asian startup ecosystems are distinct from those in many Western contexts (e.g., USA/Silicon Valley) as a consequence of governmental involvement, often with explicit national goals, as opposed to a more *laissez-faire* and bottom-up approach that primarily relies on private enterprise, venture capital, and academic research, and with less direct governmental guidance or industrial policy steering.

In many ways, this distinctiveness is an outcome of the adoption of different models of capitalism compared with, for example, the USA. Japan developed a form of corporatism ("Japan Inc.") with close coordination between the state and organised business interests, integrating large businesses into policy design. This ensured broad support but could slow responses and marginalise independent voices. In Korea, the government practiced 'guided capitalism' from the 1960s, providing preferential support to *chaebol*s, which effectively constrained opportunities for new startups until later policy shifts. Similarly, Chinese incubators were deeply linked to the country's "Science and Technology for National Strength" strategy, driving regional economic development and industrial upgrades, rather than being purely market-driven like many Western counterparts. China's government-aligned approach means that policies for major technology companies are deeply integrated into national strategies, and sometimes this can lead to unpredictable regulatory environments, and even crackdowns.

At the same time, the distinctiveness of East Asian startup ecosystems is also a consequence of the responses of countries to crises and strategic imperatives. While Western governments of course also respond to economic challenges, the East Asian cases often show a more direct and comprehensive re-orientation of national economic strategy towards startups in the wake of major challenges and crises (e.g., Japan's long-term stagnation from the 1990s after the burst of its 'bubble economy' and the Asian Financial Crisis in Korea) or to address concerns about future competitiveness (e.g., China's shift to an innovation-driven economy, and Japan's push for deep-tech). It also derives from the prioritisation of industrial upgrading and self-reliance. East Asian policies frequently connect startup policies to broader industrial upgrading, regional development, or national self-reliance goals. One example is Chongqing, which is transforming its traditional manufacturing base into an innovation-driven economy focused on smart technologies, robotics, and new energy vehicles through government initiatives like "Made in China 2025". Another example is Shenzhen which, in response to US sanctions on China from the late 2010s, has restructured its industrial chain for security and control, investing heavily in semiconductor companies to increase localisation rates. A national-level example is Japan, which is shifting focus to deep-tech and cross-tech sectors, integrating traditional industries with advanced technologies, supported by government institutions such as the New Energy and Industrial Technology Development Organisation (NEDO). All this stands in contrast with a perceived Western emphasis on market-driven innovation, even if defence or other government funding is available.

In sum, government policy in East Asia has been influential and often prescriptive in shaping startup ecosystems across the region, moving beyond merely facilitating market conditions to actively constructing the environment for innovation and entrepreneurship. Taken together, this consistent, deliberate, and sometimes crisis-driven governmental involvement serves as a key distinguishing factor when compared to the more decentralised and market-centric approaches that are typically found in equivalent Western contexts.

7.5 Market Dynamics and Internationalisation

The fourth key observation emerging from our comparative analysis reveals how market dynamics and internationalisation forces have profoundly shaped the development of startup ecosystems in Japan, Korea, and China, creating patterns fundamentally different from Western models. While Silicon Valley's celebrated "born global" paradigm emphasises immediate international scaling from inception, East Asian ecosystems have evolved along more nuanced trajectories that are deeply rooted in the complex interplay between substantial domestic markets, historical corporate structures, and evolving geopolitical realities. Cultural forces in East Asia have also shaped the propensity for internationalisation. For example, the historical lack of international diversity in founding teams and management, partly due to cultural homogeneity and less emphasis on born global strategies, typically has been a challenge for East Asian startups seeking international expansion. This contrasts with the often inherently global outlook of a large number of Western startups, which often have diverse founding teams and aim for international markets from the outset. The distinctive approach of East Asian startups to market development and internationalisation represents not merely a deviation from Western norms but a sophisticated adaptation to unique regional conditions that merits careful examination.

The defining characteristic across all three East Asian countries is the predominance of domestic-first strategies, where startups typically establish robust home market foundations before contemplating international expansion. This sequential approach reflects multiple interconnected factors that distinguish East Asian markets from their Western counterparts. First, the sheer size and sophistication of domestic markets—Japan's affluent and discerning consumer economy, Korea's globally leading digital infrastructure and tech-savvy population, and China's vast internal market with over a billion potential users—provide startups with substantial growth opportunities without an immediate need for cross-border ventures. Second, the pervasive role of government in shaping market access through industrial policies, regulatory frameworks, and strategic guidance has historically favoured domestic market development. Third, the legacy of large corporate structures—Japan's *keiretsu* networks, Korea's *chaebol* conglomerates, and China's state-owned enterprises—initially created formidable barriers to market entry, compelling startups to develop creative strategies for survival and growth within domestic boundaries rather than pursuing risky international expansion.

In Japan, the market dynamics for startups have been profoundly shaped by institutional structures that date back to the post-war economic reconstruction period. The Main Bank system, which provided stable long-term financing to established corporations, and the intricate *keiretsu* networks of cross-shareholdings and preferential business relationships, created what many describe as a "valley of death" for new ventures seeking capital and customers. Early internet startups faced additional challenges from a conservative business culture that valued established relationships and proven track records over innovative but unproven business models. In response to these constraints, successful Japanese startups like Rakuten and CyberAgent developed distinctive strategies of extensive diversification and acquisition, building comprehensive service ecosystems that could compete with traditional corporate groups. However, this domestic focus has contributed to persistent internationalisation challenges. High-profile ventures from mobile gaming pioneers DeNA and GREE to more recent unicorns like Mercari in e-commerce and SmartNews in content aggregation have repeatedly demonstrated a pattern of strong domestic performance followed by struggles to achieve sustained global penetration. These difficulties often stem from deeply ingrained organisational cultures that prioritise perfectionism, extensive localisation, and consensus-building—valuable traits in the Japanese market but potential impediments to the speed and adaptability required for international expansion.

Korea's startup ecosystem tells a different but equally instructive story about market dynamics and internationalisation challenges. The historical dominance of *chaebol* conglomerates created a highly concentrated economic structure where a handful of family-controlled business groups commanded the majority of resources, talent, and market opportunities. This landscape underwent dramatic transformation following the 1997 Asian Financial Crisis, which shattered the myth of *chaebol* invincibility and created space for entrepreneurial ventures as displaced professionals sought new opportunities. Despite Korea's subsequent development of world-leading digital infrastructure, sophisticated consumers eager for innovative services, and strong government support for startups, the ecosystem continues to exhibit what can be characterised as an aspiration-achievement gap in internationalisation. While Korean entrepreneurs increasingly recognise the importance of global expansion—particularly given their relatively small domestic market of 50 million people—structural impediments persist. Research reveals that founding teams typically lack international diversity, with only about 25% including members with substantial overseas experience and foreign participation remaining exceptionally rare. This homogeneity constrains the development of cross-cultural competencies essential for navigating diverse global markets. The paradox deepens when considering the global success of Korean cultural exports through the Korean Wave (*hallyu*)—from K-pop and

K-dramas to Korean beauty products—which has generated unprecedented international interest in Korean content and lifestyle but has not systematically translated into globally competitive technology startups.

China's approach to market dynamics and internationalisation presents yet another model, characterised by the unique interplay of state guidance, massive domestic scale, and rapid technological leapfrogging. The state-led transformation of China's economy through successive waves of reform created a distinctive ecosystem where market forces operate within carefully managed policy frameworks. Early initiatives like the "Torch Plan" established science parks and incubators as instruments of regional development, while the more recent "Mass Entrepreneurship and Innovation" initiative unleashed entrepreneurial energy on an unprecedented scale. This vast domestic market, combined with rapid adoption of digital technologies, provided Chinese startups with a massive testing ground where they could achieve scale before considering international expansion. The success stories are impressive—ByteDance leveraged algorithmic innovation and massive user data to create TikTok, achieving global reach that few Asian startups have matched. This internationalisation was facilitated by unique Chinese advantages: "sea turtle" returnees who studied and worked abroad brought back technical expertise and global perspectives, government programs like the "Digital Silk Road" created infrastructure for expansion into developing markets, and the compressed development cycle allowed Chinese firms to leapfrog directly from manufacturing to platform-based digital services. However, the escalating Sino-US tensions and technology decoupling have fundamentally altered this trajectory. Chinese startups now navigate an increasingly complex landscape where geopolitical considerations shape market access, leading many to adopt a "dual circulation" strategy that balances continued domestic growth with selective and strategic international engagement in politically compatible markets.

The internationalisation story of East Asian startups cannot be fully understood without examining the profound impact of inbound foreign investment and the presence of global technology companies in reshaping local ecosystems. Since the early 2000s, the entry of global technology giants like Google, Amazon, Microsoft, and Apple into East Asian markets has created transformative ripple effects beyond simple competition. These companies introduced new operational models that challenged traditional hierarchical structures, compensation frameworks that disrupted established salary systems, and talent development practices that emphasised individual initiative and rapid skill acquisition. Perhaps most significantly, they created what researchers term "alumni effects"—as employees of these global firms gained experience with international best practices, many subsequently launched their own startups with inherently more global perspectives and operational capabilities. This bidirectional flow of influence—domestic startups learning from global companies while foreign firms adapt to local markets—has created hybrid entrepreneurial environments that blend international best practices with deep local market knowledge and cultural understanding.

Contemporary developments in market dynamics and internationalisation present both unprecedented opportunities and formidable challenges for East Asian startups. On the opportunity side, digital infrastructure has dramatically lowered barriers to international market entry. E-commerce platforms, cloud services, and digital payment systems enable even small startups to reach global customers without massive upfront investments in physical infrastructure. Moreover, the rise of East Asian soft power creates unique advantages—Japanese anime and gaming culture provides natural entry points for entertainment and gaming startups, the Korean Wave opens doors for lifestyle and beauty ventures, and Chinese innovations in e-commerce and digital payments offer models for emerging markets. Government policies across all three countries have also evolved to explicitly support internationalisation through funding programs, regulatory sandboxes for cross-border services, and strategic partnerships with other nations. Yet structural impediments remain stubbornly persistent. Regional capital markets continue to be fragmented, making it difficult for startups to raise growth capital for international expansion. The limited "born global" mindset means many entrepreneurs still view international expansion as a later-stage activity rather than a core strategic imperative from inception. Perhaps most critically, the historical East Asian approach of sequential expansion—perfecting products in domestic markets before venturing abroad—may prove increasingly disadvantageous in winner-take-all platform markets where network effects reward first movers and global scale trumps local optimisation.

Looking toward the future, the imperative for East Asian startups is not simply to copy Silicon Valley's internationalisation playbook but to develop distinctively regional models that transform unique characteristics into competitive advantages. This might involve leveraging substantial domestic markets as innovation laboratories while maintaining global ambitions from inception, utilising government support and corporate partnerships to accelerate international expansion while maintaining entrepreneurial agility, combining manufacturing excellence with digital innovation to create products that are both physically and digitally sophisticated, and harnessing emerging soft power and cultural exports as beachheads for technology ventures. The increasingly multipolar nature of the global innovation landscape, accelerated by geopolitical tensions and the rise of regional technology blocs, suggests that multiple models of internationalisation can coexist and thrive. East Asian startups that successfully navigate this complex terrain—balancing domestic strength with global ambition, managing geopolitical risks while seizing new opportunities, and creating hybrid models that combine the best of Eastern and Western approaches—will not only succeed commercially but also contribute to a more diverse and resilient global innovation ecosystem. The challenge and opportunity for researchers, policymakers, and entrepreneurs is to understand these evolving patterns and support the development of internationalisation strategies that are both globally competitive and authentically rooted in East Asian strengths and contexts.

7.6 Conclusion

The preceding three chapters explore the unique historical developments and evolutionary paths of startup ecosystems in Japan, Korea, and China, showcasing their profound transformation from industrial powerhouses to emerging innovation hubs. This chapter, in its role as a critical juncture between major parts of this book, has brought these individual narratives into comparative dialogue, revealing a complex tapestry of convergent trends and persistent divergences across the East Asian region. We have observed that while a shared emphasis on technological advancement and state-led development has been a common thread, the specific characteristics of startup ecosystems in each country have evolved distinctively. Korea, for instance, has cultivated a supply-centric ecosystem, often driven by government support for high-tech ventures, whereas Japan has maintained a technology-centric focus, leveraging its deep industrial and research capabilities. China, in contrast, has forged a dynamic, market-centric ecosystem, propelled by its vast domestic market and rapid digital adoption. These distinctions underscore that there is no singular "East Asian Way" to unleashing innovation, but rather a spectrum of effective, context-specific approaches.

One key takeaway from this comparative analysis is the complex and nuanced interplay between historical legacies, government involvement, and (shifting) societal characteristics. We have seen how deep-seated cultural values, such as varying degrees of risk aversion and the emphasis on social status or collective harmony, have profoundly influenced entrepreneurial activity and the structure of support networks in East Asia. Moreover, the differing scales of domestic markets have compelled distinct strategies for the establishment, scale-up, and internationalisation of startups. The role of government, too, has been paramount, with each nation deploying a diverse array of policies—from direct funding and incubation programs to regulatory frameworks—to catalyse startup growth.

As we transition into the next major part of this book, our comparative foundation provides an essential lens through which to explore specific thematic drivers that cut across the national boundaries of our focal East Asian nations. The next chapter on culture will further unpack the intricate ways in which societal norms, values, and educational systems shape entrepreneurial aspirations, risk-taking propensity, and collaborative dynamics in East Asia. The chapter that follows will examine in more detail the role of government policy, exploring in detail the diverse and often highly interventionist strategies employed by East Asian nations to nurture their startup ecosystems. Finally, the chapter on internationalisation will further deepen our understanding of how East Asian startups are navigating global markets, forming strategic alliances, and adapting to international competitive pressures, building on the recognition that global outreach and tapping into overseas talent and networks are crucial for further strengthening these ecosystems. By dissecting these cross-cutting themes, we aim to provide a more holistic and actionable understanding of the forces that continue to shape the vibrant and ever-evolving landscape of startup ecosystem development across Japan, Korea, and China.

Notes

1. Since this chapter bridges the content between the country study and thematic parts of the book, it does not introduce new evidence. We therefore refrain from inserting citations to avoid duplications. The relevant citations are provided in the chapters referred to.

Chapter 8
Culture and Entrepreneurship in East Asia

8.1 Introduction

Culture—the tapestry of shared norms, values, and beliefs within a society—is a powerful, though often invisible, force in shaping economic processes and outcomes. This is particularly true in the dynamic world of startup entrepreneurship. This first thematic chapter of the book explores the profound and nuanced influence of culture on the startup ecosystems of Japan, Korea, and China. For decades, the Western model of entrepreneurship—closely associated with Silicon Valley and characterised by individualism, a high tolerance for risk, and non-hierarchical values—has been lauded as the global standard of excellence. From this perspective, the traditional cultures of East Asia, with their emphasis on collectivism, hierarchy, and long-term orientation rooted in Confucian traditions, would seem to be infertile ground for entrepreneurial success.

In this chapter, we argue against such a simplistic view. Throughout, we treat culture as a key condition for the performance of startup ecosystems embedded in national coordination mechanisms rather than a stand-alone causal driver. Through our discussion of how culture influences startup entrepreneurship and startup ecosystems in East Asia, we demonstrate that while East Asian entrepreneurship differs significantly from the Silicon Valley model, new ventures have been able to leverage the region's distinct cultural conditions to achieve remarkable success.

To build this argument, the chapter is structured as follows. We begin by defining the concepts of culture and "entrepreneurial culture", establishing the Western archetype as a point of comparison. We then delve into the core tenets of East Asia's shared Confucian heritage, explaining how values like relationalism, respect for seniority, and long-term perspectives have historically shaped societal structures. The main body of the chapter presents a detailed analysis of the evolving entrepreneurial cultures in Japan, Korea, and China. We explore how each nation has undergone immense economic and social transformations, leading to the emergence of vigorous startup ecosystems that blend tradition with modernity. Through specific examples,

Y. Cheng et al., *Unleashing Innovation the East Asian Way*,
https://doi.org/10.1007/978-981-95-6513-9_8

from the consensus-building of Japanese innovators and the aggressive strategies of Korea's *chaebol* founders to the paradoxical "enlightened authoritarianism" of Chinese technology giants, we show how cultural values have been reinterpreted and harnessed to fuel, rather than hinder, entrepreneurial ambition in the region. Ultimately, we provide a nuanced perspective on the role of culture in entrepreneurship, challenging the notion of a one-size-fits-all model for entrepreneurial success, and highlighting how the diverse cultures of East Asia provide a powerful and distinct foundation for unleashing innovation across the region.

8.2 What is Culture?

Generally speaking, culture is believed to strongly affect entrepreneurship and its outcomes, as institutional structures and organisational strategies are nested in culture. But what is culture in the first place?

From a sociological perspective, culture is broadly defined as the shared norms, values, beliefs, and practices in a society.[1] This means that culture is the result of a socialisation process. Individuals acquire norms, values, beliefs and practices from other individuals whom they interact with and who wield influence over them, such as family members, friends, teachers, and colleagues.

Culture has different levels. Specifically, culture research distinguishes between group culture, organisational culture, national culture and global culture.[2] Group culture refers to the shared norms and practices of individuals who closely interact within a group, such as a team of colleagues within an organisation. Organisational culture refers to shared norms and practices within an organisation, such as a company or a government agency. National culture refers to shared norms and practices within a country. Finally, global culture refers to norms and practices shared by all people in the world. There are also further levels of culture that are located in-between the aforementioned levels and that are highly relevant, depending on the context. One such intermediate level are regional cultures that refer to sub-regions within countries. For example, Saxenian's influential comparative work on Silicon Valley and the Greater Boston area highlighted regional cultural differences between high-tech clusters within the USA that were highly consequential for economic outcomes.[3] Furthermore, research has also identified clusters of countries that exhibit cultural similarities and that are thereby situated between the national and global levels of culture. For example, a "Confucian Asia" cluster that consists of Japan, Korea, Mainland China, Hong Kong, Taiwan, and Singapore has been identified by cross-cultural research.[4]

In business studies, national cultures and cultural differences between countries have attracted most research attention. In particular, individual-level survey data have been collected across many countries through several large-scale research projects, followed by the identification of underlying cultural dimensions from these survey data and an analysis of country-level differences as regards to these dimensions. Table 8.1 provides an overview.

Table 8.1 Major global studies on cultural dimensions

Lead researchers	Survey participants	Number of countries	Cultural dimensions identified
Geert Hofstede	Company-affiliated professionals	107	Individualism/collectivism, power distance, masculinity, uncertainty avoidance, long-term orientation, indulgence
Fons Trompenaars and Charles Hampton-Turner	Company managers and employees	43	Universalism-particularism, individualism-communitarianism, specific-diffuse, neutral-affective, achievement-ascription, short term-long term, sequential-synchronic
GLOBE (global consortium of more than 150 researchers)	Company-affiliated professionals	62	Institutional collectivism, in-group collectivism, power distance, assertiveness, gender egalitarianism, future orientation, performance orientation, humane orientation
Shalom Schwartz	Teachers and students	80	Intellectual autonomy, affective autonomy, mastery, hierarchy, conservatism, harmony, egalitarianism

Sources Hofstede et al. (2010), Trompenaars and Hampden-Turner (2020), House et al. (2004), Schwartz (1999)

These studies on national cultures and cross-country cultural differences have met considerable criticism. Some of this criticism is related to the underlying data samples, which are often quite old and relatively small in some countries, and which are arguably not all highly representative of professionals or populations at large. For example, the pioneering cultural framework developed by Geert Hofstede was based on initial survey data collected between 1967 and 1973 from employees of a single multinational firm in different countries: IBM. Furthermore, bearing in mind within-country cultural heterogeneity across locations and regions, the interpretation of average survey data values in each country as national culture has also been questioned.[5]

Regardless of the extensive criticism that these multi-country studies have met, they have nonetheless been highly influential, and they do offer insights on cultural dimensions that differ across countries. While the cultural dimensions identified by the different studies are not all identical, they broadly converge on culturally embedded preferences with regards to individual orientation versus group orientation, hierarchy versus equality, long-term orientation versus short-term orientation, and risk taking versus risk avoidance. We will revisit these underlying core issues when discussing entrepreneurial culture and the influence of culture on entrepreneurship in East Asian countries in the following sections.

8.3 What Is Entrepreneurial Culture?

As for culture in general, entrepreneurial culture can be observed on different levels, such as an organisation, a region, or a country. However, regardless of the level of observation, entrepreneurial culture can be broadly understood as the norms, values, beliefs and practices that support entrepreneurial behaviour, such as taking initiative and starting a new business. Entrepreneurship studies have converged on the view that at least in highly advanced economies, entrepreneurial culture can be associated with individualism, high tolerance of risk, and egalitarian, non-hierarchical values.[6] In other words, entrepreneurship thrives when individuals feel free and encouraged to pursue their personal goals, are willing to take risk, and are not constrained by social hierarchies.

Importantly, national uncertainty avoidance does not map one-to-one onto individual risk preferences; the two are conceptually and empirically distinct. In collectivist settings, team-based founding, reciprocal ties, and prosocial motives can substitute for pure individualism in motivating entrepreneurial entry.

Cultural norms and values of individualism, risk-taking and egalitarianism are thought to be prevalent in North America. In fact, according to the data collected by Hofstede and GLOBE, North American countries as well as some European countries tend to score high on individualism, and low on power distance and uncertainty avoidance. Conversely, East Asian countries score relatively lower on individualism, and higher on power distance and uncertainty avoidance.[7] Thus, these data suggest that entrepreneurial culture may be stronger in Western countries than in East Asia.

However, data on entrepreneurial activity and entrepreneurial intention from the Global Entrepreneurship Monitor, which is based on large-scale surveys of working age individuals across 46 economies, offer a more nuanced picture (see Table 8.2). They show that the percentage of working-age adults who engage in early-stage entrepreneurial activity (i.e., who are either nascent entrepreneurs or owner-managers of a new business) is higher in North America than in Europe or East Asia. Furthermore, the percentage of adults with entrepreneurial intentions (i.e., who intend to start a business within the next three years) is also quite high in the USA and Canada. However, the rates of entrepreneurial intention are even higher in Korea and China—two East Asian countries. Overall, data suggests that while individualistic, risk tolerant, and egalitarian cultural norms and values in North America may indeed support entrepreneurship, entrepreneurial intentions are even more widespread in two East Asian countries with relatively collectivistic, hierarchical and long-term oriented cultures. In other words, it cannot be inferred that entrepreneurship is generally stronger in relatively individualistic, egalitarian, and risk-taking Western countries than in more collectivistic, hierarchical, and risk-avoiding East Asian countries. The underlying mechanisms that explain how entrepreneurship is supported in the cultural context of Japan, Korea, and China is discussed later in this chapter.

Beyond entrepreneurial activity in general, the spatial context of startup entrepreneurship tends to be discussed primarily on the level of cities, as our review of startup ecosystems in Japan, Korea, and China in Chaps 4–6 already has shown.

Table 8.2 Entrepreneurial activity among adult population in major countries, 2023

Indicator	USA	Canada	Germany	UK	France	Italy	Japan*	Korea	China
Early-stage entrepreneurial activity rate (% of adult population)	15.6	18.7	5.0	8.2	6.1	4.2	5.3	14.7	10.4
Rate of entrepreneurial intentions (% of adult population)	12.2	14.5	5.9	7.2	18.6	9.0	5.0	31.0	15.3

Source GEM (2024, * 2022)

The globally most prominent examples of successful startup ecosystems are located in North America. Global startup ecosystem rankings by Startup Genome and StartupBlink invariably rank Silicon Valley (the San Francisco Bay area) and New York City as first and second, respectively.[8]

Silicon Valley in particular stands out as a globally admired startup ecosystem role model. The beginnings of Silicon Valley as a successful startup ecosystem can be traced back to the foundation of Hewlett-Packard (HP) by William Hewlett and Dave Packard in Palo Alto in 1937. Hewlett and Packard both graduated from Stanford University and were encouraged by their advisor, engineering professor Frederick Terman, to commercialise ideas they developed in their Master's thesis. Their firm originally produced oscilloscopes before expanding into radar and artillery technology during the Second World War and eventually, into computer technology. In 1956, William Shockley, a co-inventor of transistor technology at Bell Labs, founded Shockley Semiconductor Labs nearby—the first company to produce transistors using silicon. A few years later, eight Shockley employees left the firm and founded Fairchild Semiconductor. Subsequently, many Fairchild employees created their own companies. They included Gordon Moore and Robert Noyce, who in 1968 founded Intel in Santa Clara. In total, 31 semiconductor firms were established in the area throughout the 1960s. Through such entrepreneurial activities by leading scientists and engineers, an agglomeration of IT companies rapidly evolved in the San Francisco Bay area. It was commonly named "Silicon Valley" from the early 1970s onwards.[9]

The continuous growth and success of the Silicon Valley startup ecosystem has been attributed to a high extent to its regional culture of unhindered flow of talent and knowledge between companies, universities and research laboratories, which were successively joined by venture capital investors who supported entrepreneurial activity.[10] Competent and entrepreneurial individuals continuously sought to exploit new opportunities and were quick to change their employers or to found their own startups if they assessed that such moves helped them to achieve their goals. Famous entrepreneurs such as Steve Jobs and Mark Zuckerberg pulled out of college without graduating and founded their companies in Silicon Valley, which became the giant multinational firms Apple and Facebook (later Meta), respectively. In Silicon Valley, they could effectively leverage their entrepreneurial vigour and capabilities, regardless of their young age or lack of university degrees.

Aside from strong individualism, risk-taking, and egalitarian meritocracy, another important feature of Silicon Valley's entrepreneurial culture is a widespread tendency to engage in serial entrepreneurship. In other words, startup entrepreneurs often leave their companies and sell their ownership in these companies after having successfully scaled up their business, while founding new companies, sometimes in quick succession. While serial entrepreneurship is by no means limited to Silicon Valley entrepreneurs,[11] it is a behaviour that is commonly attributed to entrepreneurs in the San Francisco Bay area. Many of these entrepreneurs tend to consider entrepreneurship as a project-based activity, implying that their engagement with particular companies is often temporary.

As a result of the exceptional success of the Silicon Valley startup ecosystem and of many companies that are located in this ecosystem, Silicon Valley has become a global role model for startup ecosystem stakeholders and policymakers. Moreover, from a cultural perspective, the entrepreneurial culture of Silicon Valley—with its focus on individual action, risk-taking and meritocracy—is now widely perceived as the type of culture that is most supportive for startup entrepreneurship and that should be nurtured in startup ecosystems anywhere. Furthermore, when applying this stance, it follows that startup ecosystems in locations with different cultural traditions such as East Asia need to change their culture to enhance their success.

However, is Silicon Valley's entrepreneurial culture really superior to entrepreneurial culture in East Asian startup ecosystems? Do ecosystem stakeholders in East Asia really need to heed the Silicon Valley cultural role model and adopt the norms, values, beliefs and practices that have evolved in this region? Not necessarily—the influence of culture on entrepreneurial success is more complicated than a stereotypical focus on the Silicon Valley role model suggests. In particular, the confluence of various cultural and other contextual factors for entrepreneurial success needs to be carefully considered. In the following sections, we explore in more detail the cultural traditions of East Asia, and discuss the development of entrepreneurial culture in East Asian countries and its influence on entrepreneurial outcomes.

8.4 Cultural Traditions and Entrepreneurial Culture in East Asia

East Asian cultural traditions are built substantially on the thoughts of ancient Chinese philosophers who lived between 600 and 200BC—a period of political and social turmoil in China that produced "a hundred schools of thought" of highly diverse ideas that competed for the attention of kings and warlords who sought advice on how to establish and maintain order.[12] Among the globally most well-known of the philosophers who lived during this period are Laozi (the founder of Daoism), Kongzi (Confucius), Menzi (Mencius), and Sunzi (author of "The Art of War").[13] Arguably, the most consequential among these thinkers are Confucius (551-479BC), who founded a new school of thinking, and Mencius (372-289BC), who built on and further developed Confucius's ideas.

What are core Confucian ideas? The basic tenet of Confucianism is the establishment of social order through values such as *ren* (humanity), *yi* (moral responsibility), *li* (ritual), *zhi* (knowledge), *xin* (trustworthiness), and *xiao* (filial piety).[14] If everyone observes these values, social order and harmony in society is established, it is argued. In essence, more experienced and knowledgeable individuals should share their knowledge and wisdom with less experienced others, and the less experienced individuals should follow the advice of more experienced individuals. Though Confucianism assumes that the nature of human beings is good, its core ideas seek to establish harmony based on an inherently unequal status of individuals. Furthermore, Confucianism emphasises relationalism, as its core values are always applied in relationships between individuals, as opposed to principles that individuals could follow by themselves, without particular regard of their relationships with others.

These Confucian core principles and ideas became the dominant doctrine of government in China from the third century until the end of the Chinese empire in 1911.[15] Confucianism also dominated Korean state doctrine and society throughout the Chosun dynasty (1392–1910).[16] In Japan, Confucianism became highly influential during the Edo Period (1603–1868).[17] Taken together, Confucianism has had a very strong and lasting cultural influence in all three countries, not least because it was a central tenet of government doctrine, society, and education systems for many centuries.

In various ways, the Confucian cultural values that dominated East Asian countries until the relatively recent past have not been supportive for entrepreneurship. First, in alignment with Confucian thought, Japan, Korea, and China all established and maintained class societies until the nineteenth century whereby a differential social status was given to individuals based on their occupations. Among these occupation-based classes, merchants and traders were given low social status, since generating income through commercial activities was not seen as a valuable way of living. Furthermore, class-based societies in which the social status and range of opportunities given to individuals have been ascribed and mostly inherited over generations based on occupations made it very difficult for individuals to seek new opportunities.

Second, various Confucian values countervail Western entrepreneurial culture (as discussed in the previous section). Specifically, the emphasis on unequal relationships between individuals based on their relative amount of experience and knowledge makes it difficult to challenge and change the status quo in East Asia. For example, social status is often assessed through the relative age of individuals. This means that you should always follow the advice given to you by more senior individuals, and the superior status of these senior individuals versus yours will never change. Confucian relationalism also results in an emphasis on social relationships that counteracts individual ambitions and aspirations, particularly those of young individuals.

Furthermore, East Asian education systems that have been influenced by Confucian values have focused on rote learning—essentially following the instructions of teachers and memorising contents given by them. In contrast, critical thinking by students has been strongly discouraged. Finally, and supported by relationalism, Confucian cultural values encourage taking a long-term perspective on activities and outcomes. In essence, what individuals should consider most important is the extent to which they have really supported their children and other junior individuals by the end of their lives. Conversely, pursuing short-term financial or other opportunities is frowned upon.

Overall, it is clear that Confucian cultural traditions in East Asia countervail Western-style and, in particular, Silicon Valley-style entrepreneurial culture. The free-wheeling, individualistic quest for new ideas and business opportunities by Western entrepreneurs is certainly at odds with the values, beliefs, and practices that have dominated East Asian societies for centuries.

Does this mean that, from a cultural perspective, there is no fertile ground for startup entrepreneurship in East Asia? Not necessarily. In recent times, East Asian countries have undergone major cultural change, and this change has resulted in more favourable conditions for entrepreneurship. Furthermore, regardless of their shared cultural traditions, there is considerable cultural variety across the East Asian countries, and therefore their cultures should not be viewed as monolithic.

In the following section, we first take a look at some recent indicators of cultural preferences and entrepreneurship in Japan, Korea, and China, and then review how entrepreneurial culture has evolved in each of the three countries.

8.5 Evolving Entrepreneurial Culture in East Asia

Japan, Korea, and China have each undergone major political, economic, and societal upheavals since the late nineteenth century. All three countries experienced dramatic change and emerged as major global manufacturing and innovation powers in recent decades. Therefore, the following question arises: how and to what extent do Confucian values, which have been previously dominant in the three countries, continue to influence their culture in general and entrepreneurial culture in particular?

Irrespective of their somewhat diverse methodologies and findings and their limitations, the aforementioned four major global studies on cultural values offer some observations on recent cultural values in Japan, Korea, and China from a global comparative perspective.[18] First, collectivism is relatively strong across all three countries. Second, the cultures of the three countries are relatively top-down, with hierarchical values being particularly strong in Korea and China. Third, findings on risk-taking attitudes in the three countries are somewhat inconsistent across the studies, particularly as regards China. Overall, however, the results suggest that on average, most individuals in the three countries tend to avoid risk. Fourth, there is a strong long-term orientation in the three East Asian countries.

Taken together, these observations suggest that, regardless of major societal and economic change, Confucian cultural values such as relationship orientation, hierarchy and deference, and a preference for taking a long-term perspective, are still prevalent in East Asia. These values, and a tendency to avoid risk, do not seem to be conducive for vibrant startup entrepreneurship from a Western perspective and, in particular, from a Silicon Valley perspective.

As we already have seen in Chaps. 4–6, however, there are major and rapidly growing startup ecosystems in Japan, Korea, and China. Furthermore, data on entrepreneurial activity in general also do not indicate that entrepreneurship is weak across East Asia (see Table 8.2). Instead, the data point towards considerable differences between Japan, Korea, and China. In Korea, the rate of entrepreneurial intention is extraordinarily high, and the rate of early-stage entrepreneurial activity is almost as high as in North America and much higher than in European countries. For China, both indicators are somewhat lower, but they are still higher than in most major European countries. In contrast, the entrepreneurial activity indicators for Japan are below average among the large industrialised economies.

In summary, our review so far has shown that despite cultural values in East Asia differing from those in Western countries—and appearing less supportive of entrepreneurship from a Western lens—startup activity in the region remains vibrant. Moreover, significant variations exist in entrepreneurial activity levels among Japan, Korea, and China. Next, we explore how entrepreneurial culture has evolved in each of these three countries and examine the role of cultural values in shaping entrepreneurship within their distinct socio-cultural contexts.

8.5.1 Japan

Before turning towards industrialisation and Westernisation in the late nineteenth century, Japan in the Edo Period followed a Neo-Confucian social order adopted from China through Korea. Neo-Confucianism in Japan placed merchants in the lower ranks of social hierarchy, below peasants who were seen as self-sufficient and more productive. Furthermore, strongly collectivistic values were widespread in Japan, reinforced through arrangements such as shared water irrigation systems for paddy fields where farming villages became tight-knit communities.[19] However, historians show that the socioeconomic structures that upheld such official social order kept undergoing various changes, in effect creating the basis for the remarkable modernisation and economic growth of Japan in the Meiji Period (1868–1912). Despite formal distinctions between social groups (e.g., merchants and samurai), the realities of growing urbanisation in practice blurred these divisions. A degree of intermingling emerged, reflected in shared urban spaces and participation in new forms of culture such as *kabuki* theatre.[20]

The new Meiji government started pursuing capitalism for the "national interest," elevating the social status of those involved in business activities. Nevertheless, since old perceptions did not completely disappear, former samurai—previously the group at the top of Neo-Confucian social hierarchy—tended to favour joining the government as it was the centre of power and the occupation was held in particularly high public esteem. In face of such attitudes, leading Meiji era reformers such as Eiichi Shibusawa were worried that if the public image of businessmen could not reach the levels of appreciation of politicians and administrators, recruiting top talent would be very difficult, especially because going into business tended to be risky and did not necessarily yield high monetary rewards. Thus, reformers worked towards creating a more attractive cultural perception of businesspeople—contrasting new entrepreneurs with old merchants while simultaneously portraying them as heirs of esteemed samurai values. New entrepreneurs were depicted as honest and educated men who applied modern knowledge for the purpose of national interest. Professed ideals of loyalty and (public) service—echoing the *bushidō* (samurai code of chivalry)—were also portrayed as distinguishing the new Japanese entrepreneurs from Western capitalists who focused on their own profits.[21]

After the Second World War, Japan experienced another era of transformation and economic growth. Previously dominant business conglomerates (*zaibatsu*), seen as one of the backbones of militarism of the Japanese Empire, were targeted with anti-monopoly reforms initiated by the US occupying forces. While the *zaibatsu* conglomerates were dissolved, there was an increase in activities of smaller enterprises and entrepreneurs, including those that successfully shifted their products and operations to meet peacetime demands (e.g., Soichiro Honda).[22] However, as the post-war recovery progressed, the old *zaibatsu* were reconfigured as horizontal, loosely connected *keiretsu* business groups, characterised by cross-shareholdings and directors of member companies sitting on each other's boards. Consequently, the role of big business was prominent again, especially in light of its collaboration with the Ministry of International Trade and Industry (MITI) that spearheaded hugely influential industrial policy.[23]

A distinctive Japanese management system that solidified in the post-war era had important characteristics in the areas of finance (e.g., the main bank system) and labour (e.g., lifetime employment, seniority-based pay, and corporate unions). These characteristics promoted long-term orientation, stability, and loyalty.[24] Also, the gap in remuneration between employees and top managers, even in large Japanese enterprises, was much lower than in rival US firms.[25] These various features of the system could be argued to support more harmonious group relations and echo traditional Confucian cultural values—including strong relationship orientation, a focus on social hierarchy, and an emphasis on taking a long-term perspective.

Small and medium enterprises (SMEs) were abundant and contributed in important ways to innovation in Japan. However, and especially in manufacturing, many of them functioned primarily as subcontractors of large companies, being in close and long-term relationships with them.[26] Overall, large companies held a dominant position in the society and economy of Japan, which was also reflected in, for instance, the preference of graduates of top universities to join large firms, or in small firms sometimes being considered a "problem" (as supposedly being too numerous and less efficient).[27] However, over time, when Silicon Valley-style innovation gained prominence and when entrepreneurship started to be viewed globally as a promising engine of economic growth and new job creation, Japan too began placing increasing hopes on fostering a specific type of entrepreneurship—growth-oriented "venture business" or, in other words, startups.[28]

Indeed, since the 1990s—particularly after the collapse of Japan's bubble economy—various attempts to adapt to the forces of globalisation and rapid technological change, including the gradual decline of the post-war industrial policy and implementation of neo-liberal policies, propelled a certain level of convergence towards the Silicon Valley innovation model in Japan, empowering more individualistic types of entrepreneurial actors, including founders themselves and their support networks, such as angel investors and independent venture capitalists.[29] Nevertheless, despite these changes and the development and strengthening of a large startup ecosystem in Tokyo, as well as more nascent ecosystems in several other cities, entrepreneurship in Japan continues to be strongly influenced by cultural values and institutional arrangements that have been long present in the country.[30]

For example, increased fluidity in employment systems has engendered a culture that is more permissive to mid-career transitions (in contrast to the post-war ideal of staying in the same—preferably large—company for life) as well as some level of entrepreneurial risk taking. METI (the Ministry of Economy, Trade and Industry—the successor of MITI) has created various policies and initiatives to support startups, including those aimed at promoting an entrepreneurial culture. However, given the enduring emphasis on social order, Japanese policymakers tend to prioritise sustaining large corporations over the pursuit of "creative destruction", even as they simultaneously seek to foster startup entrepreneurship.[31] This points to a focus on more harmonious collective dynamics, in alignment with Japanese cultural traditions.

Moreover, while many Japanese startups today adopt flatter organisational structures or Silicon Valley-style fundraising, Confucian values—such as focus on relationships, strong hierarchies, and long-term orientation—continue to shape the entrepreneurial landscape of Japan. One of the important ways in which entrepreneurs in Japan differ from their Western counterparts is by frequently embracing the "lifework" approach to entrepreneurship versus the "project" orientation approach. In the "lifework" approach, founders tend to commit to their venture with a long-term perspective in mind rather than treat it as a more temporary activity—a project—from which one can move on or adjust one's commitment. Japanese entrepreneurial founders also tend to act more like a "locomotive" (rather than a "conductor") of their company, meaning that they put more focus on having control.[32] Furthermore, Japan's startup founders often self-describe as belonging to a "village" (*mura*) of people involved with startups and venture capitalists, thereby highlighting the relational focus within relatively tight-knit communities.[33] Additionally, there is a perception that Japanese founders must demonstrate resilience and drive to earn favour with local investors.[34] Given that Japanese startups remain predominantly led by native male entrepreneurs, the relationships and personal traits they emphasise are often embedded in social hierarchies where people with these characteristics hold a dominant position.

Overall, while recent decades have witnessed a general trend of rising individualism in Japan, certain features of such individualism are clearly less desirable in the local cultural and institutional context. One illustration of what constitutes a code of conduct violation in Japan is the story of Takafumi Horie, the founder of the Internet company Livedoor. Takafumi Horie led a flashy lifestyle, interacted with established business elites in a confrontational way and, after engaging in certain grey areas, was imprisoned for securities fraud, with his company being delisted from the Tokyo Stock Exchange (TSE).[35] This triggered the so-called Livedoor Scandal of 2006 that negatively impacted TSE Mothers (a section of the TSE focused on startup companies) and made some people nervous about pursuing entrepreneurial activity. While arguably the most important issue in the fall of Horie was his attempt at a hostile takeover of Nippon Broadcasting System Inc., this story was also portrayed in Western media as an exemplification of the attitude that in Japan "the nail that sticks out gets hammered down".[36] In the Japanese media there were also numerous commentaries and narratives, but even if one was to look for comments centred on the aspect of individualism, certain prominent outlets would often present the situation quite differently than in the Western media. For example, the behaviour of Horie was contrasted with the more humble attitude of doing business demonstrated by other young entrepreneurs who, rather than having an office in the central, costly, and fashionable Roppongi Hills have chosen to be located in an inconspicuous building on the outskirts of Tokyo.[37] Such narratives could be argued to also link to public concerns about *kakusa shakai* (disparity society) in Japan, in addition to the key issue of Horie acting in a confrontational way towards incumbents.

Conversely, many other well-known and individualistic startup entrepreneurs have behaved in more culturally acceptable ways. Examples include Masayoshi Son, the founder of SoftBank; Hiroshi Mikitani, the founder of Rakuten, and Tomoko Namba, the founder of DeNA. These successful entrepreneurs distinguished themselves not by rejecting the establishment, but by strategically engaging with and reshaping it. Rather than adopting a purely confrontational stance, they pursued influence through constructive, collective action and integration. A prime example is Hiroshi Mikitani's role in founding the Japan Association of New Economy (JANE). This organisation, acting as a "new Keidanren" (Keidanren being the Japanese Business Federation) for the digital age, provided a formal and powerful collective voice for advanced technology companies and their industry representatives to lobby the government and interact with traditional business federations. This demonstrated a commitment to systemic evolution rather than lone-wolf disruption. By deliberately positioning the association as a constructive counterpart rather than an open antagonist to the traditional Keidanren, Mikitani could promote policy change while avoiding the confrontational style that had undermined Takafumi Horie. Over the past decade JANE has submitted dozens of white papers, organised high-profile "New Economy Summits", and secured concrete concessions—including simplified procedures for cashless payments and sandbox frameworks for mobility services—demonstrating that institutional entrepreneurship can coexist with culturally endorsed modesty in Japan.

This discussion confirms the overall observation that the human capital of founders in East Asia (including education and prior experience), in combination with networks built while studying and working in established companies, can strongly enhance their startup performance.[38]

In sum, even if many startup entrepreneurs have an outsider status in Japan (since they take risks and deviate from the idealised social norm of working for a large company), it is still important for them not to behave too confrontationally, and to conform to some extent to Japan's cultural norms. At the same time, the overall trend of cultural change is clearly favourable to startup entrepreneurship, as individualism is increasing, and there is a certain level of convergence towards a Silicon Valley-style of entrepreneurship, albeit with many distinct Japan-specific features. The public image of entrepreneurs is becoming more attractive, and there is an increasing policy support for startups. Also, various educational institutions have introduced courses to cultivate "entrepreneurial spirit" (*kigyōka seishin*), which can be expected to further propel entrepreneurial culture in Japan.

8.5.2 Korea

A strictly Neo-Confucian social order was maintained in Korea prior to the end of the nineteenth century, and entrepreneurship could not thrive under these conditions. However, this began to change after Japan gradually took control of Korea around the turn of the twentieth century and formally annexed the country in 1910. The subsequent period of colonial control by Japan (which ended in 1945) generally does not invoke positive memories in Korea due to political suppression and economic colonisation. Nonetheless, entrepreneurial activity began to grow during this period, as the Japanese rulers dismantled the pre-modern Korean state and replaced it with a capitalist system that emulated the structure that had been established in Japan after the Meiji Restoration of 1868. While Korean entrepreneurs and their companies were discriminated against under colonial rule, it now became possible to engage in business entrepreneurship under modern, rule-based conditions. Therefore, numerous Koreans, the majority of whom were from poor or modest backgrounds, seized this opportunity and created new businesses. Some among these early Korean entrepreneurs were highly successful and they accumulated considerable wealth.[39]

After Korea was liberated from Japanese rule in 1945, subsequent years brought chaos and devastation to the country. Upon its liberation, Korea was divided into a communist North under Soviet, and later, Chinese influence, and a capitalist South under American influence. This division resulted in an implosion of economic activities, followed by millions of deaths and the destruction of much of the country's infrastructure during the Korean War between 1950 and 1953. Thereafter, Korea was ruled by military dictatorships from 1961 to 1987.

Improbably and remarkably, business entrepreneurship continued to thrive in Korea throughout this highly volatile period. Numerous entrepreneurs sought opportunities in chaos, and some among them were extremely successful. They created business conglomerates which grew rapidly in size and scope. In the following decades, some of these conglomerates became leading global competitors in knowledge-intensive industries such as information and communication technology (ITC) and automobiles.[40] For example, Lee Byung-chul, who founded Samsung in 1938, turned his business into a leading Korean conglomerate that subsequently became one of the world's largest competitors in the ITC industry under the leadership of his son, Lee Kun-hee.[41] Similarly, Chung Ju-yung founded Hyundai Group in the late 1940s. Hyundai quickly became Korea's largest construction business and ventured into automobile manufacturing in 1967. Under the leadership of Chung, and later his son and grandson, Hyundai Motor became a leading global automobile manufacturer.[42]

Industrial policies from the 1960s that focused on expanding the manufacturing sector and promoting exports have frequently been mentioned as the main reason for the explosive growth of Korean conglomerates (*chaebols*) in the second half of the twentieth century.[43] However, while governmental support policies certainly helped the *chaebols*, some conglomerates were also highly successful on global markets even after the Korean government wound down export subsidies and other support measures. More generally, and aside from policy support, culture needs to be considered if we are to fully understand the remarkable success of Korean business groups.

Although Korea transitioned from a pre-modern economic system to modern capitalism in the twentieth century, traditional cultural values were still highly influential. Importantly, types of human relationships based upon Confucian principles have been transposed to the company and workplace context. Specifically, two of the Confucian cardinal relationships prescribe that within a family everyone has to follow the father, and within a country everyone has to follow the monarch. In Korea, these principles were commonly reinterpreted in such a way that everyone has to follow the manager within the "family" of a workplace team, and that everyone has to follow the Chief Executive Officer (CEO) or the chairman within the larger context of a company or business group.[44] As a result, *chaebol* leaders had enormous leverage over their associates. They could effectively apply bold and aggressive business strategies in the knowledge that all employees would follow and implement their directions unconditionally, quickly and enthusiastically. Senior managers could even deliberately instil crises on their companies to push workers to a higher performance level.[45] In other words, traditional cultural values strongly supported Korean entrepreneurs in very different ways to their Western counterparts. Being at the pinnacle of corporate organisations gave Korean business leaders extraordinary influence over their followers, and they could use this influence effectively to enhance the success of their businesses.

As discussed in Chap. 5, startup entrepreneurship once again took off in Korea in the 2010s, with strong policy support playing an important role in creating favourable conditions for the growth of major startup ecosystems. However, aside from policy support, the cultural context also needs to be considered for a deeper understanding of why so many startups have been established in Korea in recent years, and why so many of them are thriving.

Korea has become a rich country over the last decades, and millions of Koreans study or work abroad for years, mostly in the USA and other Western countries. This high level of economic development and income, combined with the widespread exposure of Koreans to Western countries and cultures, have engendered a profound cultural change, particularly among younger generations. Specifically, younger Koreans no longer accept the authoritarian leadership style that has been the norm among entrepreneurs and business leaders over many decades. Nowadays, young Korean professionals show far less enthusiasm for working at major conglomerates, viewing their corporate cultures as overly hierarchical and conservative. Valuing workplace autonomy, many now leave these companies when it is lacking, choosing instead to launch or join technology startups.[46] A growing number of Korean graduates are also now choosing startup careers over traditional employment, driven by the same pursuit of workplace freedom. These trends illustrate the growing willingness among young Koreans to trade higher salaries and social prestige for greater autonomy and professional fulfilment.

The growing allure of startup entrepreneurship to recent generations of young Korean professionals has been further amplified by high-profile success stories that serve as powerful role models of entrepreneurial achievement. One example is Kim Beom-su, who grew up in abject poverty in Seoul with eight family members sharing one room. After having worked for a few years for a subsidiary of Samsung, Kim Beom-su started his first own business in 1997 and subsequently founded Kakao, which became Korea's dominant text messaging and social media platform after just a few years.[47] Another example is Kim Bom Suk, who returned to Korea after studying and working in the USA to found the social commerce company Coupang in 2010. Subsequently, he boldly transformed the business into an integrated e-commerce platform, relying on a global team of executives and professionals that included more than 200 non-Koreans. Despite strong resistance from Korea's entrenched business community, Kim Bom Suk succeeded in growing the company into the country's largest and market-dominating e-commerce business.[48]

What all this means is that Korean technology startups now face significantly fewer challenges in recruiting highly skilled and motivated technical and managerial talent—a critical shift given that talent acquisition previously was very difficult and served as a major growth bottleneck in Korea. In short, aside from governmental support policies, cultural change in Korea constitutes a key driving force for the growth of startup ecosystems in the country.

Overall, while traditional cultural values in Korea previously supported *chaebol* entrepreneurs in important ways, cultural change is now a major driving force of the growth of startup entrepreneurship. This demonstrates that the cultural context, which is very different from Western countries, has been crucial for enabling and supporting entrepreneurship in Korea. It further illustrates that entrepreneurship can thrive under very different conditions, and that Korean entrepreneurs need to be responsive to the cultural context in which they are embedded instead of blindly pursuing a Western (or Silicon Valley) entrepreneurial culture that is less relevant in Korea.

8.5.3 China

China's entrepreneurial culture was shaped by Confucian traditions, socialist suppression, and post-reform resurgence. Its evolution reveals a paradoxical coexistence of hierarchy and innovation, where entrepreneurial vitality persists despite various institutional constraints.

Despite the emphasis of Confucianism on hierarchy, collectivism, and risk aversion, China's history reveals a resilient undercurrent of entrepreneurial activity that operated within, rather than against, Confucian norms. For example, during the Ming and Qing dynasties (1368–1840), regional merchant groups like the Shanxi and Huizhou clans built vast trade networks rooted in familial ties and localised credit systems.[49] These enterprises thrived by leveraging Confucian ethical principles such as *xin* (trustworthiness) and *yi* (moral responsibility) to sustain long-term collaborations, demonstrating how commerce could flourish by co-opting, rather than rejecting, dominant cultural frameworks. Nevertheless, this adaptability existed in tension with Confucianism's rigid social stratification, which relegated merchants to the bottom of the "scholar-farmer-artisan-merchant" (*shi nong gong shang*) hierarchy, systemically marginalising entrepreneurship for centuries. This duality underscores a historical paradox: China's commercial traditions persisted not through overt resistance to Confucian values but via informal networks and moral bargains that granted them extra-institutional legitimacy. Merchants navigated this contradiction by embedding their practices in Confucian ethics to secure internal cohesion while remaining politically invisible, a strategic ambivalence that fundamentally shaped Chinese entrepreneurial culture.

Following the establishment of the People's Republic of China in 1949, the socialist planned economy fundamentally restructured the economic framework. Private enterprise was denounced as a "capitalist remnant", and the 1956 public–private joint state-private ownership campaign effectively nationalised privately-owned businesses, nearly eliminating individual entrepreneurship.[50] During this period, entrepreneurial activities were confined to the underground economy, such as rural "black market" transactions, surviving through the circumvention of collective systems. This era of suppression not only severed commercial traditions but also instilled a profound risk aversion in society—entrepreneurship came to be viewed as both politically incorrect and fraught with uncertainty. A cultural mindset was created where independent business initiatives were seen as dangerous deviations from state-mandated economic models.

Deng Xiaoping's Reform and Opening-Up Policy in 1978 marked a turning point in China's entrepreneurial culture. The policy shift catalysed two distinct entrepreneurial pathways: grassroots entrepreneurship and institutional transition. First, grassroots entrepreneurship enabled rural entrepreneurs such as Lu Guanqiu (the founder of Wanxiang Group) to leverage local resources and policy ambiguities to transform family workshops into manufacturing giants. Second, institutional transition was triggered by the restructuring of state-owned companies, spurring a wave of officials and professionals to "jump into the sea" (*xiahai*)—state employees who left secure jobs to pursue private ventures.[51] One example is Liu Chuanzhi, who left the Chinese Academy of Sciences to establish Lenovo, converting state-backed research and development (R&D) into market-driven products. This resurgence was further fuelled by Deng Xiaoping's Southern Tour in 1992, which accelerated market liberalisation and legitimised wealth creation. Success in this era relied on two factors: policy arbitrage and *guanxi* (a fundamental concept in Chinese society and business that refers to a system of social networks and bonds, long term relationships built on trust and loyalty, and reciprocal obligations that combine to underpin personal and professional interactions).[52] Entrepreneurs adeptly navigated regulatory grey zones to secure licenses, land, and financing, while *guanxi* effectively facilitated access to government-controlled resources, blending traditional social structures with market pragmatism.

A true watershed moment that unleashed modern China's entrepreneurial culture came in 2001 when President Jiang Zemin announced the historic decision to admit private entrepreneurs into the Chinese Communist Party. This ideological breakthrough fundamentally legitimised business ownership, dismantling decades of political stigma against capitalists and creating a new paradigm in which "getting rich is glorious" became compatible with socialist ideals.[53] This policy shift was amplified by Premier Zhu Rongji's sweeping market-oriented reforms (1998–2003), which turbocharged entrepreneurial activity through three key mechanisms: (i) the privatisation of state housing (creating personal capital for business startups), (ii) the restructuring of state-owned enterprises (releasing millions of skilled workers into the private sector), and (iii) China's accession to the World Trade Organisation (opening global markets to domestic entrepreneurs). These changes coalesced to kickstart China's venture capital market in the early 2000s—a foundation that would enable the meteoric rise of internet-era entrepreneurs.

It was against this institutional backdrop that the post-2000 internet revolution spawned a new generation of Chinese entrepreneurs who leveraged the country's huge market size while carefully balancing autonomy with global compliance norms. This cohort includes Jack Ma, whose Alibaba Group revolutionised commerce through Taobao and Alipay—digital platforms that succeeded not just through technological innovation but by addressing China's trust deficit in transactions. Alipay's escrow payment model—whereby payment is withheld until buyers confirm they have received their purchased goods—subtly echoed the Confucian value of *xin* (trustworthiness).

The success of entrepreneurs such as Jack Ma paved the way for the entrepreneurial momentum to reach new heights a decade later with Premier Li Keqiang's 2014 "Mass Entrepreneurship and Innovation" campaign. This top-down mobilisation created an unprecedented infrastructure for startups—from streamlined business registration processes to tax incentives for angel investors. The policy effectively socialised risk-taking, with local governments competing to launch innovation hubs modelled on Beijing's Zhongguancun science park. While the campaign generated some speculative bubbles, it altered career aspirations: the rate at which university graduates founded startups increased by 240% from 2014 to 2018 according to Ministry of Education data.[54]

The multi-stage evolution of entrepreneurialism in China—from ideological emancipation under Jiang, to market liberalisation under Zhu, and systematic enablement under Li—transformed entrepreneurship from being a politically suspect activity into a celebrated driver of national rejuvenation. However, this process did not reduce corporate reliance on hierarchical structures; instead, it spawned a unique governance paradox amid market liberalisation. As external constraints weakened, entrepreneurs increasingly relied on authoritarian decision-making to navigate policy uncertainties (such as sudden industry crackdowns). Hierarchical systems became the primary risk-hedging mechanism by compressing decision chains and enforcing execution discipline.

Ren Zhengfei's "corps-model" architecture at Huawei demonstrates that even while internal innovation is encouraged through "horse race mechanisms", ultimate strategic direction and resource allocation in China typically remain strictly dictated from the pyramid's apex.[55] This "enlightened authoritarianism" reflects Chinese entrepreneurs' profound obsession with control—they crave decentralised vitality yet refuse to relinquish final authority over commercial outcomes. The system permits controlled experimentation but never uncontrolled emergence, creating organisations that are simultaneously agile and autocratic. Similarly, Xiaomi, which initially thrived under flat management, rapidly adopted hierarchical structures as it scaled up, with founder Lei Jun packaging "internet thinking" to hardware ecosystems while maintaining traditional pyramid structures in supply chain management.

The cultural expression of this hierarchy is the "wolf culture" that is pervasive in China's advanced technology sectors where relentless ambition, long working hours, and intense internal competition are framed as necessary for global success.[56] Huawei's "spare tire plan" (developing domestic alternatives for key components to mitigate supply chain disruptions and a reliance on foreign technologies) and "survival mode" rhetoric transformed external sanctions into internal mobilisation tools, while ByteDance achieved rapid product iteration through "alternating six-day work weeks" and algorithm-driven "data horse races". Unlike Silicon Valley's individualism, Chinese entrepreneurship often operates within structured hierarchies that grant founders near-absolute authority—similar to Korea's *chaebol* system discussed above. Chinese entrepreneurs like Lei Ming (Xiaomi) and Zhang Yiming (ByteDance) wield this hierarchical influence to drive rapid scaling, blending Confucian notions of paternalistic leadership with market-driven ferocity, and leveraging vertical authority to fuel scaled-up expansion.[57]

However, the resistance of younger generations to the "996" work schedule (working from 9 am to 9 pm, 6 days a week), exemplified by the recent "lying flat" movement in China, is forcing corporations to recalibrate. Tencent's "Tech for Good" initiative and Alibaba's reduced overtime policies reflect attempts to balance efficiency with sustainability. These adjustments soften hierarchical expressions without dismantling their foundations—much like SHEIN's centralised control over its agile supply chain being masked by a "small-order rapid-response" model. Nevertheless, China's entrepreneurial ecosystems reveal an anti-Silicon Valley path: hierarchical and collectivist frameworks not only accommodate high-growth innovation but may even catalyse it, albeit at the cost of constraining creativity to the single dimension of execution speed and often exerting considerable pressures on the workforce.

8.6 Conclusion

In this chapter, we argue that entrepreneurial culture in East Asia rests on very different foundations than in Western countries in general and in Silicon Valley in particular. Confucian cultural values that emphasise the importance of relationships, loyalty to senior individuals, and taking a long-term perspective, combined with the rigid social class systems based on these values, caused entrepreneurship to be suppressed in East Asia up to the nineteenth century. However, when Japan, Korea, and China successively industrialised, these Confucian values enhanced the effectiveness of capable entrepreneurs who established themselves at the top of social and organisational hierarchies as business founders, thereby gaining strong authority over employees who followed their directions enthusiastically and swiftly. Through such effective top-down leadership, Japanese, Korean, and Chinese entrepreneurs have tended to grow their companies at a pace unheard of in Western countries, gaining competitive advantage through the rapid development and commercialisation of new products and services.

In recent years, cultural change has contributed to the growth of startup entrepreneurship in East Asia, while also creating new challenges for startup entrepreneurs. Confucian cultural values have gradually weakened, and the acceptance of strict, hierarchical organisational cultures is rapidly declining, especially among younger generations. Consequently, many young professionals now join startups or establish their own in the expectation that they may enjoy more freedom and autonomy in their professional lives, though not necessarily shorter working hours than in major established companies. For these reasons, startup founders in East Asia often find it easier than in the past to recruit top-notch talent for their companies. However, founders nowadays also need to apply a different leadership style from the highly autocratic East Asian entrepreneurs of earlier generations. While startup founders are still very much perceived as leaders who are expected to lead from the front, and to design and communicate their companies' overall strategies effectively, they also need to provide sufficient autonomy to their followers in order to boost their motivation and effectiveness.

In summary, the fact that entrepreneurial culture in East Asia differs strongly from the Silicon Valley role model does not mean that it is less effective. On the contrary, the combination of strong top-down leadership, strong ambition, and strong collective organisational spirit often found in Japanese, Korean and Chinese startups enable them to not only grow quickly, but also to increasingly challenge Western competitors. In other words, there are blends of entrepreneurial culture in East Asia that strongly deviate from the entrepreneurial culture of Silicon Valley but nonetheless drive major entrepreneurial success.

Notes

1. This sociological view of culture is non-normative, assumes a close linkage between culture and society and emphasises the persistence and durability of culture. The sociological perspective contrasts with traditional humanities which took a more normative stance on culture and considered it to be fragile. For a more in-depth discussion, refer to Griswold (2012, 3–10).
2. Erez and Gati (2004), 587–588.
3. Saxenian (1994).
4. Gupta and Hanges (2004), 183–203.
5. For a more detailed review and critique of the foundations and limitations of the major survey-based comparative studies of national culture, see Smith (2006) and McSweeney (2015).
6. Hayton and Cacciotti (2015), 715.
7. House et al. (2004), Hofstede et al. (2010).
8. City-level ecosystem rankings by Startup Genome and StartupBlink can be found here: https://startupgenome.com/report/gser2023 and here: https://www.startupblink.com/, respectively.
9. A detailed account of the genesis of the Silicon Valley startup ecosystem is offered by Saxenian (1994, 20–27).
10. Saxenian (1994), 30–57.
11. Plehn-Dujowich (2010), 377.
12. For a concise overview of ancient Chinese philosophers and their core ideas, refer to Chen and Lee (2008), 1–11.
13. In this book, we use the Latinised names of Kongzi and Menzi (Confucius and Mencius) because these are the names under which the philosophers are most well-known globally.
14. Chen and Lee (2008), 2.
15. Yang et al. (2008), 33.
16. Hemmert (2018), 16.
17. Boot (2013).
18. As the studies by Hofstede, Trompenaars and Hampden-Turner, GLOBE and Schwartz are based on different methodologies and datasets and the cultural dimensions they have identified are not all identical, their findings are not straightforward to compare. Therefore, we do not offer tabulated data on cultural values in East Asian countries by these studies. Instead, we would like to refer readers who have a further interest in the studies and their findings to the online resources they provide. Hofstede data can be found here: https://geerthofstede.com/culture-geert-hofstede-gert-jan-hofstede/6d-model-of-national-culture/.

    Trompenaars/Hampden-Turner data can be found here: https://www.thtconsulting.com/culture-factory/culture-explore/compare-countries/.

    GLOBE data can be found here: https://globeproject.com/results.html#country.

    Schwartz data can be found here: https://www.researchgate.net/publication/304715744_The_7_Schwartz_cultural_value_orientation_scores_for_80_countries.
19. Hanada and Tomita (2025).
20. Tipton (2016), 1–23.
21. Hirschmeier (1970).
22. Tipton (2016), 168–175.
23. Johnson (1982).
24. Aoki and Dore (1994).
25. Inagami and Whittaker (2005).
26. Ueno et al. (2006).
27. Kapturkiewicz and Kotosaka (2019), Whittaker (1997a).
28. Lechevalier (2014), Whittaker (1997b).
29. Lechevalier (2014), 121–137.
30. Kapturkiewicz (2022), Kapturkiewicz (2025), Kotosaka and Sako (2017).
31. Klingler-Vidra and Pardo (2025), 38–60.
32. Whittaker et al. (2009).

33. Frenkenberger (2023), Kapturkiewicz (2016).
34. Frenkenberger (2023).
35. Hayakawa and Whittaker (2009).
36. Forbes (2009).
37. Nihon Keizai Shimbun (2014).
38. Hemmert et al. (2024).
39. Hemmert and Kim (2021), 14–23.
40. Hemmert (2018), 28–32, 44–53.
41. Hemmert and Kim (2021), 30–34.
42. Hemmert and Kim (2021), 34–40.
43. See, for example, Amsden (1989) and Clifford (1998).
44. Hemmert (2018), 16–18.
45. Hemmert (2018), 115–120.
46. Hemmert and Kim (2021), 131.
47. Hemmert and Kim (2021), 57–59.
48. Hemmert and Kim (2021), 59–61.
49. Li et al. (2019).
50. Chinese Academy of Social Sciences (2013).
51. Chen (2012).
52. A frequently used English translation of *guanxi* is "relationship"; others include "social ties," "social capital," and "social network". However, in the literature that studies China, *guanxi* is a widely acknowledged term to use instead of a translation. See Li et al. (2022).
53. Dang (2009).
54. Ministry of Education (2018).
55. Farh and Pi (2018).
56. Liu (2024).
57. Chen and Li (2022).

Chapter 9
Political Context Conditions: The Role of Government in East Asian Startup Ecosystems

9.1 Introduction—What Role for Government?

Silicon Valley was the outcome of "spontaneous order".[1] It did not grow out of a grand design, nor was it orchestrated by a central planning unit. Instead, it evolved from decentralised entrepreneurial activities that leveraged the new profit opportunities created by digital technologies, the synergies resulting from proximity to established high-tech firms and universities, and the ability to attract a large pool of talent. In the dominant Silicon Valley narrative, the role of government was minimal. The main contribution by public authorities was to not interfere, to not subject the new disruptive business models to regulatory scrutiny, and to not obstruct the inflow of global talent.[2] However, the story of the private market-driven ecosystem is incomplete, even in the case of the prototypical model of Silicon Valley. The brief history of the digital revolution outlined in Chap. 2 has already alluded to the pivotal role played by the public sector in the USA, and especially the US government, by creating demand for Herman Hollerith's tabulating machine, by investing in telecommunication networks, or by laying the foundations of digital networks, including the internet. Other examples of the USA's "entrepreneurial state" include investments in space exploration, satellite communication and, more recently, the support for electric vehicles and autonomous driving.[3]

The success of Silicon Valley inspired many countries to develop their own domestic startup ecosystems. In the process of catching up, governments took a more active and visible role. This holds especially true for East Asia, as we discuss in the country cases presented in Chaps. 4, 5 and 6. East Asian policy initiatives were partly motivated by the inherent potential for learning that derives from being in a latecomer position. The role of the state in East Asia has not been entrepreneurial in the sense of directly expanding the frontiers of new technologies. Instead, the focus has been on improving support structures, and on overcoming national barriers for entrepreneurial activity. East Asian ecosystems have been shaped by policies in various ways, which enabled faster ecosystem assembly as latecomers.

Y. Cheng et al., *Unleashing Innovation the East Asian Way*,
https://doi.org/10.1007/978-981-95-6513-9_9

State support for entrepreneurship is typically motivated by the observation that there are not enough domestic high-tech startups combined with an assumption that the government can and should do something to improve the situation. This assumption stems from an assessment that domestic support infrastructures have deficiencies or shortcomings, making decentralised entrepreneurial initiatives insufficient for developing a vibrant startup scene. But how should support policies be designed and implemented? Arguably, entrepreneurship has little in common with the bureaucratic procedures applied within governmental institutions or the conservative nature of legislative processes dominated by status-quo interests. Entrepreneurs are successful because they ignore precedents and break away from established routines. They take high risks, indicating they are not afraid of failure. In contrast, bureaucrats rely on precedents and routines. They are risk-averse and try to avoid mistakes. Entrepreneurial activity seems to be similarly alienated from politics. Political decision-making favours the status quo. It is shaped by the interests of established businesses with preferential access to policymakers. Entrepreneurs are outsiders who challenge the status quo. Who would promote policies in support of such outsiders?

The model of the "developmental state" may provide an answer to these questions. The term was coined by Chalmers Johnson in his historical study of Japan's Ministry of International Trade and Industry (MITI).[4] The underlying ideas can at least be dated back to the German writer, policy adviser and entrepreneur, Friedrich List (1789–1846).[5] The developmental state became a central concept in the analysis of the economic success not only of Japan, but of other economies in East Asia and beyond.[6] It seemed especially well-suited to the late developing economies that sought to quickly upgrade their industrial structure and technological capabilities. The model has been hailed as a pragmatic middle way between a market economy and a planned economy. On the theoretical side, it stimulated comparative analyses of national economic policies, which contributed to a better understanding of their embeddedness in wider historical and socio-cultural national context and the acceptance of the logical consequence that capitalism comes in a variety of forms.[7] But to what extent does the developmental state model help us understand the role of government in the evolution of East Asian startup ecosystems?

The next three sections examine the evolution of startup ecosystem policies in Japan, Korea, and mainland China from a wider historical perspective. We then summarise and compare the three country cases, and discuss our findings in light of the three questions raised above.

9.2 Japan—Promoting Startups to Revitalise an "Aging" Economy

Japan was by no means a latecomer in the field of digital technologies. Much of its post-war success related to its ability to exploit the business potential inherent in digitalisation. Prominent examples are the successful miniaturisation of the transistor in consumer electronics and office equipment, whereby Japanese companies conquered world markets; the global success of Nintendo and Sony in console video games; the early introduction of numerically controlled machines, whereby Japanese companies ushered in the era of flexible automation in manufacturing; and NTT Docomo's i-mode, which pioneered the mobile internet. Japan was also able to establish a strong e-commerce platform company, Rakuten, and it hosts a major social media platform, LINE. Statistics with regards to business expenditures on research and development (R&D) and the ownership of international patents attest to Japanese companies a leading role in the development of new and innovative products and services, including digital technologies. Why then did the government come to conclude that Japan's national innovation system was lacking startups?

One major concern for policymakers was Japan's relatively poor growth performance entering the 1990s. Also, the population was rapidly aging and had started to decline after 2010. The legacy of Japan's pre-1990 economic success continued to be strongly felt in the economy's institutional setup, and its downsides became increasingly apparent. In particular, the preferential access of large corporations to domestic talent via the coordinated nationwide hiring of university graduates put smaller companies at an even greater disadvantage as graduate numbers declined.[8] Meanwhile, long-term orientation supported by employee loyalty made Japan the country with the largest share of long-lived companies globally. The flip side was a low rate of new company formations.

Against this backdrop, the Japanese government sought to break away from the economy's "low metabolism" and to revitalise economic activity. The digital transformation described in Chap. 2 was perceived as an opportunity, and high-tech startups were considered to be an important ingredient within a policy mix that initially did not explicitly focus on new ventures, but instead on reforms to improve innovation, regional revitalisation, internationalisation, and structural change. To illustrate, towards the end of the 1990s, the reforms of national research universities that were directed towards improving the transfer of technology between university research and private businesses, and at facilitating the exploitation of new inventions through university spinoffs and university-industry collaborations, also improved the conditions for startups to flourish.

Startups explicitly entered the spotlight under "Abenomics", the economic policy framework launched by Shinzo Abe during his second term as prime minister from 2012 to 2020.[9] Abenomics consisted of three "arrows". The first two addressed monetary and fiscal policy, while the third one targeted structural reform, which was meant to also improve the business environment for startups. "Society 5.0", which was introduced by the government in 2016 in response to Germany's "Industry 4.0" as Japan's vision of a digital future, constituted another important policy shift, and it was originally conceived as the guiding theme of Japan's 5th Science and Technology Basic Plan. However, it soon became referenced in other policies and endorsed by Japanese industry. As a framework to allocate public funding to basic research, "Society 5.0" did not address startups in particular, but through its wider impact on public policy discourse, the potential of digital technologies became broadly understood, and their diffusion through startups was emphasised as a political priority.

Japan's regulatory framework needed to be adjusted to the needs of digital business models. In 2013, the Abe government revived an experimental approach to deregulation already tested under the Koizumi administration by designating specific cities or regions as National Specific Strategic Zones (NSSZ).[10] In 2014, the city of Fukuoka became an NSSZ for "Global Startup and Job Creation". In 2018, "regulatory sandboxes" were introduced to temporarily test the viability and impact of innovative business ideas. By March 2023, 29 projects had been approved in areas such as fintech, AI and the Internet of Things, mobility, and healthcare.[11]

In June 2018, METI launched the J-startup platform to offer systematic support to promising startups with respect to branding, networking, mentoring, and internationalisation (see Table 9.1). The program adopted a "select and concentrate" approach: from over 10,000 Japanese startups, 30 to 50 high-potential firms—typically in deep tech, platforms, or Sustainable Development Goal (SDG)-oriented areas—were rigorously evaluated by private-sector advisors and an external review panel. Selected firms received clear benefits in visibility and ecosystem connectivity. Nonetheless, founders have noted that beyond the "branding lift," deeper engagement—such as substantial funding, improved customer access, or significant business development opportunities—was often modest. Still, it was acknowledged that the program's primary value was the public recognition of the importance of startups for innovation, not post-selection growth support. The 2021–2026 Basic Plan's expansion of the Small Business Innovation Research (SBIR) support scheme to startups partially addressed this gap by tying public procurement to early commercialisation, but scale and ministry adoption remain binding constraints.

In 2019, Japan's Cabinet Office initiated the complementary Startup City program with the aim to develop "world-class startup ecosystems". In addition to Fukuoka, three other cities and regions were designated as Global Startup Cities: Tokyo, Kansai (Osaka), and Central (Nagoya), and four more under the category of Startup Cities: Sapporo, Sendai, Hiroshima, and Kitakyushu. The designated cities had to commit to develop strong startup support infrastructures (see Table 9.2). They were the first to be allowed to issue startup visas for foreigners. The visa program started in 2019 and sought to attract foreign entrepreneurs to Japan in order to strengthen the diversity and international linkages of domestic startup ecosystems.

In 2020, the Basic Act on Science and Technology enacted in 1995 as a framework for Japan's technology policy and implemented through five-year "basic plans", was substantially revised by expanding its coverage to the social sciences and humanities, and by emphasising the role of "innovation creation". The act was consequently renamed as the Basic Act on Science, Technology and Innovation. The present 6th

Table 9.1 Support program of the J-Startup platform

– Select: Competitive selection of promising startups with help of private experts
– Connect: J-Startup community, policy support, private sector support
– Go global: Supporting global expansion with Japan External Trade Organization

Source J-Startup, https://www.j-startup.go.jp/en/about/

Table 9.2 Strategy initiatives under Japan's Startup City project

– Creation of startup cities through research, specific support measures, landmark programs, internationalisation (networks, visas)
– Empowerment of universities
– Cutting edge acceleration programs
– Gap funding for deep tech startups
– Public procurement for startups
– Enhancement of network and community
– Increasing mobility of human resources

Source Cabinet Office, https://www8.cao.go.jp/cstp/openinnovation/ecosystem/index.html

Plan (2021–2026) under the theme "Realising Society 5.0" refers to the formation of innovation ecosystems as an explicit goal. It opened the (SBIR) support scheme introduced in 1999 to startups. The SBIR obtained a JPY 200bn (USD 18.5bn) budget to support public procurement from startups by various ministries. The 6th plan also emphasises entrepreneurial education, the promotion of startup hubs in cities, and co-creation projects by industry, universities and government.

Building on these initiatives, the Kishida government (2021–2024) adopted a five-year plan for promoting startups that was targeted towards: "(1) fostering human resources and building networks that facilitate the creation of startups, (2) strengthening the supply of funding for startups and diversifying exit strategies, and (3) promoting open innovation" (see Table 9.3).[12] The plan grew out of PM Fumio Kishida's vision of a "New Form of Capitalism". The plan, which received a record high earmarked budget of JPY 1 tn (USD 10bn) continues to be implemented under the government of Prime Minister Shigeru Ishiba, although his policy speech of November 29th 2024 mentioned startups only once.[13] The five-year plan also established a Minister in Charge of Startups, as one of the policy fields of the Minister of State for Economic and Fiscal Policy.

Overall, the Japanese government has ramped up its support for high-tech startups and startup ecosystems by addressing various deficiencies and shortcomings of domestic support infrastructures, such as entrepreneurship education, university startups, startup-business ties, and internationalisation. However, it did not fully endorse the idea of market disruption. For example, the US ride-sharing provider Uber has so far only been allowed to operate in Japan through tie-ups with Japanese taxi companies. Using an Uber-Taxi comes with a reservation surcharge, which does no harm to Japan's taxi industry. Similarly, Airbnb is subject to Japanese private lodging (*Minpaku*) regulations. Moreover, it is estimated that around 90% of government funding of corporate R&D continues to be received by large corporations.[14]

Table 9.3 Support measures under Japan's 5-year plan

1. Pillar—Building human resources and networks for startup creation
– Improve entrepreneurship education at Japanese universities and other higher education institutions
– Develop startup incubation facilities at universities with national research institutes and experts from large corporations
– Aim at "one exit from 50 startups" at each research university across Japan by 2027
– Commercialize 5000 university projects in Startup cities by 2027
– Improve commercialisation of universities' intellectual property
– Establish a 100-billion-yen fund by the Japan Science and Technology Agency
– Improve access to and support by experienced mentors
– Attract more foreign entrepreneurs and investors
– Establish entrepreneur development hubs overseas
– Expand study abroad programs
– Establish global startup campus concept with international universities and global companies
– Focus funding for research on the development of younger researchers
2. Pillar—Enhancing funding, diversifying exit options, and public procurement
– Redirect existing public organisations and programs towards startup support, such as SME and Regional Innovation, Japan; Japan Investment Corporation; Development Bank of Japan; NEDO; AMED; redirect R&D related subsidies
– Measures to encourage investments in and financing of startups by individuals, crowdfunding, banks, GPIF and foreign investors
– More flexible use of stock options
– Improve IPO environment
– Increase public procurement from startups
3. Pillar—Open innovation, promoting collaboration between large companies and startups
– Tax measures to promote open innovation and M&A exit strategies
– Improve restructuring regulations
– Support labour mobility
– Using J-Startup and Japan Open Innovation Council to strengthen collaboration between large companies and startups

Source Cabinet Secretariat, https://www.cas.go.jp/jp/seisaku/atarashii_sihonsyugi/pdf/sdfyplan2022en.pdf

9.3 Korea—Startups to Break Away from Conglomerate Industrial Structures

Korea's startup support policies evolved from the late 1990s and were informed by the interventionist mindset of industrialisation and export promotion policies prevalent in previous decades. After regaining independence in 1945 and following the Korean War, the government initially focused on import substitution policies to strengthen the domestic manufacturing base. The Korean market was closed for imports of basic consumer goods such as textiles and processed food. Furthermore, selected companies received substantial government support to ramp up production in these industries, including the provision of hard currency at favourable exchange rates to import raw materials (e.g., cotton, flour, and sugar) for processing in Korea, as well as non-repayable loans and tax exemptions.[15]

Following a coup in 1961, Korea was led by military governments until the 1980s. During this period, industrialisation policies became even more interventionist, with five-year economic plans stipulating production targets in specific designated industries. The targets changed over time from labour-intensive industries (e.g., textiles and apparel) to capital-intensive basic industries (e.g., steel, cement, chemicals), and then to knowledge-intensive assembly industries such as electronics and machinery.[16] Furthermore, the policy focus shifted from import substitution to export promotion. However, the policy interventions, while becoming more proactive and aggressive, resembled those from the 1950s: a focus on the development of specific industries and the selection of specific companies to implement economic development plans. Again, the selected companies were comprehensively supported through a variety of measures, including low-interest loans, tax credits, preferential tariffs, and export subsidies. In contrast to the 1950s, the industrialisation policies during this period were spectacularly successful. Industrial production, exports and income levels increased dramatically. While the government stepped back from explicit industrialisation planning and the direct support of designated companies from the 1980s, its highly interventionist policy approach gained strong legitimacy.

The industrialisation policies of the Korean government could initially be regarded as resembling startup support policies in some important aspects, though the term 'startup' and the concept of startup ecosystems did not exist at the time: relatively young and promising companies with initially modest resources were comprehensively supported to achieve rapid growth. However, as a result of their success, the supported companies rapidly evolved from "startups" into large, diversified conglomerates that dominated entire industries and had privileged access to capital and highly skilled professionals. Consequently, governmental support policies for small and medium-sized enterprises (SMEs) during the 1980s and 1990s primarily focused on protecting such firms from the unfair business practices of large conglomerates, and on providing them with tax and financial benefits to help them survive in a business environment dominated by *chaebols*.[17] However, there were no dedicated startup support policies at this time.

The policy direction in Korea changed suddenly during the Asian Financial Crisis of 1997, as an initial liquidity crisis turned into a general economic crisis that forced numerous Korean conglomerates to restructure and reduce their workforces in order to survive. While rolling out emergency measures to help conglomerates overcome these shocks, the Korean government also desperately sought other ways to improve the nation's economic situation and restore growth. As an outcome of this search for new sources of economic growth, a Special Law to Promote Venture Capital Companies was enacted in 1997 (see Chap. 5). Based on this Law—which constituted the first major startup support policy measure in Korea—SMEs could seek registration as new ventures when they had received investments from venture capitalists, were R&D intensive, or were mainly engaged in a high-tech industry. Registered venture firms became eligible to a number of privileges, such as tax cuts.[18]

Evidently, the Law and its associated incentives were highly relevant from the perspective of companies, as more than 11,000 companies became registered as venture firms by 2001.[19] Indeed, and as discussed in Chap. 5, Korea experienced its first startup boom around the turn of the millennium, since many skilled professionals founded their own companies after having been laid off by conglomerates or having left them voluntarily. While this initial startup boom collapsed following the US dotcom crash in 2000, the foundations for startup support policies in Korea had been laid.

More comprehensive policies to support startups have subsequently been rolled out in Korea since the late 2000s, as a consensus emerged among policymakers that the nurturing of technology startups offered a promising means of diversifying the Korean economy away from large conglomerates and to strengthen economic growth. Since then, the volume and scope of the programmes have been continuously expanded. To illustrate this, Table 9.4 provides an overview of the Korean government's startup support programmes in 2024, which amounted to KRW 3.7tn (USD 4.4bn).

Table 9.4 Startup support programmes by the Korean government, 2024

Support type	Purpose	Number of programmes	Budget (in billion KRW)	Budget ratio (%)
Loans and guarantees	Providing start-ups with basic funding	7	2054.6	55.3
Commercialisation	Funding support for start-up commercialisation	166	793.1	21.4
Mentoring and consulting, and personnel	Business start-up support through systematic mentoring and consulting; providing personnel	69	49.8	1.3
Facilities, space, and education	Supporting infrastructure, working space and education programmes for new firms	98	134.1	3.6
Global expansion	Supporting start-up's expansion to foreign markets	23	113.8	3.1
Events and networks	Creating networks for effective communication to establish an open innovation ecosystem	28	22.6	0.6
R&D	R&D funding for new start-ups	6	544.2	14.7
Total		397	3712.1	100.0

Source Ministry of SMEs and Startups (2024)

In terms of budget allocation, the primary policy focus has been on the provision of startup funding at both an early stage and in the commercialisation and growth stage. However, there are also programmes that provide startup entrepreneurs with mentoring and consulting services and enhanced access to facilities and working space, and which offer support for global expansion efforts and network building. Such initiatives demonstrate that Korean policymakers are aware of the need to nurture and strengthen startup ecosystems beyond the provision of funding to individual firms. Furthermore, in order to facilitate the search for relevant support programmes, and similar to Japan's "J-Startup", the Korean government has established "K-Startup" as an integrated information platform that lists a large number of programmes offered by various ministries and government agencies.[20]

Notably, not all of the governmental startup support programmes in Korea are directly administered by government agencies, indicating an awareness that private investors and entrepreneurship experts are often more qualified to evaluate startups applying for support. One programme that has received widespread recognition is TIPS (Tech Incubator Program for Startups). This was specifically designed to combine private and governmental funding. Promising start-ups are selected by accelerators, which invest KRW 100 mn (USD 118,800) of venture or angel capital into them. This private investment is then matched by up to KRW 1200 mn (USD 1.43 mn) in government funding for R&D and other business expenses. Selected start-ups are also offered professional support by the accelerators that have invested in them. In other words, the Korean government has outsourced the selection of start-ups eligible for TIPS grants to accelerators, which need to be certified by the government to participate in the programme.[21]

Another major example of indirect government support for startups is the Korea Venture Investment Corporation (KVIC), which was created in 2005 as fund-of-funds to inject liquidity into startup ecosystems by providing venture capital firms with governmental funding. The government initially budgeted USD 1bn as working capital. However, KVIC's funding volume has since steadily increased. At the end of 2024, the Corporation had USD 8.2 bn of assets under management. Venture capital companies can apply for KVIC funding on a regular basis, and then use these funds to finance startups.[22]

The startup support policies of the Korean government are widely credited with having effectively kickstarted startup ecosystem development. Despite some initial criticism that governmental funding was so dominant that it distorted market mechanisms, private funding has substantially increased over time. While it has been estimated that governmental programmes provided up to 90% of external funding for Korean startups in the early 2010s, experts have assessed that the proportion of private funding has increased to approximately 50% by the early 2020s. Government support programmes have also been criticised for burdensome bureaucratic requirements, from complex application documentation to extensive post-funding reporting obligations. Whilst it is understandable that public policymakers and administrators should set strict standards to prevent the misappropriation of public funds, there should also be scope to reduce the administrative burden for startups. Alternatively, more governmental support could be given by indirect means, as discussed above.

Finally, the supportive policy stance towards technology startups in Korea includes only a partial willingness to allow startups to disrupt business models and industries, in the spirit of Schumpeter's "creative destruction". Here, the Korean government has a mixed track record, mirroring Japan. While startups enjoy relative freedom to scale in emerging industries and sectors, incumbent firms in mature industries have successfully lobbied government for protectionist measures. A telling example is the 2020 shutdown of Tada, the van-hailing service, following intense pressure from taxi companies.[23]

9.4 China—Startup Ecosystems as Part of Economic Development Strategies

China's policy framework for startup ecosystems has undergone a major transformation, moving from a model dominated by state control toward a more refined approach that incorporates market-oriented principles and holistic ecosystem construction. The reform and opening-up policy initiated in 1978 gradually introduced market mechanisms, which gave birth to the rise of township companies such as Lu Guanqiu's Wanxiang Group and laid a preliminary foundation for the private economy. In the 1990s, the establishment of Shenzhen, Xiamen, and other Special Economic Zones (SEZs) represented a key breakthrough. They acted as laboratories for market-oriented reforms, attracting foreign direct investment and facilitating technology transfer through preferential policies and relaxed regulations. The Foxconn Shenzhen Base, for example, demonstrated the potential for large-scale manufacturing and technology absorption.

In 1988, Beijing established Zhongguancun Science and Technology Park, as discussed in Chap. 6. Although this government-led park model sowed the seeds for future startup ecosystems, a fully market-orientated model had to wait for breakthroughs achieved by private companies within the system. Typical examples are Huawei and ZTE. Huawei was founded in 1987, relying on the strategy of "localisation of program-controlled switchboards" of the Ministry of Posts and Telecommunications (1980s). However, constrained by the national monopoly of communications equipment, the company was forced to adopt the strategy of "encircling the cities from the countryside" (occupying county-levels market first).[24] This development reveals the double dilemma of startup ecosystems for high-tech companies at that time. First, the state mainly implemented the strategy of "exchanging market for technology" and communications and energy sectors were monopolised by the state, binding technology transfer with import equipment quotas. It was not until 1988 that the "supplementary" status of private economy was recognised for the first time. This meant that the development of private high-tech companies faced strict administrative barriers, not least in terms of industry and market access. Second, under the guidance of the "rejuvenating the country through science and education" strategy, the main purpose of government policy was to address key technology gaps via state-ownership. Consequently, a lack of resources and the absence of a market orientation presented major challenges to the creation of startups.

A major policy shift accompanied by startup ecosystem construction began in China around 2010. It was driven by the need to address limitations such as restricted market access, limited funding for private ventures, and an overall lack of dynamism, and it sought to unlock the potential of private innovation. The origins of this policy shift can be traced back to the Outline of the National Medium and Long-term Science and Technology Development Plan (2006–2020) issued in 2006 (*hereafter "the 2006 plan"*), which marked a major upgrade of the national strategy. The document signalled a fundamental shift along three dimensions. First, there was a goal shift—for the first time the Chinese government established "independent innovation" as a pillar of national competitiveness, replacing the previous "market for technology" strategy. Second, there was a shift in focal actors. The 2006 plan emphasised the "dominant position of companies in innovation activities", recognising that the majority of R&D investment needed to be made by companies. Third, there was a shift in policy tools. The plan set a hard target of 2.5% of GDP in R&D investment by 2020, and stipulated that more than 50% of the technology transfer income of universities should belong to R&D personnel. This incentivised researchers to commercialise their inventions and contribute to a market-oriented innovation ecosystem. Although this programmatic policy document did not directly support start-ups, it laid the foundation for subsequent policies by prioritising the transfer of scientific research achievements to companies.

In 2014, and to maintain the economic growth momentum in face of the structural challenge of industrial overcapacity, Premier Li Keqiang put forward the policy of "mass entrepreneurship and innovation", indicating that China's innovation-driven development strategy had entered a new stage of national mobilisation. The policy was not only a strategy to cope with the short-term downward pressures on the economy, it also reconfirmed and strengthened the core concepts of "independent innovation" and "companies as main actor" established by the 2006 plan. In 2015, the State Council issued the Opinions on Several Policies and Measures for Vigorously Promoting Mass Entrepreneurship and Innovation, which established a comprehensive policy support system covering fiscal, taxation, financial, service and talent dimensions. In order to ensure the coordinated implementation of policies, a joint inter-ministerial meeting for promoting mass entrepreneurship and innovation was established at the national level, led by the National Development and Reform Commission (NDRC) and with the participation of 25 ministries and commissions.[25] Now, the focus of policy had shifted significantly towards stimulating the vitality of market players, in an attempt to exploit the innovative potential hidden in the private sector and to make it the new engine of economic development.

The policy of "mass entrepreneurship and innovation" has since become the core national economic strategy of China. In 2017, the report of the Nineteenth National Congress of the Communist Party of China clearly pointed out that "innovation is the first driving force leading development", and postulated the need to "stimulate and protect entrepreneurship, and encourage more social subjects to engage in innovation and entrepreneurship". It shows that the policy objectives shifted from state-led technological catch-up to the construction of a market-oriented innovation ecosystem with the participation of multiple stakeholders, and to accelerate the transformation of China to a knowledge-intensive and technology-driven economic structure. Strategic transformation also led to a comprehensive upgrading of policy tools. The landmark policies and their innovative breakthroughs are summarised in Table 9.5.

In terms of institutional environment, the revised Company Law in 2014 eliminated paid-in minimum capital requirements, and in 2020 the Regulations on Optimising the Business Environment institutionalised the reform of "separate operating permits and business licenses", reducing the start-up time of companies to four working days, as well as shortening the administrative list of items for approval by more than 1000. These regulations significantly reduced the threshold for entrepreneurship, enabling more individuals and small teams to formally register

Table 9.5 Major policy tools in China (2015 to 2020)

Field	Core policy	Major content and aims
Institutional environment	– Company Law (revised in 2014) – Market Access Simplification, such as the Notice of the State Council on Promoting the Reform of "Separating Permits from Business Licenses" Nationwide (2018) – Regulations on Optimizing Business Environment (2020)	– Eliminating paid-in minimum capital requirements – Lower the threshold of entrepreneurship
Financial support	– State Council Opinions on Several Policies and Measures for Vigorously Promoting Mass Entrepreneurship and Innovation (2015) – The registration-based IPO system of the STAR Market (2019) – Beijing Stock Exchange (2021)	– Building "startup-growth-maturity" full cycle financing chain
Carrier network	– The 14th Five-Year Plan (2021–2025) – Guideline for the General Office of the State Council on Developing Public Space to Promote Mass Innovation and Entrepreneurship (2015)	– Promote Mass Innovation and Entrepreneurship
Talent mechanism	– Implementation Plan for Deepening the Reform of Science and Technology System (2016) – National Thousand Talents Program (2008) and local versions such as the "Haiju Project" in Beijing, and the "Peacock Plan" in Shenzhen – Reform Plan for the Management of the National Key Research and Development Program during the 14th Five-Year Plan Period (2020) – Open bidding for selecting the best candidates (2020)	– Attracting global talents, especially returnees – Unleash the entrepreneurial enthusiasm of R&D personnel

businesses. In response, the daily average number of newly registered companies rose from 10,000 in 2013 to 27,000 in 2023.[26] At the same time, the negative list management model, first piloted in the Shanghai Free Trade Zone in 2013, permitted wholly foreign-owned companies to set up data centres and artificial intelligence (AI) companies.[27] This reform marked a partial breakthrough in China's "selective opening" system, accelerating the transition of foreign investment access from a "case-by-case examination and approval system" to a "filling-based opening" system.[28] This type of regulatory sandbox is increasingly utilised in China as a mechanism to accelerate the commercialisation of emerging technologies and it has created synergies with Free Trade Zones in promoting innovation and entrepreneurship. For example, after completing testing in the Lingang Sandbox (Shanghai), the autonomous driving company Momenta accelerated its technology verification and secured over CNY 2bn (approximately USD 279 mn) in funding in 2023–2024 for mass production deployment. Meanwhile, sandbox test data also empowered regulators to optimise cross-border data rules in the Lingang zone.

The financial support system in China focuses on building a full-cycle capital chain. In 2015, the National Venture Capital Guidance Fund for Emerging Industries was set up, with its scale expanding from CNY 40bn (approximately USD 6.22bn) initially to approximately CNY 300bn (approximately USD 42.5bn) in 2023.[29] Through the three-level leverage of "financial capital, state-owned capital and social capital", investments in strategic areas such as semiconductor chips and AI were promoted, driving Shenzhen Venture Capital, Hillhouse Group and other institutions to invest in Cambricon (an AI chip producer) and AMEC (Advanced Micro-Fabrication Equipment, a semiconductor chip producer). At the same time, reform of the stock market was undertaken. In 2019, the pilot registration-based initial public offering (IPO) system of the STAR Market was implemented, and in 2021, the Beijing Stock Exchange, focusing on cultivating "specialised, sophisticated, distinctive and innovative companies" was formed, closing the investment loop of the "angel-venture capital-stock market".

The strategic construction of innovation carrier networks catalysed regional technological clusters. Continuing the "Torch Plan", 178 high-tech zones were built in 2023.[30] Among the startups to emerge, ByteDance and Megvii came out of Beijing's Zhongguancun, while Shenzhen Nanshan High-Tech Zone gave rise to UBTECH and DJI, with the latter today accounting for around 70% of the global drone market.[31] Both zones formed a bipolar "North AI, South Hardware" innovation pattern across China. This "bipolar pattern" can be seen as the product of spatial agglomeration externalities in innovation. Meanwhile, national level incubators were established across the country in response to political demands for a more balanced regional development. This spatial governance model was further strengthened during the 14th Five-Year Plan period from 2021 to 2025. The 14th Five-Year Plan focuses on the support of core technologies such as quantum computing and commercial aerospace. Government procurement targets domestic substitution, such as the Huawei Kunpeng chip replacing Intel's central processing units (CPUs). The policies also helped to create the Shenzhen-Dongguan-Guangzhou global unmanned aerial vehicle (UAV) industry belt accounting for 70% of the national output value and the "Quantum Avenue" in Hefei, the capital of Anhui province.[32,33]

Talent mechanism policies in China have focused on releasing the potential of intellectual capital. The government has actively pursued the "National Thousand Talents Program", which has attracted thousands of top talents to the country. The Beijing "Haiju Project" inspired Robin Li (co-founder of Baidu) and Wang Xiaodong (co-founder of BeiGene, now BeOne Medicines) to return home and fill the top talent gaps in the fields of AI and biomedicine. In response to the 2016 Science and Technology System Reform Plan, which stipulated that more than 50% of the income gained from the commercialisation of scientific research should go to researchers, Tsinghua University incubated Megvii (an image recognition and deep-learning software developer that operates the world's largest computer vision platform), and a team at the Chinese University of Hong Kong founded SenseTime, one of Asia's leading AI software companies.[34] In 2021, Zhejiang Laboratory (Hangzhou) gathered 300 industrial engineers to develop key technologies for AI chips. Taken together, these measures have led to an explosive growth of university spin-offs across China.

Despite the notable advancements in China's startup support policies and startup ecosystems, some structural contradictions persist. Primarily, the surge in venture capital, often lacking adequate oversight, has created capital bubbles and inefficient resource allocation. Further exacerbating these inefficiencies, local governments in their pursuit of investment and talent have implemented overlapping and homogenous industrial policies, resulting in a "tournament-style" dynamic that fosters duplicated efforts, as evidenced by the proliferation of semiconductor industrial parks despite limited national chip self-sufficiency. This phenomenon is compounded by policy-driven capital misallocations, wherein certain sectors, particularly semiconductor chips and artificial intelligence, attract a disproportionate amount of investment, thereby diverting resources away from critical but less favoured domains like basic materials and high-end equipment. Such imbalances enhance the emergence of "pseudo-hard technology" firms that are reliant on government subsidies to sustain profitability, raising concerns regarding their long-term competitiveness and genuine innovation capabilities. This constellation of factors suggests that the transition of China's startup ecosystems remains incomplete, with continued government involvement potentially distorting market mechanisms and hindering the development of fully competitive, market-driven companies and systems of innovation.

The trade frictions between China and the USA in 2018 uncovered another major shortcoming in China's innovation policies, because it highlighted systemic vulnerabilities in critical technologies, such as lithography machines and electronic design automation (EDA) tools. This necessitated a shift in policy focus from application layer innovation (e.g., Internet business models) to innovation in underlying technologies (e.g., semiconductors, industrial software) in order to address, in part, China's over-reliance on foreign technology and the lack of indigenous innovation capacity (see Table 9.6).

In response to the call for "self-reliance and strength in science and technology," there were policy breakthroughs along three dimensions. With regards to the strengthening of technological capabilities, the second phase of the National Integrated

Table 9.6 Major policy tools in China (2021 to 2025)

Field	Core policy	Major content and aims
Institutional environment	– Anti-Unfair Competition Law (revised in 2022, 2025) – Regulations on Data Security Management (2024) – Ministry of Industry and Information Technology Guidelines for Optimizing Business Environment in the Context of High-Tech Innovation (2024)	– Strengthen protection of intellectual property and fair market competition, especially in high-tech sectors vulnerable to external interference – Standardize data-related operations for startups, ensuring security while facilitating innovation – Streamline approval, improve regulatory flexibility for innovative business models, reducing impact of external uncertainties
Financial support	– Sci-tech Innovation-Oriented Relending and Rediscount (2024) – Expansion of REITs for Sci-tech Industrial Parks (2023) – Special Funds for Technological Self—Reliance Startups (2021)	– Provide targeted low-cost capital to startups in "bottleneck technology" areas, countering external capital access obstacles – Mobilize social capital for long-term investment in sci-tech infrastructure, building financing chain for innovation-driven parks – Directly subsidize or provide risk compensation for startups focusing on independent R&D to break foreign technology monopolies
Carrier network	– 14th Five-Year Plan for the Development of National Innovation-Driven Zones (2021–2025)	– Strengthen construction of innovation clusters, concentrating resources to tackle core technology gaps – Upgrade grassroots innovation carriers, enhancing service capacity for startups facing external pressure

(continued)

Table 9.6 (continued)

Field	Core policy	Major content and aims
Talent mechanism	– Outline of the Plan for Building a Strong Education Nation (2024–2035) – Several Measures on Further Strengthening the Cultivation and Utilization of Young Scientific and Technological Talents (2024) – Ten support measures to encourage high-level talents to serve enterprises (2024)	– Concentrated recruitment of overseas talents in fields like semiconductor, AI, reducing dependence on foreign-sourced talent blockages – Systematically cultivate local young talents, building reserve force for long-term innovation against external constraints – Break institutional barriers, encourage talent circulation between academia and industry to speed up tech conversion, countering external technology lockdowns
International cooperation response	– Administrative Measures for International Joint Innovation Platforms in Yunnan Province (2025) – Science and Technology Innovation Action Plan for the Belt and Road Initiative (Revised 2023) – Guide for Chinese Enterprises on Overseas Safety Risk Prevention (revised 2022)	– Standardize the process of international cooperation, and on the basis of ensuring security, retain necessary global innovation exchanges (such as open-source technologies, academic conferences) – Deepen scientific and technological innovation cooperation with countries along the Belt and Road, and open up alternative technology exchange and market synergy channels – Guide overseas R&D centres of enterprises to avoid geopolitical risks and ensure the continuity of R&D projects

Circuit Industry Investment Fund, commonly known as the "Big Fund" with a scale of RMB 200bn (approximately USD 27.59bn) injected capital into SMIC (Semiconductor Manufacturing International Corporation) and YMTC (Yangtze Memory Technologies) to accelerate the construction of 28 nm de-Americanised production lines.[35] The Ministry of Science and Technology upgraded the "Nuclear High-End Basic Project" special project to include photoresist and other materials in the priority list. In the business cultivation dimension, the "Little Giant" plan supports 14,600 SMEs (2024), of which 5000 are working in new technologies including AI.[36] Along the regulatory dimension, the government implemented the Data Security Law (2021) and the Generative AI Service Management Measures (2023) to ensure a balance between innovation and security.

Geopolitical pressure has also given birth to the "dual circulation" strategy, which fostered divergent pathways for startups. Technology-driven companies, such as

ByteDance (owner of TikTok), exemplify this trend, with their success attributable, in part, to algorithmic innovation bolstered by the compliance framework set forth in China's Ministry of Commerce Guidelines for Foreign Investment Cooperation in Digital Economy. This reflects an evolution from restrictive data control measures to proactive adherence to global governance standards, thus enabling startups to operate in international markets within a well-defined regulatory structure. In the domestic sphere, initiatives such as the Rural Revitalisation Strategy and the Ministry of Agriculture's "Internet + Agricultural Products" policy facilitate the modernisation of agricultural supply chains through investments in cold-chain logistics and digital payment systems, as demonstrated by Pinduoduo's AI-enhanced "farm-to-table" business model. This dual approach—driven by both state-led infrastructure modernisation and algorithmic innovation—underscores a hybrid model wherein domestic policy supports tech-enabled structural improvements, while market-led supply chain innovation is leveraged globally within state-defined compliance boundaries. This balance between strategic policy direction and market-based flexibility characterises the unique developmental pathway for Chinese startups.

In summary, China's startup ecosystem policy has undergone a dynamic and multifaceted evolution, uniquely shaped by state-led initiatives, market forces, and geopolitical pressures. From an initial emphasis on technology transfer to a more recent focus on technological self-reliance, the government has played a central role in directing innovation and entrepreneurship across the country. Building on the principle of "seeking autonomy in opening up" introduced in 2006, the current policy framework is designed to promote foundational technological autonomy while striking a dynamic equilibrium between security and innovation. Moving forward, it will be crucial to find a balance between further enhancing the openness and inclusiveness of China's innovation system, while safeguarding national security.

9.5 Evaluation of Startup Ecosystem Policies in East Asia

The policy rationale for the support of startup ecosystems mentioned in the introduction to this chapter has already hinted at the importance of national context. Policies in East Asia are motivated by and directed towards the intention to resolve specific weaknesses in national support infrastructures for technology intensive startups. Therefore, they address country-specific weaknesses such as limited internationalisation in Japan, venture capital shortages in Korea, or technological capability challenges in China. Differences relating to historical background, socio-economic conditions, and political-administrative structures create additional specificities. Accordingly, while East Asian governments pursue the same goal of fostering startup ecosystems, they choose different strategies and employ various tools. In the case of China, startup support programs evolved more or less naturally out of the government's general strategy to enhance domestic technological capabilities and economic growth. They represented a continuation of the government's strategic role in economic development. What changed were the concrete targets and instruments in response to past achievements, new technological regimes and, more recently, geopolitical shifts.

In Japan, the heydays of industrial policy were already past when startup ecosystems emerged. Entering the 1980s, the government came to abandon industrial and trade policies in favour of less interventionist technology and innovation policies. Deregulation and administrative reforms weakened both the independence and influence of the elite bureaucracy, which had formed the institutional core of the concept of the developmental state.[37] Neoliberalism became a new feature of Japan's economic policy.[38] In this sense, the growing support for startups appears as a revival of developmental policies. However, we can also detect continuities as startup support measures became integrated into existing policy fields such as regional revitalisation, research and technology, or SME support programs.

In Korea, too, neoliberal ideas had replaced the developmental orientation of economic policy as the country recovered from the Asian Financial Crisis in the late 1990s. In this respect, the support of startups and the promotion of ecosystems may seem contradictory. However, they do not contradict, but rather question the general applicability of the label "neoliberal". Korea's startup support policies not only resembled previous industrialisation policies in important ways, but they also proved similarly effective. While the nascent Korean manufacturing sector needed active government support in the 1960s and 1970s to scale up quickly and gain global competitiveness, the country's nascent startup ecosystems also benefited from government policies to get off the ground in the 2000s and 2010s.

This brief recapitulation answers the question about the role of the developmental model in East Asia. Whereas startup support policies represent a continuation of the developmental state in the Chinese context, they constitute a revival for Japan and Korea. Even in these latter two countries, governments benefited from the legacy of earlier developmental policies, such as institutional memory and the fact that a large portion of the general public was probably still familiar with and ideologically not opposed to the government playing a more active role in economic development.

This still leaves open the question of how such policies could successfully be pursued given the contrast between the cultures usually associated with entrepreneurship and bureaucracies, and the outsider status typically attributed to entrepreneurs. Must such conditions not strongly constrain the effectiveness of startup support schemes? As noted in Chap. 2, entrepreneurship in the digital age is very different from Schumpeter's classical characterisation. Entrepreneurial activity in startup ecosystems is integrated in a highly professional, functionally specialised superstructure. This does not eliminate fundamental entrepreneurial risks, but makes entrepreneurial activity more amenable to the logic of bureaucratic systems and policy making since policy targets, beneficiaries, support criteria, and key performance indicators can be more easily specified and traced.

In addition, the continuity of the developmental state or—as in the case of Japan and Korea—its legacy, can also provide some clues. First, the developmental model is based on a broad political consensus that the government bears responsibility for economic growth. Therefore, East Asian governments did not need to specifically justify why they engaged in the support of startup ecosystems. Second, developmental strategies benefit from "the virtue of backwardness".[39] Being a follower comes with various advantages. The existence of leading examples reduces fundamental uncertainties and provides the precedents that politicians and bureaucrats need to justify their actions. Whereas China's relatively stable political structure allows for the implementation of long-term development strategies, democracies, with four-to-five-year election cycles, require an elite bureaucracy that is sufficiently shielded from short-term political pressures. Although the Japanese METI no longer has the same degree of independence as its predecessor MITI, it can still claim its role as the Ministry responsible for the development of industry. In Korea, while policies in some areas may change when the ruling party and government changes, there is a remarkable degree of continuity in other areas, including startup support. Although the ruling party has changed three times since the 2010s, startup support policies have largely remained in place, reflecting a broad cross-party consensus about their importance for economic performance.

Suppose we consequently apply the logic of startup ecosystems and developmental policies. In that case, we come to realise that startups can no longer be characterised as outsiders of the socio-political system, but instead—at least in East Asia—as an integral part of it. As startups became endorsed and supported by economic policies, their disruptive potential became "domesticated". It was subordinated to innovation and growth strategies along politically acceptable trajectories. This domestication manifests itself in regulatory sandboxes and in specially designated economic zones that serve as testing fields for the social acceptance of potentially disruptive innovative business models.

9.6 Conclusion

This chapter has taken a closer look at government support policies as an important contextual factor in the development of East Asian startup ecosystems. The policies pursued have addressed weaknesses perceived in national ecosystems. They are strongly influenced and shaped by national histories, socio-economic conditions, and the characteristics of the political system, as well as by legal and administrative structures. As a result, national policies differ, despite the fact that they pursue similar goals. In China, government involvement in startup ecosystems is in full alignment with its strategic economic development strategy, and in Japan and Korea it is related to the model of the developmental state that was applied during the successful economic catch-up of the two economies. The effectiveness of startup support measures very much benefited from the professionalisation and functional specialisation within entrepreneurial ecosystems. However, by bringing startup ecosystems into the realm of economic policy, their disruptive potential became domesticated and instrumentalised for the realisation of regional, technological, and economic growth strategies.

Looking ahead, we may expect that government policies in support of East Asian startups will continue to be relevant, but at the same time, they will likely further evolve. As ecosystems mature, government policies will need to focus more on indirect measures that strengthen the business environment for startups in general, and that enhance their global connectivity. This means winding down direct support and relying more on private sector initiatives in the further evolution of ecosystems.[40] The question remains how policymakers will be able to transition their support programmes in this direction.

Looking beyond startup policies, we may also ask what implications should be drawn from the three country cases with regard to the future role of governments in economic development. Startup ecosystems do not represent the only policy field where the developmental nature of government policies has resurfaced. Climate change, the recent pandemic experience, and economic security have similarly brought the role of government in economic affairs to the forefront, not only in East Asia but more widely, although in East Asia this might have been less ideologically charged. The fundamental challenges that economies worldwide are facing warrant a re-evaluation of the role of government. In this respect, startup support policies can be expected to remain an important field of study and interest.

Notes

1. Hayek (1964) distinguishes natural, artificial and spontaneous order. The first is produced by nature, the second by human design, and the third is the unplanned outcome of decentralised interactions.
2. Saxenian (1994).
3. Although Saxenian acknowledges the role of government funding, the role of public policy is given much more weight in the concept of the "entrepreneurial state" introduced by Mazzucato (2013).
4. Johnson (1982). In 2001, MITI was reorganised as part of a general overhaul of the government's administration and is since then known under the name Ministry of Economy, Trade and Industry (METI).
5. See Levy-Faur (1979).
6. Ramirez (2024).
7. Hall and Soskice (2001).
8. Waldenberger (2016).
9. Kushida (2018).
10. https://www.chisou.go.jp/tiiki/kokusentoc/english/index.html.
11. https://www.cas.go.jp/jp/seisaku/s-portal/pdf/underlyinglaw/Japans_Regulatory_Sandbox_presentation.pdf.
12. https://japan.kantei.go.jp/ongoingtopics/policies_kishida/newcapitalism.html.
13. The passage reads "By leveraging digital transformation (DX), we will promote innovation and support startups in strategic fields where Japan has significant potential, including AI, quantum technology, biotechnology, space, fusion power, and GX. We will also invest in people by supporting skills improvement. Now is the time to realise a growth-driven economy led by wage increases and investment and to establish Japan as a prosperous nation that continually generates world-leading innovation". https://japan.kantei.go.jp/103/statement/202411/29shoshinhyomei.html.

14. Katz (2023).
15. Hemmert (2018), 29.
16. Chang (2003), 47–54.
17. Hemmert and Kim (2021), 50.
18. Ko and Shin (1999).
19. Hemmert (2018), 83.
20. K-Startup (2025).
21. OECD (2023), 167.
22. Gompers and Chan (2024) and KVIC (2025).
23. Korea Times (2020).
24. Zhang (2017).
25. https://english.www.gov.cn/policies/latest_releases/2015/08/20/content_281475171912944.htm.
26. https://www.gov.cn/lianbo/bumen/202402/content_6935083.htm.
27. Chinese Academy of International Trade and Economic Cooperation (2024).
28. Hsueh (2011).
29. https://www.cnbc.com/2023/02/08/worlds-largest-drone-maker-dji-is-unfazed-by-challenges-like-us-blacklist.html.
30. https://www.gov.cn/lianbo/bumen/202312/content_6919803.htm.
31. CNBC (2023).
32. https://com.gd.gov.cn/attachment/0/580/580526/4713607.pdf.
33. https://www.news.cn/liangzi/20250428/1bda0422949e49da915ef62a9eb4c277/c.html.
34. https://www.sensetime.com/en/news-detail/51169068?categoryId=1072&gioIndex=1.
35. https://www.bloomberg.com/news/articles/2024-03-08/china-readies-27-billion-chip-fund-to-counter-growing-us-curbs.
36. https://www.scmp.com/economy/china-economy/article/3288996/chinas-strategic-little-giant-firms-quickly-rise-14600-surpass-2025-goal.
37. Introduced by Johnson (1982).
38. Lechevalier (2014).
39. Gerschenkron.
40. Brown and Mawson (2019), 360–361.

Chapter 10
Internationalisation and the Development of East Asian Startup Ecosystems

10.1 Introduction

Although startup ecosystems rely on local or regional clusters and support infrastructures, international linkages also play an important role. Silicon Valley continues to benefit very much from the global talent it has been able to attract, both in terms of entrepreneurial and technical skills. The enormous success of Silicon Valley startups has also depended upon the ability to scale their business beyond the US market. Again, this required and enforced international linkages, including venture capital from abroad or collaborations with multinational companies, as in the case of Tesla and Toyota back in 2010, when the US startup was developing its production capacity.[1]

As discussed in Chaps. 4–6, such linkages have not been as strong in the case of startup ecosystems in East Asia. Although China has partly benefited from the skills, experiences and networks of returnee entrepreneurs (or "sea-turtle founders", as they are known in China), Chinese, Japanese, and Korean ecosystems have not managed to attract high levels of global talent. This is not so much because of geographic distance, but more to do with language barriers as well as differences in entrepreneurial culture and work styles, as we discuss in Chap. 8. In addition, the international background of entrepreneurial teams in East Asia tends to be limited, and intentions to scale business across borders are usually weak. As a consequence, business models are typically designed primarily to serve domestic markets.

The underdevelopment of international linkages has been recognised not only by research, but also by policy-makers and other actors engaged in the promotion of startup ecosystems in East Asia. As we discuss in Chap. 9, this has led to the implementation of specific policies designed to attract global talent, and to support the international expansion of promising startups.

As emphasised throughout this book, startup ecosystems are embedded in a particular national environment. This also applies to their international linkages, which

Y. Cheng et al., *Unleashing Innovation the East Asian Way*,
https://doi.org/10.1007/978-981-95-6513-9_10

reflect the internationalisation of their respective economies. Internationalisation in East Asia has been a dynamic process shaped by three key factors:

- historical industrial pathways, where Japan's *keiretsu*, Korea's *chaebol*, and China's state-linked "national champions" have created distinct templates for global market entry.
- geopolitical realignments, particularly US-China tensions that are currently bifurcating supply chains and venture capital flows.
- hybrid innovation models, exemplified by Shenzhen's hardware-software ecosystems that attract both regional startups and multinational corporations (MNCs).

This macro-economic dynamic has shaped significantly the internationalisation of startup ecosystems in East Asia. They do not apply the Silicon Valley's "born global" paradigm, however, where startups often scale internationally from inception. Instead, the internationalisation of East Asian startup ecosystems appears as a thread that connects adaptive tactics along historical trajectories, as can be seen in Japanese companies' combining legacy manufacturing strengths with startup-driven open innovation, Korea's gaming and software firms leveraging K-pop culture for soft power, and China's "dual circulation" strategy that simultaneously promotes domestic innovation and selective global integration. As a consequence, East Asia's startup scene has transformed from a fast-follower in the shadow of Silicon Valley to a multi-polar engine that is both shaped by globalisation's fault lines while at the same time testing and adjusting them.

This chapter is organised to make that distinction explicit. The first main section provides a historical review of East Asian firms' internationalisation trajectories, using the "Flying Geese" framework to show how earlier export surges and industrial upgrading created the institutional and policy environments that later shaped entrepreneurial opportunities. This contextualisation deliberately focuses on large firms rather than startups, since their experiences defined the templates of capital formation, talent development, and regulatory engagement that today's startups inherit. The following sections then turn to the internationalisation of startup ecosystems themselves. Section 10.3 examines outbound internationalisation, outlining the opportunities created by policy support, corporate venture capital, digital infrastructure, and cultural soft power, as well as the persistent challenges around funding, talent, geopolitics, currency, and perceptions. Section 10.4 analyses inbound internationalisation, showing how foreign information and communication technology (ICT) MNCs and accelerator programs have reshaped entrepreneurial culture, talent flows, and funding structures. The chapter concludes with three scenarios that link these dynamics to the future evolution of East Asian startup ecosystems.

Throughout the chapter, we do not limit ourselves to present day startups. The following pages firstly revisit the trajectories of firms that began as startups but have since grown into established MNCs. While the internationalisation challenges they faced differed from those confronting today's ventures, their experiences provide essential context. These cases illustrate how earlier generations of entrepreneurs navigated capital constraints, regulatory shifts, and market entry barriers, thereby shaping the institutional and cultural conditions within which contemporary East Asian startup ecosystems now operate.

10.2 Historical Context

10.2.1 The "Flying Geese" Pattern and Beyond

According to the Japanese economist Kaname Akamatsu,[2] sequential industrial upgrading after World War II followed a remarkably ordered cadence in East and South East Asia. In the 1950s, Japan rebuilt its export base around light-manufacturing staples such as cotton yarn, apparel, and simple plastics. Subsequently, rising wages and a strong yen pushed Japanese firms up the value curve in the 1960s and 1970s to steel, shipbuilding, and later consumer electronics—epitomised by Sony's Trinitron TV (1968) and the Walkman (1979). Korea embarked on the same development path roughly one and a half decades later,[3] starting with footwear and sweaters in the late 1960s and early 1970s, moving to automobiles and white goods in the 1980s, and dominating memory semiconductors and mobile phone handsets by the mid-1990s.[4] China, arriving another decade later, leveraged World Trade Organisation (WTO) accession in 2001 to master labour-intensive assembly of computers and smartphones, and by the 2010s was exporting a home-grown digital-platform economy spearheaded by companies such as Alibaba, Tencent, and ByteDance. This neat relay—from textiles, to consumer electronics, then to an information technology and platform economy—validated Akamatsu Kaname's "Flying Geese" metaphor of successive regional leadership in which the production of commoditised goods moves from the more advanced economies to the less advanced ones.[5,6]

Hard numbers underscore this developmental pattern. UNCTAD trade statistics show that electronics as a share of total manufactured exports peaked sequentially in East Asia over the past four decades: Japan at 29% in 1986, Korea at 24% in 1995, and China at 38% in 2019. Over the same period, outward foreign direct investment (FDI) surged in lockstep: Japanese FDI stock abroad expanded from US$49bn in 1975 to US$263bn in 1985; Korean FDI stock jumped from just US$2bn in 1985 to US$95bn in 1997, and Chinese outward FDI soared from US$29bn in 2000 to more than US$2.3tn by 2022. Currency movements amplified the transitions—yen appreciation after the 1985 Plaza Accord, Won liberalisation in 1993, and gradual RMB internationalisation after 2005 all nudged firms to outsource or offshore production and marketing.[7] Taken together, these data on trade composition and capital flows effectively portray in an empirical way the economic upgrading of East Asian economies from the 1980s onwards.

Knowledge diffusion and entrepreneurial learning were equally sequential during this period. Classic Japanese management texts—such as Konosuke Matsushita's "Path" essays, Soichiro Honda's autobiographies, and the Toyota Production System manuals—were translated wholesale into Korean and Chinese by the late 1980s.

Study tours sponsored by the state-funded trade and investment promotion organisations such as the Japan External Trade Organisation (JETRO), the Korea Trade Promotion Corporation (KOTRA), and later China's Ministry of Commerce (MOFCOM) allowed factory managers from Busan and Shenzhen to observe the workings of kanban scheduling and total-quality circles on the shop floors of Nagoya and Hamamatsu.[8,9,10] By the early 1990s, Samsung engineers had reverse-engineered Panasonic's video cassette recorders (VCRs) and Huawei's early routers copied Cisco chassis dimensions to fit into the same 19-inch racks favoured by Japanese telecom carriers. These episodes of micro-imitation created a tacit curriculum for thousands of would-be founders across East Asia.[11,12]

Yet, when the Japanese economy slid into its "Lost Decade" after the 1991 asset crash, Korean and Chinese entrepreneurs confronted a new reality: Japan's script offered fewer answers for software, services, or global branding in the Internet age. Consequently, each country sought fresh role models for its startup ecosystems—Korea borrowed from Silicon Valley's fabless-chip example and China leapfrogged straight to mobile Internet monetisation.[13]

The ensuant divergence in approach across East Asia became stark in the 2000s. Japan doubled-down on precision hardware and deep-tech niches such as robotics (led by FANUC and Cyberdyne), advanced materials (Toray's carbon fibre), and biopharma platforms (such as PeptiDream), banking on proprietary intellectual property (IP) and long product cycles rather than exploiting rapid scaling effects. Korea, in contrast, fused design-centric hardware with cultural content, with the same supply chains that produced Galaxy smartphones also manufacturing light-sticks for K-pop concerts, while Webtoons (digital comics) IP fed both Netflix originals and metaverse avatars. China, buoyed by a nearly one-billion-user domestic payment network and state-directed mega funds, transformed from being the factory of the world into an architect of digital ecosystems—exporting super-apps (such as WeChat clones in Africa), fintech platforms (such as Ant Group's Alipay), and state-backed cloud infrastructure across Belt-and-Road corridors, crafting digital economy alliances to stand against the US-dominated landscape.

The availability and expansion of entrepreneurial finance across the region mirrored these shifts. By 2022, 71% of Japanese venture capital (VC) still funded domestic hardware or life-science ventures, whereas Korea's VC industry deployed nearly one-third of available funds to cross-border e-commerce and creator-economy deals. Chinese capital followed two tracks: globally ambitious sovereign funds (e.g., China Investment Corporation [CIC] and the Silk Road Fund) backed infrastructure projects and strategic minerals mines abroad, (such as CIC's investments in the US private equity firm Blackstone and the Pakistani hydropower projects financed by the Silk Road Fund), while private VCs concentrated on exploiting network effects within China's vast domestic market (e.g., Alibaba and Meituan).

Economic policies similarly adjusted. Japan's Ministry of Economy, Trade and Industry (METI) pivoted from export insurance in the 1950s to global startup acceleration program such as J-Startup in the late 2010s. Korea rolled out the K-Startup Grand Challenge in 2016 to attract foreign founder talent to support *chaebol* supply chains. China embedded entrepreneurship into grand strategy: the "Go Global"

(1999) and "Made in China 2025" blueprints tied startup incentives to geopolitical ambitions, offering tax holidays, fast-track initial public offering (IPO) lanes in Hong Kong, and subsidised cloud credits for outbound Software as a Service (SAAS) startups. These policy architectures, while disparate, all trace their lineage to the original developmental-state toolkit.

10.2.2 Japan's First Outward Surge (1950s to 1990s)

In 1957, a post-war startup named Tokyo Tsushin Kogyo—soon to be Sony—shipped 10,000 units of its TR-63 "Transistor Six" on a Pan-Am Clipper bound for New York. Priced at US$39.95 (equivalent to around US$420 in 2023) and weighing just 160 g, the pocket radio sold roughly 100,000 units, prompting industry rivals such as Regency, Philco, and RCA to cut prices by up to 20%. LIFE magazine called the device a "miracle in miniature," recasting Japanese goods from dime-store curiosities to precision electronics.[14] By 1965, exports generated 55% of Sony's revenue, and this success story was replicated by Matsushita's colour TV sets for the US market (in 1966) and Sharp's microwave ovens for Europe (in 1968).

By late 1970s, Japanese companies had established themselves as global brand names. TIME magazine featured Akio Morita (the co-founder of Sony) on its May 10 1971 cover. With sales of music cassettes levelling, Sony engineers fitted a stereo head, a metal chassis, and AA batteries into a 390 g body and launched the TPS-L2 Walkman, a portable audio player, in 1979, which went on to become a major hit in the U.S. market.

Currency turbulence soon rewired the strategy for international markets. The 1985 Plaza Accord forced a 54% yen appreciation within two years, vaporising export profit margins.[15] To counter lost export competitiveness and rising trade frictions, Japanese companies intensified outward FDI. UNCTAD data show Japan's outward FDI stock jumped from US$21bn in 1984 to US$107bn in 1989.[16,17]

Japanese original equipment manufacturers (OEMs), especially in the automotive sector, drove the growth of the internationalisation among much smaller, younger companies as the suppliers of lead MNCs. Honda's Marysville, Ohio line (launched in November 1982) rolled out 883 Accord vehicles in its first month with one car leaving the production line every 57 s—matching Suzuka's benchmark.[18] Toyota's US$800mn Georgetown, Kentucky plant followed in 1988 and by 1993, it was North America's most productive factory at 11.55 labour hours per vehicle.[19] More than 150 suppliers—Denso, Aisin, Yazaki, Nissin Kogyo—shadowed the assemblers, erecting R&D centres, die-casting shops, and just-in-time (JIT) operations within a 300-mile radius.[20,21]

Hardware prowess soon spilled into intellectual property exports. Nintendo's "Family Computer" (1983) became the Nintendo Entertainment System when it launched in New York on 18 October 1985: more than 50,000 units were sold before Christmas, reviving a moribund US video-game industry. Sega's 16-bit

Genesis (1988) and Sony's disc-based PlayStation (1994) extended the hardware-plus-IP business concept, enabling global franchises such as Super Mario, Sonic the Hedgehog, and Final Fantasy that later underpinned film, merchandising, and mobile-game spin-offs.[22] By 1999, JETRO reported 3146 Tokyo- and Osaka-based small and medium sized enterprises (SMEs) earning character-goods royalties, double the number in 1994, illustrating the multiplier effect whereby startup studios piggy-back on console-installed bases—a dynamic discussed in Chap. 8 on soft-power leverage.

The Japanese government, though rarely in the spotlight, provided critical scaffolding in the 1990s. MITI's Machinery and Information Industries Bureau produced a 4000-page English translation of the EU Low Voltage Directive within eight weeks, saving SMEs an average of JPY 12mn per certification cycle.[23]

Feedback loops into entrepreneurship were also evident. By 2000, overseas production accounted for 34% of Japanese manufacturers' output compared with 9% in 1980. Sony, Panasonic, and Toyota each derived a majority of revenue abroad, and Nikkei's "Emerging 100" list featured 61 startups with more than 30% of foreign sales, from PeptiDream's peptide-drug partnerships with Roche to Takara Tomy's Beyblade toy ecosystem.[24] A new generation of Japanese startups were once again testing their abilities to expand into global markets.

10.2.3 Korea's Chaebol-Driven Globalisation (1980s to 2020s)

Korea's strategy for scaling startups overseas is inseparable from the outward march of its *chaebols*. In 1997, Samsung Electronics shipped the world's first commercial mobile handset to Sprint in the United States, proving that a Korean device could succeed in a demanding Western market.[25] Overseas revenue soon overtook domestic sales at Samsung and, more importantly, the breakthrough signalled that Korean engineers could set global wireless standards.[26] Alumni from the CDMA handset program later launched or mentored component and software ventures, embedding an export mindset in Korea's startup ecosystems.[27] It also demonstrated Korea's capacity for rapid product development under crisis conditions.[28]

During the 2000s, Korean conglomerates institutionalised this knowledge spill-over. Samsung, LG, Hyundai, and SK Telecom created open-innovation units offering capital, supply-chain access, and introductions overseas.[29] Samsung Next, launched in Silicon Valley in 2013, completed more than seventy equity and merger and acquisition (M&A) deals.[30] LG's research centre in California, opened in 2021, followed the same strategy for health and climate-related technology. Hyundai's CRADLE labs in Boston and Tel Aviv, and SK Telecom's Partner Fund round out the corporate-VC web, focusing on smart mobility and cloud infrastructure, respectively.[31] These arms operate with independent governance so that Korean founders can raise follow-on rounds from international investors and pursue foreign listings.

Policy in Korea soon matched corporate ambition. Under President Park Geun-hye, almost two billion dollars a year was allocated to create seventeen Creative Economy Innovation Centers in the mid-2010s, each co-managed with a leading *chaebol* and equipped with subsidised R&D laboratories, regulatory sandboxes, and mentors.[32] The complementary K-Startup Grand Challenge, launched in 2016 at Pangyo Techno Valley, internationalised the scene by inviting foreign teams to build the brand alongside Korean peers. The influx of talent to Korea raised standards in English fluency, cross-border compliance, and global product-market fit across startup ecosystems.[33]

Korean soft power provided the final accelerant for the internationalisation of Korean companies. The Korean Wave (*hallyu*)—K-pop, dramas, webtoons and e-sports—has turned the country into a cultural magnet. The Korea Creative Content Agency estimates that Korean exports of cultural content stood at US$12.45bn in 2020, surpassing home appliances. The expansion of cultural content has cascaded within supply chains: for example, the ed-tech firm CLASSUM has contracts with foreign universities eager for K-content. At the same time, direct-to-consumer (D2C) beauty label Glow Recipe tops shelves at Sephora after viral TikTok challenges. Even hardware benefits, an example being a Galaxy smartphone launch featuring the girl group Blackpink that showers attention on accessory startups that bundle augmented reality (AR) face filters or light sticks.[34]

The synergy of *chaebol* market volume, policy scaffolding, and cultural magnetism has produced an unusually outward-oriented startup cohort in Korea. Founders treat Korea's fifty-million-person market as a sandbox, and presentations for seed-stage pitches already frequently target customers in Southeast Asia, North America, and the Middle East.[35] The Korean state supports this stance with export insurance, tax credits covering 25% of overseas marketing expenses, and preferential loans for foreign receivables. Alumni of Samsung Next and the Grand Challenge maintain hubs in Palo Alto, Tel Aviv, and Singapore, giving new companies plug-and-play access to foreign talent and capital.[36] Two decades after that first mobile crossed the Pacific, Korea has evolved from fast-follower to fast-globaliser, offering a compelling blueprint for startups in other mid-sized economies.

10.2.4 China: From Manufacturing Hub to Algorithmic Platforms (1990s to 2020s)

China has effectively condensed the Japanese and Korean internationalisation trajectories into a single generational cycle, progressing from sub-contract manufacturing to global manufacturing leadership.[37,38] The Pearl River Delta served as the initial locus of transformation: following Deng Xiaoping's 1992 "Southern Tour", a corridor of approximately thirty kilometres between Shenzhen and Dongguan attracted Taiwanese tooling companies and migrant labour, producing components for Sony Walkmans in one year and glass panels for Apple iPhones in the next. By

2007, China's merchandise exports had increased fourfold relative to 2000, reaching 35% of gross domestic product (GDP), and generating the cash flow that would subsequently finance new venture investment.[39]

Phase One of this transition (early-1990s to mid-2000s) was characterised by accelerated industrial learning.[40] Chinese original equipment manufacturers such as BYD—then supplying batteries for Motorola pagers, and now a leading electric vehicle manufacturer, and the electronics company TCL—assembling television sets for Thomson—mastered ISO-9000 audits and Federal Communications Commission (FCC) labelling requirements demanded by Western buyers.[41] Having internalised these standards, leading Chinese companies embarked on strategic acquisitions: Lenovo's 2005 purchase of IBM's personal-computer division provided immediate retail access in roughly 160 countries, while Huawei rapidly displaced Alcatel and Ericsson in third-generation (3G) base-station markets.[42,43] Consistent with this outward orientation, UNCTAD data indicate that China's stock of outward FDI expanded from US$29bn in 2000 to US$317bn in 2010, a multiple comparable to that of Japan's post-Plaza Accord surge and Korea's post-1997 crisis acceleration.[44,45]

China's central government actively facilitated this trajectory. The 1999 "Go Global" initiative re-framed overseas expansion as a patriotic imperative.[46,47] Policy banks—most notably the China Development Bank—provided multi-billion-dollar credits that enabled, for example, ZTE to secure Nigerian telecommunications tenders and Haier to construct refrigeration plants in Egypt. China's accession to the WTO in 2001 reduced average tariffs by roughly two-thirds, while regulatory tolerance for variable interest entity (VIE) structures allowed Chinese internet firms such as Sina (2000) and Baidu (2005) to list on NASDAQ. Although these initial public offerings (IPOs) yielded limited immediate capital, they generated valuable intangible assets: chief financial officers versed in the US, understanding of Generally Accepted Accounting Principles (GAAP), boards familiar with Securities and Exchange Commission (SEC) disclosure practices, and an international investor base capable of pricing "China risk" more systematically.[48]

Phase Two (mid-2000s to early-2020s) of China's internationalisation unfolded primarily within data centres rather than dockyards. Protected by the Great Firewall yet supported by a domestic user base exceeding one billion people, companies such as Alibaba, Tencent, and Baidu optimised e-commerce, super-application, and search models behind substantial home-market barriers before exporting these capabilities to foreign markets. External financing remained favourable. For example, Alibaba's 2014 New York Stock Exchange (NYSE) listing raised a record US$25bn, and Tencent's post-2011 issuances secured sub-3% interest rate on its U.S.-dollar dominated bond. By 2016, WeChat Pay had overtaken UnionPay in mobile-payment volume, providing Chinese entrepreneurs with an on-device laboratory for fintech experimentation that G7 economies were only beginning to contemplate.[49]

Geopolitical dynamics have nevertheless introduced significant constraints to the development of Chinese startups. In hardware, Chinese suppliers enjoyed an extended period of permissive access—Huawei's exclusion from fifth-generation (5G) networks did not commence until 2019, whereas data platforms had already earlier encountered resistance. India prohibited 224 Chinese mobile applications following the 2020 border confrontation, and the United States expanded the remit of the Committee on Foreign Investment in the United States (CFIUS) and enacted the 2022 CHIPS and Science Act, thereby intensifying scrutiny of artificial intelligence (AI)-related mergers and acquisitions. Despite these headwinds, several structural advantages persist: a domestic market valued at approximately USD 11tn that supports large-scale user reaction testing, public banks willing to extend US-dollar credit lines, and a cohort of "sea-turtle" founders bilingual in English and programming languages such as Python.[50,51]

10.2.5 The Lessons of History for the Internationalisation of East Asian Startups

East Asia's "Flying Geese" arc, described above, can be viewed as a relay race in which Japan, Korea, and China have each sprinted through a cycle of export dominance, overseas investment, and entrepreneurial diffusion before handing the baton on to the next economy.

In the first leg of this metaphorical relay, Japan coupled obsessive craftsmanship with bold brand storytelling: Sony's pocket radio and Walkman, Toyota's Kentucky assembly line, and Nintendo's NES convinced global consumers that "Made in Japan" meant speed and precision. When the Plaza Accord sent the yen soaring, Japanese firms redeployed capital abroad and the state rushed in with credit guarantees, translated technical standards, and subsidies that made offshore production feasible. The second leg began when Korean *chaebols* matched Japanese quality but added crisis-honed urgency. Samsung's CDMA handset breakthrough proved that Korean engineers could commercialise global wireless standards, while corporate-venture funds, state-run innovation centres and a rising wave of K-pop and webtoons provided young startup firms with cheaper paths to foreign users. What took Japan four decades to accomplish compressed into two for Korea.

The anchor leg of our metaphorical relay sees China condense the entire script again. Shenzhen OEMs such as BYD and TCL learnt from Western buyers, the "Go Global" mandate unlocked cheap policy-bank dollars, and outward FDI surged almost immediately. A huge and protected home market allowed companies such as Alibaba, Tencent, and ByteDance to refine platform models before projecting them overseas.

The internationalisation story of East Asian companies has followed a repeating rhythm. First, a macro-shock pushes companies to look abroad: Japan faced the post-Plaza yen surge, South Korea the 1997 Asian financial crisis, and China its 2001 WTO accession. Governments then stepped in with soft loans, fast-track regulations, and export incentives that removed friction. Leading breakout products such as Sony's Walkman, Samsung's CDMA handset, Alibaba's e-commerce platform, and later TikTok's short-video platform provided a strategy template, inspiring thousands of founders to copy, adapt and extend it. Over time, each country has crystallised distinctive edges such as Japan in precision hardware, Korea in design fused with pop-culture branding, and China in data-driven digital platform business. Learn, leap, teach—history demonstrates that the metaphorical baton has kept moving down the East Asian value chain.

10.3 Outbound Internationalisation Opportunities and Challenges

10.3.1 Contemporary Internationalisation

The post-pandemic years have acted as a stress-test for startup ecosystems in the three countries, accelerating some historical tendencies while muting others. We now describe and synthesise the most recent developments to have emerged between 2020 and 2025 concerning the internationalisation of East Asian startup ecosystems.

Japan still leads with a "profit-first, step-out-later" logic that echoes its Walkman-era discipline. Roughly 82% of venture capital remains directed towards the domestic market. This capital structure nudges Japanese founders to reach cash-flow break-even before they look to expand overseas. The recent trajectories of SmartNews (which relaunched its US advertising business in 2022), Astroscale (which entered into orbital-debris and on-orbit servising contracts with the United Kingdom (2022) and the USA(2023), and Spiber (which established a biomanufacturing joint venture in Thailand in 2022) illustrate the gradual shift toward more global-centric Japanese startups. However, the large majority of Japanese startups follow the prevailing sequence: monetise at home, invest surplus earnings abroad, and only then raise equity for foreign growth.

For the most part, Korean startups continue to treat their home market of fifty million people as a proving ground, then scale abroad almost immediately—a mindset traced to the *chaebol* spill-overs. To illustrate, Coupang's US$4.6bn New York IPO in 2021 is financing fulfilment centres in Taiwan and Japan; MUSINSA's 2021 Sequoia-led round earmarks capital for Southeast Asia; and Naver Webtoon adaptations have become important intellectual property for Netflix originals. Government schemes still channel roughly one-third of available public money into overseas growth and reimburse twenty-five percent of qualifying foreign-market expenses.

Young Chinese firms have pivoted from headline-grabbing outbound M&As—common in the 2010s. ByteDance pushed TikTok past one billion monthly users in 2021; Pinduoduo took an e-commerce site, Temu, into the United States in 2022; and Shein was widely reported to have surpassed US$30bn in global sales during 2023. At the same time, capital controls have kept most mid-sized funds onshore, and even Tencent has confined itself to minority stakes in Western game studios rather than full acquisitions. The result is an outward reach measured more in daily active users than in overseas head-count or greenfield investments.

Across all three economies, the dominant motif today among startups is revenue-led internationalisation underwritten by corporate co-investors and diaspora networks, rather than the milestone-driven, hyper-burn model that defined Silicon Valley in previous decades. The region is therefore converging on a pragmatic middle path: disciplined domestic monetisation first, capital-efficient cross-border expansion second, and only selective use of venture debt or late-stage 'mega-funds' to finance truly global roll-outs.

10.3.2 To Further Exploit Opportunities

East Asian founders currently enjoy a convergence of supportive forces that was unimaginable even a decade ago. The cost of testing foreign demand has dropped significantly thanks to global digital infrastructure (as we discuss in Chap. 2). Online marketplaces such as Amazon, Shopee and Shopify, social channels like TikTok and YouTube, and PC-gaming platforms such as Steam and Epic allow a Shenzhen gadget maker, a Tokyo VTuber studio, or a Seoul indie game developer to reach millions of users overnight without sinking capital into bricks-and-mortar distribution. Embedded logistics networks, such Fulfilment by Amazon (FBA), cross-border e-parcel lanes on Cainiao, and Coupang's Dawn Delivery clones in Taiwan, convert these digital impressions into same-week delivery, giving early-stage companies a working capital profile that would have shocked their predecessors in the Walkman era.

On the policy front, each government is competing to internationalise its young companies. The Japanese government's "New Form of Capitalism" launched in 2021 targets a ten-fold increase in startups and unicorns, and has seeded a network of urban innovation hubs backed by generous R&D tax credits and relaxed stock-option rules. Likewise, Korea's 2023 Global Startup Expansion Strategy provides a sophisticated toolkit—venture-debt guarantees, SAFE (Simple Agreement for Future Equity) notes aligned with Silicon Valley terms, and a streamlined visa regime—to help propel domestic ventures into North America, Europe, and the Middle East. Collectively these measures lower regulatory friction, subsidise learning costs, and signal long-term state commitment to outward growth. In a similar vein, China's revamped "Go Global" and "Digital Silk Road" programmes frame overseas expansion as a patriotic contribution to national development, offering cloud credits, outbound M&A fast tracks, and diplomatic cover for founders exploring Belt-and-Road markets.

Abundant capital across East Asia reinforces this policy tailwind. Deep corporate balance-sheets—from SoftBank's Vision Fund and the *chaebol* Corporate Venture Capital web (e.g., Samsung Ventures, Hyundai CRADLE, LG Technology Ventures, SK Telecom Ventures) to Tencent, Alibaba, and a widening constellation of Chinese government guidance funds—provide late-stage investments that match the size of U.S. or European investments. While China's on-shore markets continue to supply mega-rounds for consumer-internet startups, tightening domestic liquidity in Korea has spurred many founders to "flip" their headquarters overseas locations like to

Singapore or Delaware and tap cross-border investors. Japan, for its part, is experiencing record foreign LP (Limited Partners) interest in home-grown funds as the weak yen and a maturing exit market improve internal rate of return (IRR) arithmetic or other forms of investment returns.

Talent flows amplify these structural advantages. Silicon Valley, Singapore, Toronto and London now function as revolving doors through which various engineers, returnees, and K-Startup Grand Challenge alumni cycle expertise back into East Asia. Statistics on Chinese unicorns (a term referring to particularly large startup companies as defined by each country), show that more than four-fifths of founding teams have at least one returnee with overseas study or work experience. Korea's startup visas and soft-landing packages replicate this pattern. Japan's startups have begun poaching English-speaking product managers from Rakuten, Mercari, or other earlier generations of startups that have already internationalised to learn the go-to-market expertise. The result is a growing managerial class across East Asia that is fluent in both local context and global best practices, building a talent pipeline for global business expansion.

Finally, culture itself has become a strategic asset in the outward expansion of East Asian startups. The worldwide resonance of K-pop, Japanese anime and manga, and short-video memes generated on Douyin from China has dramatically reduced customer-acquisition costs for adjacent digital products, from HYBE's fandom gaming spinoffs to SHEIN's fast-fashion drops. Japanese VTuber agencies can soft-launch game IP on Twitch to a pre-sold audience before committing to a full console rollout, while Korean beauty brands can utilise K-drama visibility straight onto marketplace shelves. Soft power turns fans into first adopters and, increasingly, into unpaid marketers—an advantage that no government subsidy can replicate.

Taken together, these interlocking infrastructure, policy, financing, talent, and cultural vectors create a historically favourable environment for East Asian startups to internationalise rapidly and capital-efficiently, provided they can navigate growing geopolitical and regulatory headwinds, which we now discuss.

10.3.3 Remaining Challenges

Capital remains a double-edged sword for founders across Japan, Korea, and China. Despite record funding size at home, Japanese venture funds still are conservative: they recycle capital through modest domestic IPOs rather than unicorn-scale funding, leaving growth-stage companies hunting overseas for larger funding. China, by contrast, has plenty of Renminbi liquidity but stringent outbound controls; only a heavily regulated filing system—introduced in 2023—now channels capital to offshore vehicles, adding months of compliance for any start-up eyeing an overseas listing. Korea suffers the opposite situation: post-2021 contraction of domestic VC has punched a mid-stage funding challenges that forces founders to court foreign funds or "flip" headquarters abroad. The net effect is a patchwork funding landscape in which timing a cross-border capital raise is often as strategic as timing a product launch.

Human capital is no easier to marshal for East Asian new ventures. Japanese startups often struggle to break linguistic and cultural barriers that limit foreign hires to accelerate internationalisation. China draws a steady stream of sea-turtle returnees to gain access to international markets, yet their global networks are increasingly filtered by geopolitical tension. Korean firms, meanwhile, must reconcile an intense work culture with the flexibility demanded by international employees; Seoul's new start-up visa helps, but retention hinges on re-tooling management norms as much as on immigration policy.

A further structural headwind is the relative paucity of "born globals"—ventures that internationalise from or near inception—across Japan, Korea, and China. Three mechanisms reinforce this pattern: (i) financing logics that reward early domestic IPOs or on-shore scale before foreign execution, (ii) human-capital frictions (language, cross-jurisdictional sales and compliance skills) that are costly to build at seed and Series A, and (iii) regulatory and data-localisation regimes that raise the fixed costs of early cross-border activity. While outliers exist, the opportunity cost of going global too early remains high for the average startup, which in turn depresses international investor visibility and loops back into conservative domestic capital deployment—amplifying the constraints described above.

Geopolitics is also a critical, and often the most unpredictable, constraint. Heightened US–China technology rivalry has turned export-control lists and data-localisation rules into daily reading for founders; even innocuous consumer apps can be swept into CFIUS (Committee on Foreign Investment in the United States) review or India-style bans. Korean and Japanese startups feel the squeeze as well: Korean chips shipped to China now attract US licence scrutiny, and Japanese SAAS vendors must ring-fence European user data under GDPR (General Data Protection Regulation). Compliance engineering and legal counsel therefore claim a growing share of early-stage cash usage speed.

Currency risk adds another layer of complexity to the outward internationalisation of East Asian startups. A whiplash Yen raises hedging costs just as Japanese start-ups book their first U.S. revenues; China's partially convertible Renminbi complicates offshore treasury management and investor repatriation; and the relative illiquidity of the won inflates spreads on cross-border financing. Sophisticated cash-management desks—common in MNCs—are only beginning to migrate to the start-up world, creating a knowledge gap that can erase margin gains overnight.

Finally, perception itself can be a bottleneck. Other than marquee deals such as Coupang or Alibaba, global investors still see few US$10bn exits from East Asia and often reduce valuations or demand earlier profitability milestones. This scepticism loops back into the capital challenge: lower mark-ups dampen local fund returns and reinforce conservative deployment at home. Breaking this cycle will require a new cohort of headline exits, as well as more visible secondary markets.

In short, the same region that offers fertile policy support and cultural tailwinds also presents East Asian founders with a minefield of capital, talent, regulatory, currency, and perception hazards. Mastering this contradiction—turning headwinds into competitive advantages—will determine which East Asian startup graduates from regional champion to truly global contender.

10.4 Inbound Internationalisation to East Asia

While we have focussed so far in this chapter on outward expansion, the concurrent inbound flow of foreign ICT multinational corporations and startups to East Asia has proven equally transformative. These global entrants have reshaped domestic startup ecosystems from within, introducing new operational models, talent practices, and funding mechanisms. Unlike the sequential "Flying Geese" export surge that moved across borders one economy at a time, inbound internationalisation has unfolded simultaneously across Japan, Korea, and China since 2000—though with strikingly different outcomes in each market. We now examine how global technology giants—such as Google, Amazon, Microsoft, Netflix, Uber, Salesforce, and others—have functioned as ecosystem catalysts, creating competitive pressures and knowledge conduits, and fundamentally altering the operational common practice of East Asian startups.

10.4.1 Inbound Internationalisation and Its Impact on East Asian Startup Ecosystems

Foreign ICT multinationals entering East Asia since 2000 have fundamentally reshaped regional startup ecosystems, though each market has presented them with distinct challenges and opportunities that yielded markedly different outcomes. These global giants arrived with proven business models but have encountered regulatory barriers, entrenched local competitors, and cultural resistance that forced creative adaptations. Their responses created unintended catalytic effects that transformed local entrepreneurial cultures, talent markets, and funding landscapes. Amazon's convenience store payment innovations in Japan and Microsoft's research investments in China exemplify how forced localisation have generated broader ecosystem benefits across East Asia.

Foreign ICT multinationals entering Japan's mature yet hierarchical business culture have tended to opt for infrastructure provision and talent development over direct market disruption.[52,53] Google established its Tokyo headquarters in 2001 and launched the Shibuya startup campus in 2019, creating new professional networks outside traditional corporate structures. Amazon's struggle with Japan's resale price maintenance system led to payment innovations at convenience stores and ATMs. These adaptations demonstrated to foreign entrepreneurs the necessity of localisation while showcasing them alternative business models. Microsoft's evolution from basic

Japanese localisation to AI leadership illustrates this pattern. The company's substantial R&D investments, including a US$2.9bn commitment through to 2025, exemplify how a persistent presence could generate spillover effects into the ecosystem.

The cumulative impact transformed workplace culture and entrepreneurial expectations in Japan. Foreign MNCs introduced alternative compensation structures—median JPY 12.5mn versus JPY 8.5mn for domestic companies—alongside flexible work practices and performance-based advancement. The "alumni effect" proved particularly significant. Former employees like Rosen Diankov, who co-founded the robotics firm Mujin, injecting international entrepreneurial spirit into Japan's traditionally risk-averse startup environment.

Korea's advanced digital infrastructure enabled foreign MNCs to pursue collaborative rather than competitive strategies.[54] For example, national security restrictions on map data exports constrained Google's direct expansion while strengthening domestic players such as Naver and Kakao. This regulatory environment encouraged partnership models. Google for Startups Campus Seoul launched in 2015 with presidential endorsement and generated remarkable returns—KRW 706bn in startup funding and with 3700 jobs created. Similarly, Amazon strategically emphasised Amazon Web Services (AWS) cloud services and cultural export acceleration through K-Beauty programs rather than challenging dominant Korean e-commerce players in their domestic market.

Microsoft's US$1.8bn KT Corporation (formerly Korea Telecom) partnership exemplified sophisticated collaboration, combining AI research, infrastructure development, and joint startup funding. Netflix's US$2.5bn content investment commitment in Korea demonstrated how global platforms could amplify Korean cultural assets while serving their own growth objectives. Selective regulations in Korea created a protective framework that paradoxically strengthened local startups. To illustrate, Uber faced ridesharing restrictions while Netflix achieved content success, providing learning opportunities to Korean startups before their own international expansion.

China has presented foreign firms with the most complex operational landscape. Internet sovereignty policies simultaneously constrained foreign operations while generating unexpected catalysts for innovation. The "Great Firewall" limited direct service access, yet enabled significant R&D contributions by inward-investing firms through research centres and strategic investments. Google's constrained presence in China still influenced mobile development through Android's open-source architecture. Amazon's marketplace closure in 2019 contrasted with AWS's continued operations through local partnerships, maintaining technology transfer channels despite the competitive advantages of domestic cloud providers.

Microsoft Research Asia (MRA), established in Beijing in 1998, arguably generated the most profound impact on startup ecosystem development in China. It functioned as what observers called "West Point for Chinese tech talent". MRA alumni now lead major Chinese technology companies, including ByteDance's Hongjiang Zhang Alibaba's Wang Jian, andnumerous AI startup founders. This "brain circulation" effect transformed foreign R&D investment into indigenous Chinese innovation capacity.[55,56]

The "forced adaptation" model—joint ventures, limited-service portfolios, and enterprise focus—inadvertently created space for domestic champions while generating knowledge spillovers, competitive pressure, and capital flows that have contributed significantly to China's technology emergence.

These varied experiences across Japan, Korea, and China have established distinct patterns of foreign MNC influence that continue to shape talent development, funding mechanisms, and entrepreneurial culture in startup ecosystems throughout the region.

10.4.2 Transformative Impact on Talent and Labour Markets

Foreign ICT multinationals have fundamentally reshaped talent dynamics across East Asian startup ecosystems. They have introduced new career pathways, compensation structures, and skill development frameworks that have gradually spread throughout the broader innovation landscape of the region.

Foreign MNCs consistently offered compensation premiums that forced domestic firms to rethink their talent retention strategies. The numbers tell the story clearly. For example, in Japan, international subsidiaries paid a median JPY 12.5mn versus JPY 8.5mn for domestic companies in 2024. This 47% premium created a divided labour market where top-tier engineering talent could command substantial wage increases by switching between sectors. The competitive pressure intensified particularly in high-demand areas, such as AI, cloud computing, and mobile application development. Crucially, these wage differentials also loosened traditionally rigid labour markets, as professionals accustomed to mobility between foreign and domestic firms increasingly considered entrepreneurial careers. In this way, the presence of foreign MNCs indirectly expanded the pool of skilled talent available to startups, especially in cutting-edge technology domains.

Google for Startups programs across the region systematically addressed the "global mindset" gap through structured entrepreneurship education. The results were measurable: Tokyo's campus emphasised AI and machine learning, and Google's AI Startup School in Seoul created professional development pathways that bypassed traditional corporate hierarchies in Korea.

Microsoft pursued technical capability upgrading through programs like the Founders Hub and Azure AI training. The scale was unprecedented. To illustrate, Microsoft globally committed to training 10 million people in digital skills in Japan by 2025—with parallel initiatives in Japan, Korea and China—representing the largest private sector workforce development investment in the region's history. These programs introduced cloud-native development, DevOps methodologies, and automated testing frameworks that previously were uncommon in traditional East Asian software environments.

The "alumni effect" proved crucial for the development of executive talent. Microsoft Research Asia graduates now lead major East Asian technology companies: ByteDance's Hongjiang Zhang exemplifies how foreign R&D experience translates into entrepreneurial leadership. Google alumni, such as Colin Huang (the founder of Pinduoduo, a Chinese online retailer), and numerous Japanese entrepreneurs who previously worked for ICT multinational companies have created visible success models for internationally oriented career paths.

Labour market practices by ICT MNCs in East Asia have evolved through three distinct phases.[57,58] The initial entry period focused on gaining basic market access and acquiring talent. Foreign MNCs adapted to local employment practices while offering premium compensation to attract top graduates. This phase established the foundational infrastructure—R&D centres, local management teams, and technical partnerships—that promoted the development of East Asian startup ecosystems.

The expansion phase that followed saw the systematic establishment of innovation hubs and accelerator programmes. Google's Campus launches in Seoul (2015) and Tokyo (2019), Amazon's Startup Loft initiatives, and Microsoft's support programs created professional communities that were independent of traditional corporate hierarchies. Startup careers gained legitimacy as alternatives to *chaebol*, *keiretsu*, or state-owned enterprise employment during this period.

The third phase—AI acceleration (2020 to present)—has an unprecedented focus on AI talent development. Microsoft's US$2.9bn investment in Japan, Google's Gemini AI integration with KDDI, and AWS's expansion of GPU-intensive cloud capacity have all targeted AI capabilities specifically in the region. This investment concentration has created specialised talent pools that serve both foreign MNCs and domestic startups, significantly accelerating regional AI development sophistication.

Language and cultural adaptation patterns evolved significantly throughout these three phases. Early approaches relied heavily on expatriate management and English-language operations. Later, successful programs increasingly emphasised local talent development and culturally adapted management practices. Salesforce Ventures from the USA exemplified this hybrid approach by maintaining US-based managing partners while developing local deal sourcing capabilities.

Current startup ecosystem dynamics in East Asia reflect two decades of accumulated foreign MNC influence.[59] Startups that emerged from international accelerator programs consistently show higher percentages of international staff, greater willingness to adopt remote work practices, and more sophisticated global market entry approaches. These practices have gradually influenced broader industry standards, particularly in Japan where traditional employment models were historically more rigid (as we discuss in Chap. 4). Importantly, the same channels of influence that reshaped major firms also affected startups: exposure to foreign MNC norms accelerated the adoption of flexible work arrangements, cross-border hiring, and global business models, creating a new generation of ventures better positioned to compete internationally.

Over the past decade, technical sophistication gaps have become pronounced in East Asia. Startups accessing AWS cloud credits through accelerator programs, Azure AI services through Microsoft partnerships, or Google Cloud platform integration demonstrate measurably higher technical capabilities in machine learning implementation, cloud architecture, and international scalability. This technical knowledge transfer from MNCs to startup ecosystems reduces the time required for startups to achieve technical maturity, enabling more ambitious product development at earlier stages of their life cycle.

Professional network effects have also given rise to new forms of inter-regional collaboration. Alumni networks from international accelerator programs facilitate knowledge sharing, business referrals, and collaborative projects across national boundaries. These networks complement rather than compete with traditional business relationships, creating additional pathways for startup collaboration and market expansion in the region. Moreover, international programs have promoted rapid prototyping and iterative development concepts that are challenging traditional perfectionist approaches in Japanese and Korean technology development. The adoption of "failing fast", a culture that is linked to Silicon Valley and Western startups, and minimal viable product frameworks have enabled faster innovation cycles and reduced time-to-market for new products and services of East Asian startups.

10.4.3 Restructuring of Funding Landscapes and Inter-Firm Relationships

Foreign MNCs have also reconfigured the financial architecture and partnership dynamics of East Asian startup ecosystems, introducing new funding mechanisms, validation frameworks, and collaboration models that complement traditional domestic financing structures.[60]

Direct financial contributions through corporate venture capital arms have created significant funding pathways previously unavailable to regional startups. For example, the Japan Trailblazer Fund of Salesforce Ventures, launched in 2018 with a US$100mn commitment, has supported more than 38 companies, making Japan the second-largest market for Salesforce Ventures investments globally after the United States. Similar commitments have also been visible in Korea, where Salesforce Ventures and other global CVCs have backed SAAS and enterprise software startups.

Google's strategic investments, including the reported acquisition of Japanese fintech Pring for an estimated US$180–270mn, established foreign acquisition as a viable exit pathway for domestic startups. Comparable dynamics are observable in China, where Google, though more constrained by regulation, has selectively participated in AI and gaming-related investments, and where other U.S. technology firms have executed minority stakes in local ventures. These cases demonstrate that foreign acquisition and investment serve as validation mechanisms beyond Japan, even if the form varies by country context.

Microsoft's M12 venture capital arm and Amazon's strategic investments, while less prominently featured in public reporting, are not solely focused on Japan. Both have active portfolios in Korea and China, with investments in cloud, AI, and mobility startups that are subsequently integrated into Microsoft's global partner networks or Amazon's marketplace ecosystems. These relationships create revenue opportunities that surpass traditional distributor channels and strengthen the positioning of startups in international supply chains.

The provision of cloud credits through accelerator programs represents a distinctive form of early-stage financial support across East Asia. AWS Activate program credits, Google Cloud startup packages, and Azure benefits are widely used by startups in Japan, Korea, and China. They effectively reduce initial capital expenditure requirements for data-intensive ventures, particularly valuable for AI and machine learning startups where computational costs represent significant barriers to experimentation and development.

The evolution of funding relationships in East Asia occurred through distinct phases that reflected changing MNC strategies and the maturation of domestic markets. Initial entry strategies emphasised market access through acquisitions and strategic partnerships with established domestic players. Amazon's acquisition of Joyo.com in China and early partnership arrangements in Japan have exemplified this approach.

The ecosystem development phase witnessed systematic establishment of accelerator programs and innovation hubs designed to nurture local talent while creating deal flow for corporate venture investments. Google's Campus model, replicated across Seoul and Tokyo, created structured environments for identifying and developing promising local startups. Microsoft's accelerator programs and Amazon's AWS Startup Loft initiatives followed similar approaches, creating standardised processes for startup evaluation and support.

The platform integration phase has emphasised deeper integration between MNC platforms and local startup ecosystems. Salesforce's AppExchange marketplace integration for portfolio companies, Google's cloud platform optimisation for accelerator participants, and Amazon's marketplace access for e-commerce startups have created symbiotic relationships whereby East Asian startups gain global distribution while MNCs benefit from locally optimised solutions.

Strategic partnerships between foreign MNCs and regional startups have evolved from simple vendor-customer arrangements toward collaborative innovation models. Microsoft's US$1.8bn partnership with KT combines technology development, market access, and startup support through joint funding mechanisms. This model demonstrates how foreign MNCs can leverage local market knowledge and infrastructure while contributing global expertise and capital resources to startup ecosystem development in East Asia.

Current funding dynamics reflect the maturation of hybrid domestic-international financing models for startups in East Asia. East Asian startups are increasingly accessing multiple funding sources—domestic venture capital, foreign corporate investors, government grants, and international accelerator programs—creating more resilient capital structures and reducing their dependence on any single funding pathway.

Validation mechanisms have evolved significantly through participation in international programs. Startups that successfully complete Google, Microsoft, or Amazon accelerator programs gain credibility that facilitates subsequent fundraising from both domestic and international investors. This validation function has become particularly important in risk-averse markets like Japan, whereby foreign program participation signals global competitiveness and scalability potential.

Cross-border partnership formation has been systematically streamlined through structured programs that provide guidance on legal, regulatory, and cultural aspects of international business development. The Microsoft for Startups programs explicitly include support for navigating international market entry, reducing barriers that previously limited regional expansion opportunities. These support mechanisms enable smaller startups to pursue global growth strategies that were previously available only to larger, well-resourced startups.

The emergence of platform-based business models, facilitated by access to MNC infrastructure and distribution channels, has created new revenue opportunity structures for all forms of companies.[61] East Asian startups developing applications for Google Cloud, integrating with Salesforce ecosystems, or leveraging Amazon marketplace infrastructure can achieve scalability and market reach that would be difficult to replicate through independent development efforts.

10.4.4 Evolution of Entrepreneurial Culture and Management Practices

The sustained presence of foreign ICT multinationals has catalysed subtle but profound transformations in entrepreneurial mindsets, management methodologies, and organisational cultures throughout East Asian startup ecosystems, creating hybrid approaches that blend global best practices with local market insights.

Foreign MNCs have introduced systematic approaches to entrepreneurship education that have complemented but diverged from traditional academic and corporate training frameworks. Google's Startup School programs delivered structured curricula covering lean startup methodologies, growth hacking techniques, and international scaling strategies across multiple regional locations. This systematic approach has standardised East Asian entrepreneurship concepts and created standard vocabularies for discussing business development strategies.

The emphasis on data-driven decision-making frameworks represented a significant departure from traditional relationship-based business development approaches in East Asia. Amazon's AWS programs promoting cloud analytics, Microsoft's AI-focused training, and Google's emphasis on user behaviour analysis introduced quantitative methodologies that enabled more precise customer segmentation and product optimisation. These analytical approaches have gradually become diffused throughout the broader ecosystem as alumni assumed leadership roles in other East Asian startups.

Work culture innovations have proved particularly influential in the traditionally hierarchical organisational environments of East Asia.[62] Google's flat organisational structures, Amazon's customer obsession principles, and Microsoft's collaborative development approaches have provided alternative models to seniority-based advancement and consensus-driven decision-making across the region. For example, Microsoft Japan's four-day work week experiment, while limited in scope, demonstrated practical alternatives to traditional overtime-intensive business cultures in the country.

Cultural transformation in East Asia has occurred through gradual diffusion rather than sudden displacement of traditional practices. At first, East Asian startups primarily affected elite technical talent who experienced alternative management approaches through direct employment at foreign MNCs. These individuals subsequently carried new practices into domestic firms or startup ventures, creating pockets of innovation within traditional organisational environments.

Gradually, East Asian startups witnessed the systematic establishment of alternative organisational models through accelerator programs and innovation hubs. Google Campus environments, Microsoft accelerator cohorts, and Amazon AWS startup communities created professional spaces where international business practices could be tested and refined within local contexts.

Currently, East Asian startups typically adopt a hybrid management approach throughout startup ecosystems. Concepts such as agile development, remote work capabilities, and equity compensation structures have become standard practices among internationally oriented startups. At the same time, traditional domestic firms have selectively adopted elements that align with their organisational cultures.

Female entrepreneurship patterns reflected the distinctive influence of international programs.[63] To illustrate, Google for Startups Campus Seoul's 37% female participation rate significantly exceeded typical domestic entrepreneurship demographics, suggesting that international programs successfully addressed barriers that limited women's participation in traditional business development pathways. This outcome demonstrates how foreign MNC initiatives can accelerate social change in East Asia in a manner that aligns with domestic policy Arguably, a large proportion of current entrepreneurial approaches in East Asia reflects the cumulative influence of two decades of international business practice exposure. Startups from international accelerator programs appear to show higher propensities for scaling faster and entering international markets. Empirical work supports these patterns, though the evidence on 'uncertainty tolerance' is less directly established, especially in East Asia.

Risk assessment methodologies have evolved significantly through exposure to international investment evaluation frameworks. East Asian entrepreneurs with international program experience demonstrate greater sophistication in analysing market opportunities, competitive landscapes, and technology risks. This analytical capability enables more informed strategic decisions and improves success rates for international expansion efforts.

The integration of social impact considerations into business models reflects the influence of global corporate social responsibility frameworks promoted by MNCs.[64] Many East Asian startups that have emerging from international accelerator programs explicitly address social challenges such as aging populations, environmental sustainability, and digital inclusion—topics that align with both local needs and global corporate priorities.

Global network utilisation has become a distinguishing characteristic of internationally-oriented startups in the region. Entrepreneurs who have participated in foreign MNC programs typically maintain professional relationships that facilitate market entry, partnership development, and knowledge sharing across national boundaries. These networks complement traditional domestic business relationships and create additional pathways for business development and growth.

Management education integration has systematically upgraded leadership capabilities throughout East Asian startup ecosystems. International programs that emphasise strategic communication, cross-cultural management, and global market analysis have created a managerial class better equipped to navigate international business environments. This capability development has proved particularly valuable as domestic markets in East Asia mature and international expansion becomes necessary for continued growth.

The cumulative effect of these cultural and practical innovations has been the emergence in East Asia of hybrid entrepreneurial ecosystems that maintain distinctive regional characteristics while incorporating global best practices. This synthesis enables East Asian startups to leverage both local market insights and international operational capabilities, creating competitive advantages that reflect the successful integration of inbound internationalisation influences.

10.5 Conclusion

This chapter has examined the evolving landscape of internationalisation for East Asian startups, highlighting both outbound and inbound dynamics across Japan, Korea, and China. We have explored the region's vast market opportunities, the unique competitive and regulatory environments, and the growing role of government policy in shaping cross-border innovation connected to startup activity.

As a concluding remark, we present three future scenarios for East Asian ecosystems—managed stabilisation, regional fragmentation, and China-centric rebalancing—each presenting distinct challenges and strategic imperatives for founders, investors, and ecosystem leaders. Ultimately, success in this era requires East Asian startups to develop regulatory agility, build resilient partnership networks, and design dual-track operational models that can adapt to shifting geopolitical and market realities. We believe that the future trajectory of East Asian startup internationalisation will unfold across three distinct yet intersecting pathways, each demanding fundamentally different strategic responses from entrepreneurs, investors, and policymakers.

The first scenario—*Stabilisation after Disruption*—envisions a managed détente where regulatory clarity emerges from current geopolitical turbulence, enabling resumed capital flows and cross-border data exchanges. Under this framework, dual headquarters strategies (for example, Shenzhen-Singapore) would hedge compliance risks. Cross-border venture syndicates would become more normalised, with sovereign funds co-leading growth rounds across national boundaries, although geopolitical risk premiums would remain priced into valuations, but no longer prove fatal to deal-making.

The second pathway—*Fragmentation and Regional Growth*—anticipates the emergence of hardened techno-nationalism, creating semi-sealed technology blocs anchored around US-centric infrastructure versus Sino-centric startup ecosystems. This fragmentation would paradoxically catalyse a boom in regulatory technology and compliance software, with Asia–Pacific privacy-software spending projected to triple. Japanese startups would monetise GDPR-plus-APPI (Japan's Act on the Protection of Personal Information) toolkits, Korean fintechs would arbitrage payment-gateway discrepancies, and Chinese software development tool providers would bridge Western encryption protocols with domestically-approved variants. Talent would localise correspondingly, with security-cleared engineers commanding premium salaries and bilingual legal engineers leading consultancies that connect and integrate systems across different systems.

The third scenario—*China-Centric Regional Rebalancing*—projects Beijing's Belt-and-Road investments and Digital Silk Road buildouts crystallising into a de facto standards regime, with the Renminbi surpassing the dollar in Asian trade invoicing and digital RMB wallets pre-installed on a majority of East Asian smartphones. Japanese and Korean startups would adapt through dual-track go-to-market strategies, maintaining one product line hosted on Chinese cloud infrastructure with Renminbi billing and another on sovereign clouds for the customers in developed countries. While this approach would unlock massive market access, it would create strategic dependency risks requiring parallel architectures—code repositories mirrored outside China, escrowed IP licensing, and contingency supply chain swapping capabilities.

Across all three scenarios, East Asian startup ecosystems must cultivate organisational agility and scenario fluency as core competencies rather than peripheral risk management tools. The region's entrepreneurs have historically excelled at rapid adaptation—from Japan's post-Plaza Accord offshore manufacturing to Korea's post-1997 digital pivots and China's pandemic-era platform exports. The coming decade will test whether this adaptive capacity can scale to navigate simultaneous technological, regulatory, and monetary fragmentation while maintaining the cross-border knowledge flows that have historically driven East Asian innovation.

Success will favour those East Asian ventures that embed geopolitical scenario forecasting and preparations into product development, maintain modular compliance architectures, and build partnership networks that are resilient to shifting alliance structures, all of which would help to transforming uncertainty into competitive advantage. The enduring message of this chapter is that internationalisation is no longer the after-market of East Asian innovation. Startups in East Asia need to take this into account from day one. Those who understand the East Asian context better and can bridge between East Asia and the global markets will grow in the following decades. They will be equipped with regulatory agility, cross-regional partnership depth, and a cross-border mindset, and they will set the pace of respective global markets beyond East Asia.

Notes

1. Nikkei Asia (2023).
2. Akamatsu (1962).
3. Amsden (1989).
4. Wade (1990).
5. Kojima (2000).
6. Ozawa (2005).
7. Ito (2015).
8. Westney (1987).
9. Kim (1997).
10. Mathews (2002).
11. Kim (1997).
12. Mathews (2002).
13. Lee (2013).
14. Nathan (1999).
15. Henning (1994).
16. Bailey et al. (1994).
17. Encarnation (1992).
18. Mair et al. (1988).
19. Kenney and Florida (1993).
20. Abo (1994).
21. Helper and Sako (1995).
22. Aoyama and Izushi (2003).
23. Okimoto (1989) and Callon (1995).
24. Porter et al. (2000) and Anchordoguy (2005).
25. Lee and Lim (2001) and Chu (2004).
26. Chang (2003).
27. Kim and Nelson (2000).
28. Hundt (2009).
29. Choung et al. (2014).
30. Song (2018).
31. Kim (2021).
32. Yoo and Kim (2015) and Moon and Yim (2018).
33. Song and Lee (2019).
34. Yoon (2021).
35. Lee and Kim (2020).
36. Park and Song (2022).
37. Naughton (2007).
38. Yusuf et al. (2014).
39. Huang (2008).
40. Sutmejer (2003).
41. Luo and Tung (2007).
42. Liu and Buck (2007).
43. Fan (2006).
44. Sauvant et al. (2010).
45. Buckley et al. (2007).
46. Voss et al. (2008).
47. Wang (2002).
48. Lin and Zhang (2009).
49. Peng et al. (2018).
50. Tschang and Almirall (2021).
51. Wang and Liu (2018).
52. Whittaker et al. (2020).

53. Lechevalier (2014).
54. Kim and Kim (2009).
55. Zweig (2006).
56. Cao (2008).
57. Lechevalier (2014).
58. Liu and Dicken (2006).
59. Whittaker et al. (2020).
60. Florida and Kenney (1991) and Kenney and von Burg (1999).
61. Parker et al. (2016).
62. Hofstede (1991) and Whittaker et al. (2020).
63. Marlow and Patton (2005).
64. Porter and Kramer (2011).

Chapter 11
Unleashing Innovation in East Asia: Key Takeaways for Stakeholders

11.1 The Need to Amend Western-Centric Frameworks

Startup ecosystems have become ever more important as drivers of innovation due to the digitisation of information and the application of digital technologies to innovation processes, resulting in lower entry barriers and easier scalability for new ventures. In our exploration of the growth of East Asian startup ecosystems in this book, and after highlighting conceptual foundations related to the key ideas of innovation and ecosystems (Chaps. 2 and 3), we analysed the startup ecosystem trajectories of Japan, Korea, and Mainland China (Chaps. 4, 5, and 6). Based on these conceptual foundations and country analyses, we proceeded to identify and discuss three major overarching themes relevant for understanding startup ecosystems in East Asia—culture, policy, and internationalisation (Chaps. 8, 9, and 10).

These three themes represent common factors that shape startup ecosystems *in the context of East Asia* in ways that make them distinct from the more extensively studied Western examples. For instance, common cultural traits influence the characteristics of entrepreneurship and its social acceptance in East Asia. The fact that East Asian governments apply explicit support policies equally impacts the nature of resulting ecosystems and the startups they foster. Last, but not least, geographic and cultural distance as well as language barriers, which in the case of China and partly Japan combine with large domestic markets, constrain the extent and depth of international linkages—a third factor which sets East Asian startup ecosystems apart from their Western counterparts. At the same time, we also find variety within East Asia as the three countries differ with regard to historical experiences and trajectories, stages of economic development, political and administrative structures, and social norms.

Importantly, differences across and beyond East Asia seem not to hamper startup ecosystem performance. While the different contextual conditions do require adaptations in entrepreneurship, support infrastructures, and business models, we observe equally vibrant startup ecosystems. This is evidenced, for example, by the growing importance of East Asia in recent international rankings, where startup ecosystems

Y. Cheng et al., *Unleashing Innovation the East Asian Way*,
https://doi.org/10.1007/978-981-95-6513-9_11

from Japan, Korea, and China are consistently found among the top 15 ecosystems globally.[1]

The observation that different organisational designs necessitated by local contingencies can produce similar outcomes is known as functional equivalence.[2] It is typical for open systems, which are exposed to competition. The high degree of functional equivalence between Western and East Asian startup ecosystems warrants a revision, or at least, an amendment of the conceptual frameworks built on predominantly Western studies. Our findings specifically demand an analytical framework that is able to incorporate the importance of: (i) cultural and historical context, (ii) government policies and regulatory environment, and (iii) international linkages.

Developing a full-fledged novel framework is beyond the scope of this book. However, based on our in-depth explorations of startup ecosystems in East Asia, we feel confident to present a more general and inclusive version than is presently available in existing literature. Figure 11.1 contains a brief overview of key elements of startup ecosystems derived from major typologies proposed by existing research.[3] In addition to entrepreneurship itself and the key elements grouped under "resource conditions" and "networks and markets", Fig. 11.1 highlights "international linkages" as an intermediary dimension. This dimension is understood to relate to entrepreneurship and all key elements within the ecosystem. In our depiction, "government policies" and the "regulatory environment", while external, interact with "support infrastructures" either through their attempt to ameliorate perceived shortcomings, or by intentionally or unintentionally imposing additional constraints. As exogenous factors, "cultural norms" and "historical experiences" also shape entrepreneurship, in addition to policies and regulations. To complete the picture, and to underscore its evolutionary nature, we also add the "outcome" or "performance dimension", together with feedback loops, into the system, as well as into the field of policy and regulation. While poor ecosystem performance is likely to stimulate corrective adjustments, positive outcomes are likely to reinforce already existing developments.

As complex, embedded and evolving systems, national startup ecosystems have manifold trajectories with different configurations of key actors and components at different moments in their development.[4] We expect that the amended conceptual framework depicted in Fig. 11.1—based on our findings from East Asia— offers ample flexibility and will prove useful and relevant for understanding the development of startup ecosystems in other regions of the world. Specifically, we hope that our framework will not only help to resolve issues around global variety, but will also facilitate conceptually grounded comparisons of startup ecosystems situated in contrasting political, economic, and social settings. The context-sensitive lens presented in Fig. 11.1 should not only help researchers to better appreciate and understand differences among national startup ecosystems. As the next sections explain in more detail, our findings also offer important takeaways for the various stakeholders directly engaged in startup systems in East Asia and beyond.

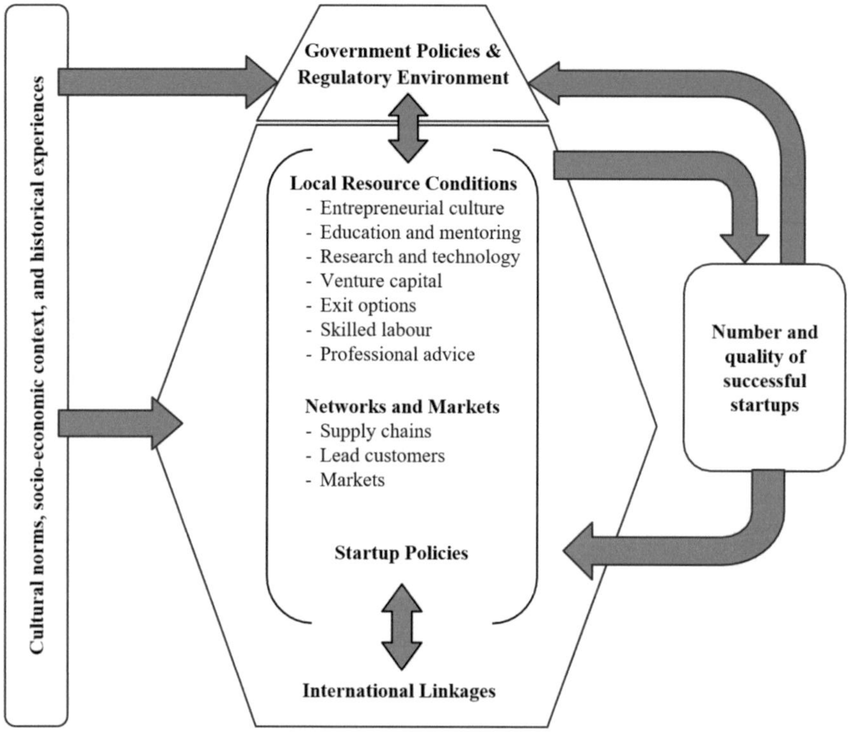

Fig. 11.1 Contextualised startup ecosystem framework. *Note* Based on the literature reviewed in Chap. 3 and our own findings

11.2 Takeaways for Startup Entrepreneurs

The growth of East Asian startup ecosystems offers ample opportunities for advanced technology entrepreneurs. First of all, local founding entrepreneurs in Japan, Korea, and China can take advantage of the changing economic landscape in these countries that is increasingly tilting in favour of startups. Attracted by more progressive organisational cultures and higher degrees of work autonomy than in large established firms, ever more university graduates as well as experienced knowledge workers are willing to seek professional careers within startups. Furthermore, there is a high degree of openness by customers towards products and services developed by startups in East Asian countries, particularly among smartphone users. All of this means that East Asia continues to offer numerous advantages to entrepreneurs interested in establishing their own business there.

As they do so, entrepreneurs are advised to strategically leverage the comprehensive government support systems and policy platforms available to them, as well as the relatively abundant investment funds now increasingly available, again partly bolstered by governmental support policies. In short, entrepreneurs need to have knowledge of, understand, and actively engage with the substantial and targeted government support available (e.g., funding grants, R&D subsidies, tax incentives, and specialised networking through national startup schemes) prior to and following establishment of the firm. At the same time, exploiting regulatory sandboxes can provide startup founders with opportunities to validate innovative business models and demonstrate feasibility to investors in the risk-averse environments of East Asia.

East Asian entrepreneurs are also advised to consider carefully the location of their new venture. Clearly, the capital cities of East Asia provide numerous benefits to young firms in terms of, for example, access to human capital, the quality of physical infrastructure, and the availability of support organisations and intermediaries (see Table 3.2). As such, these cities inevitable exert a strong gravitational pull on founders. However, we observe that secondary startup ecosystems in an East Asian country can offer distinct advantages and specialisations around focused talent pools and integrated support infrastructure that are tailored to specific industry needs. Daejeon's deep science cluster (in biotech and robotics), Shenzen's computer hardware and supply chain advantages, and Suzhou's strengths in biotechnology are just three of many examples. Choosing to locate outside of a dominant capital hub can therefore be a viable option that founding entrepreneurs should consider, especially if there is a good fit between industrial sector, business model, and firm capabilities on the one hand, and location advantages on the other.

In our analyses, we observe that the prevailing East Asian startup model prioritises achieving robust domestic scale and profitability first, reflecting the size and sophistication of local markets. This suggests that new founders should initially focus on disciplined monetisation in domestic markets, and view early international expansion as a later, capital-efficient step, rather than adhering strictly to the risky hyper-burn "born global" standard found in many Western startup contexts. In other words, founding entrepreneurs should plan for sequential expansion, using the large domestic market as a foundation for growth. At the same time, international markets should not be overlooked. Many East Asian startups will be able to leverage cultural exports ("soft power") as a marketing and entry point for international markets. The global success of East Asian cultural exports (e.g., K-pop, Japanese anime, Chinese short-video technology) lowers customer acquisition costs for associated technology products and services. Depending on industry sector, founders should consider integrating these cultural assets strategically into their business models; for example, by leveraging existing fan bases as first adopters and powerful, unpaid marketers during their international expansion efforts.

A key constraint to internationalisation that we observe for East Asian startups is the limited international background of founders and top management teams, which arguably hinders the adoption of "born global strategies". Those founders who plan to expand into international markets early after the establishment of their firm are advised to cultivate global perspectives and seek diverse team members from inception, as incorporating "returnees" or foreign talent is likely to be crucial for building the cross-cultural competencies and international networks needed to effectively navigate diverse foreign markets and unfamiliar regulations.

In order to leverage these favourable conditions effectively, East Asian startup entrepreneurs need to navigate deftly the changing business environment and cultural context found in East Asian countries. They need to practice a modern and open entrepreneurial style to attract young talent that no longer adheres to hierarchical cultural norms of previous generations. This is likely to necessitate the development of a hybrid leadership style that balances the traditional expectations of a leader with the granting of greater work autonomy, flexibility, and empowerment required to recruit and retain high-calibre technical and managerial talent amongst younger generations. At the same time, founders are advised to avoid behaviour that might be perceived unfavourably by local stakeholders; for example, those who may sense cultural transgressions when entrepreneurs live a lavish lifestyle or show little respect towards established business leaders.[5] Furthermore, because cultural norms in East Asia still place high importance on professional experience and on accumulated personal networks as sources of legitimacy, experienced technology professionals tend to be more effective than fresh university graduates—regardless of individual talent and capabilities—and this should be considered by founders in their recruitment strategies.

East Asian founders are also advised to build networks and connections with large established local and foreign firms. This is because East Asian ecosystems continue to feature strong corporate-startup symbiosis (Japan) and *chaebol*-led development (Korea), making partnerships crucial for legitimacy and scale. Collaborations with established firms, often facilitated by Corporate Venture Capital (CVCs), can provide capital, access to supply chains, and large corporate customers that might otherwise be difficult for unproven new ventures to secure.

East Asian startup ecosystems have also become increasingly attractive for foreign entrepreneurs. Startup visa programs support the immigration of foreign entrepreneurs.[6] More importantly, foreign entrepreneurs naturally tend to apply a global perspective on startup business opportunities that local entrepreneurs often lack. While many more Japanese, Korean, and Chinese startup entrepreneurs are becoming interested in global business opportunities, their ideas and business models are often strongly embedded in the national market. This embeddedness can hinder the effective launch of "born global" business models that leverage global opportunities from the outset through the creation of products and services that can be offered seamlessly across national borders. At the same time, such constraints can yield opportunities for foreign entrepreneurs in East Asian countries as they may be able to leverage globally the cutting-edge knowledge and technologies that they source locally.

East Asian countries also present challenges for foreign entrepreneurs. Japanese, Korean, and Chinese are all highly complex languages that require sustained efforts to master, and—regardless of the increasing English proficiency in East Asian countries—the effectiveness of foreign entrepreneurs will be limited by communication barriers unless they achieve a high degree of local language proficiency. Furthermore, while there is some tolerance towards cultural deviations by foreigners in East Asian countries, cultural norms are generally tight in Japan, Korea, and China.[7] This means that foreign entrepreneurs in these countries need not only to achieve a high language proficiency, but also a high cultural proficiency if they are to establish and sustain good relationships with local stakeholders. In other words, continued and substantial efforts are needed by foreign entrepreneurs in East Asia to understand the local language and cultures in order for them to be effective. They may also find it easier to navigate the local business landscape when teaming up with local entrepreneurs as co-founders.

Finally, returnees who are familiar with both the local and international perspective are particularly well-positioned to be effective startup entrepreneurs in East Asian countries if they manage to leverage and combine their global and local knowledge effectively. The role of returnees for startup ecosystems, especially in China, is well known. However, one can find prominent success stories in Japan and Korea of entrepreneurs with significant living experience abroad.

11.3 Takeaways for Knowledge Workers

Similarly to founding entrepreneurs, the continuous growth of startup ecosystems in East Asia also creates opportunities for knowledge workers—those highly educated professionals whose work is focused on the continuous expansion of knowledge through explorative activities.[8] The traditional allure of stable, lifelong careers in large conglomerates (e.g., *chaebols*, *keiretsu*) has diminished, particularly among younger generations, many of whom are dissatisfied with rigid, hierarchical corporate cultures and long work hours. As such, establishing or working for a startup is becoming increasingly attractive, which is an asset to East Asian startup ecoystems.

Startups require knowledge workers to navigate highly uncertain and challenging business environments, effectively differentiating their business models and products from competitors. Such workers are therefore in high demand, especially in East Asian megacities where major startup ecosystems can be found. Consequently, domestic knowledge workers in Japan, Korea, and China—fresh university graduates as well as experienced professionals—have the potential to develop promising career opportunities in startups. Increasingly, knowledge workers can trade social prestige for greater flexibility, empowerment, and creative freedom in the startup sector. However, they need to apply a long-term perspective when choosing this career path, as startups typically cannot offer high salaries due to financial constraints, and the work environment and culture can be intense and demanding. In practice, working for an East Asian startup can be challenging, and knowledge workers typically need to be resilient and committed. However, short-term financial sacrifices are usually rewarded by accumulating valuable knowledge, and at times a major financial reward can be gained if a startup turns out to be highly successful.

In East Asia, governments and multinational corporations (MNCs) are heavily investing in artificial intelligence (AI), deep-tech, and cloud infrastructure, as evidenced by the national AI strategy of China, and the startup-related initiatives of Microsoft and Google. Workers with specialised skills in these and related fields are in high demand, and they can command premium roles and significantly influence their employers' human resource strategies. While there tends to be a good supply of professionals with strong technical skills in fields such as software coding, accounting, or general business administration in East Asian startup ecosystems, professionals with strong critical thinking skills are in shorter supply, as the formation of such skills is still not emphasised sufficiently by the education systems of East Asian countries.[9] Therefore, Japanese, Korean, and Chinese knowledge workers who possess strong critical thinking capabilities may actively pursue professional development opportunities in startups, not least because they can leverage their skills more effectively in new ventures than in those established firms that still favour hierarchical corporate cultures.

While there are good opportunities for foreign entrepreneurs in East Asian startup ecosystems, as explained above, this also applies to foreign knowledge workers, for two reasons. First, foreign knowledge workers often can apply a valuable "out of the box" perspective when developing or implementing startup business plans that domestic knowledge workers lack due to their strong embeddedness in the economic and social systems of their home countries. Second, and similarly to foreign entrepreneurs, foreign knowledge workers often have a deep understanding of foreign markets, cultures, and business systems that can be instrumental in helping East Asian startups with their global expansion efforts. This international perspective can be highly valuable for Japanese, Korean, and Chinese startups that often lack foreign business knowledge and global networks.[10] Therefore, foreign knowledge workers who are interested in working for East Asian startups may actively explore such professional opportunities. However, as with foreign entrepreneurs, foreign knowledge workers need to be adept in the languages and cultures of their host countries, not only to receive attractive work offers by East Asian startups, but also to be effective when working for them. Foreigners, including skilled international students, often find it difficult to integrate into or found startups due to cultural and linguistic barriers. Proactively achieving high local language proficiency and understanding nuanced cultural norms will be crucial for overcoming these hurdles and securing top roles.

One group of knowledge workers who are particularly well positioned to secure interesting job offers and professional development opportunities at East Asian startups are foreign graduates of universities in Japan, Korea, and China, a group that is increasing in number.[11] Foreign university graduates are already familiar with the languages and cultures of their host countries and can therefore effectively apply their international perspective and skills at East Asian startups. They may actively seek opportunities at startups that are often more interesting and rewarding to work for than established local and foreign companies in East Asia.

11.4 Takeaways for Investors

East Asian startup ecosystems also offer attractive opportunities for investors, for various reasons. First, startup ecosystems in Japan, Korea, and China are continuously growing, and the number of successful and high-potential startups that are attractive investment targets is therefore increasing. Second, venture capital investment is facilitated by various major governmental support programs in ways that once again highlight the distinctiveness of East Asian startup ecosystems. Specifically, governmental agencies in Korea and China provide venture capital firms with working capital for startup investment through large "fund-of-funds". Furthermore, there are public–private co-investment programs for startups, such as the TIPS program in Korea that lowers the capital investment needs for angel investors who intend to invest in high-potential startups.[12] In combination, these factors result in attractive opportunities for investors in East Asian startup ecosystems. Notably, both domestic and foreign investors are targeted by governmental support policies. For example, along with domestic investment vehicles, Korea Venture Investment Corporation has created a fund-of-funds that is designed specifically to provide foreign venture capital firms with working capital to invest in Korean startups.[13] This active participation of governments in East Asian venture capital markets can significantly reduce early-stage risk for investors. Consequently, investors are advised to integrate these government-backed resources into their planning; for example, by participating in the private selection and subsequent public funding of startups within these programs.

Thus, while there are good reasons for both domestic and international startup investors, including venture capital firms and angel investors, to actively seek investment into high potential startups in East Asian ecosystems, international investors may also identify attractive opportunities in East Asian countries that are overlooked by domestic investors. Many domestic venture capital firms in East Asia tend to focus on relatively safe investments into startups with low perceived financial risks.[14] While this conservative attitude countervails the fundamental idea of high-risk, high-return venture capital investment (at least from a Western perspective), it may also result in overlooking attractive investment targets that can be effectively pursued by foreign investors. To illustrate, while the Korean e-commerce unicorn Coupang encountered scepticism from domestic startup investors in the 2010s, it received a total investment of more than US$3bn by Japan's Softbank that did not only allow Coupang to pursue aggressive growth to dominate the e-commerce industry in Korea, but also resulted in very high investment returns for Softbank.[15]

Foreign investors should also be aware and take account of those distinctive features of East Asian startups ecosystems that we identify in this book. To illustrate, foreign investors need to recognise the dominant sequential scaling model of many East Asian startups, and adjust the timing of their investment accordingly. Most East Asian startups prioritise domestic markets for early-stage income generation and growth before seeking capital for international expansion, and investment strategies should take account of this. Another distinctiveness of East Asian ecosystems is the relative lack of international experience in founding teams. This systemic weakness may impact on the scale up and performance of young East Asian ventures, especially if they intend to expand abroad. In such a context, investing in teams that include "sea turtle" returnees, former MNC employees, or globally diverse management experience should be a primary vetting criterion for investors, especially if the founding team is contemplating the prioritisation of international markets soon after establishment. Investors in general, and foreign investors in particular, should also evaluate how East Asian startups manage compliance, hedge currency risks, and adopt resilient operational strategies in a world where geopolitical tensions (e.g., US-China decoupling) and unpredictable domestic regulatory shifts (such as China's tech crackdowns) can introduce significant constraints on market access, supply chain security, and exit valuations for East Asian startups.

One final takeaway for foreign investors relates to the sub-national heterogeneity of startup ecosystems in East Asia that we identify in this book. As for founders, the gravitational pull of investors is most likely to be towards capital city startup hubs. However, and as we have shown for each of our focal countries, secondary hubs offer certain advantages and specialisations to startups in particular industries and sectors. To illustrate, Daejeon, Suzhou, and Fukuoka offer high potential for, respectively, deep-tech, biotech, and specialized manufacturing startups rooted in strong academic and research institutions. Consequently, foreign investors may find that focused investments in these clusters provides them with ready access to cutting-edge innovation and opportunities outside of the hyper-competitive and crowded investment markets of East Asia's capital cities. Certainly, we would encourage foreign investors to look beyond capital cities when designing and implementing their investment strategies for East Asia.

11.5 Takeaways for Established Firms

Given the strong growth and positive development of East Asian startup ecosystems, there are also good opportunities for established firms to strengthen their business by collaborating with local startups. There is a broad range of options for established firms to collaborate with young East Asian firms, such as being an early customer of a startup, establishing strategic partnerships for collaborative technology development, investing in startups through corporate venture capital funds, inviting startups to incorporate into company-owned incubators or accelerators, or a through combination of multiple collaboration modes.[16] Through such collaborations, established firms may enjoy valuable and efficient access to new ideas, innovative business models, cutting-edge technologies, and the specialised talent possessed by startups in ways that augment or compliment their own internal R&D capabilities. The optimal collaboration mode can be determined depending on the attributes of the specific startup partner, and the goals and needs of the corporate partner.

While such collaborations with startups can be pursued both by domestic and foreign firms, domestic firms in East Asian countries may possess more in-depth information about local startups and therefore may find it easier to identify the most promising firms with which to collaborate. However, many established firms in East Asian countries are still reluctant to work with startups, not least because major Japanese, Korean, and Chinese firms often take strong and dominant positions in their industries and command vast resources. As a result, they often struggle to understand the value of technology collaborations with young, agile firms that are commercialising new ideas and innovative business models. Arguably, some of these large incumbent firms suffer from the "not invented here" syndrome, which rejects external ideas and innovations.[17] This resistance needs to be overcome if established firms are to effectively navigate the complex technological transitions which are now being driven increasingly by startups in East Asia, especially in fields such as AI, robotics, smart manufacturing, and the biosciences. Indeed, this reluctance by some East Asian firms to engage with startups may be exploited by international firms that are more open to collaborating with new ventures and are more adept in learning from them. However, in order to enhance their knowledge about potentially valuable startup partners and the advantages of operating in an innovation 'hotspot', international firms may want to establish local organisational units in East Asian ecosystems, including local subsidiaries or corporate incubators or accelerators, in order to facilitate their interactions with startup ecosystem actors. In so doing, they not only can connect better with entrepreneurial companies, but they can also take advantage of the fact that East Asian governments actively promote university-industry links at a regional level. By positioning themselves physically within an ecosystem, established companies can leverage networks to tap into fundamental research, recruit specialised talent (e.g., PhD researchers in Daejeon), and possibly secure co-development projects with universities and academic spin-offs.

One final takeaway for established firms from our discussions in this book relates to talent retention. As we have highlighted several times, traditional hierarchical structures, seniority-based pay, and demanding work cultures (common, for example, in Japanese *keiretsu* firms and Korean *chaebols*) are increasingly driving highly skilled young professionals to startups. Should this trend continue, established firms should consider adopting more flexible work arrangements and reduce mandatory overtime to compete against the allure of startup autonomy and the attractive compensation packages offered by many foreign investing firms in East Asia.

11.6 Takeaways for Policymakers

There are also important cues for policymakers emerging from our analysis. For policymakers in East Asian countries, it is important to note that although their highly activist entrepreneurship support policies over the past two decades have strongly deviated from the Western "hands off" paradigm of minimal government intervention as possible, many of these policies have proven highly effective, not least because they were tailored to the specific context of East Asian startup ecosystems and were informed by particular national and sub-national needs. East Asian policymakers, therefore, should continue to devise policies that are contextually-relevant and informed by the situation on the ground in East Asian cities as opposed to blindly following universalist Western (or Silicon Valley) policy blueprints. In short, the effectiveness of startup-related policies relies on their contextual fit.

Notably, and as we have shown throughout in this book, East Asian startup ecosystems are rapidly evolving, and these rapid changes necessitate regular policy reviews and updates. For example, when venture capital has increased sufficiently to serve the funding needs of startups, governments may gradually phase out general funding support programs for startups and replace them with more targeted programs that address the underserved funding needs of specific types of firms. In so doing, private capital and expertise can be strategically leveraged. Moreover, policy initiatives around the further development of specialised secondary startup ecosystems that build upon local strengths (like Daejeon's science cluster and Suzhou's advanced manufacturing ties) may alleviate pressures on capital city ecosystems, and better connect startup innovation to the achievement of regional economic development goals. Similarly, greater application of regulatory sandboxes and further support of specialised startup ecosystems may allow for the controlled testing and scaling of new business models before widespread deregulation. Such an approach would help to "domesticate" the disruptive potential of startups, integrating innovation along politically and socially acceptable trajectories while mitigating risks for established industries and incumbent firms. In other words, opportunities to innovate in policy formulation and implementation continue to abound in East Asia.

There are also potentially important topics beyond startup financing that may need policy attention. For example, an innovation policy review by the OECD has found that while regulatory measures by the Korean government to help increase the low number of foreign startup entrepreneurs, such as the issue of "startup visas", were in themselves fairly effective, the biggest hurdle for potential foreign entrepreneurs and knowledge workers to settle in Korea are cultural adaptation difficulties.[18] To address this problem, Korean policymakers may need to consider how to make Korea a friendlier country for foreign residents, beyond specific regulatory measures. Indeed, governments across East Asia in general need to strengthen the implementation of systematic policies to attract, integrate, and retain diverse global talent in order to help strengthen the domestic and international competitiveness of those young East Asian firms with home country-oriented top management teams. This could include further streamlining immigration processes (e.g., Japan's Startup Visa), encouraging greater foreign student integration, and actively promoting further cultural openness. Furthermore, talent acquisition efforts should continue to prioritise bringing back experienced returnees to import global best practices and networks into East Asian startup ecosystems.

East Asian policymakers have a long and successful track record of benchmarking policies from Western countries and adapting them selectively, being mindful of their fit with the situation in their own countries and ecosystems. However, beyond benchmarking policies in Western countries, Japanese, Korean, and Chinese policymakers may also learn substantially from each other. Although we recognise that the specific conditions for entrepreneurship are not identical across Japanese, Korean, and Chinese startup ecosystems (which, indeed, is a recurrent "leitmotif" of our book), they are often relatively similar due to cultural and institutional similarities.[19] Therefore, there is an untapped potential for policy-makers to study and adopt effective policies across startup ecosystems in East Asia.

Finally, there is also a high potential for policymakers in other regions, including Western and non-Western countries, to learn from their East Asian counterparts who succeeded in kickstarting startup ecosystems within relatively short time periods. In particular, the East Asian approach demonstrates how government can move beyond merely facilitating market conditions to actively constructing and steering the innovation environment. This developmental state model, characterised by intentional policy architectures and long-term national strategic goals, provides valuable lessons for the policymakers of economies seeking rapid industrial upgrading or greater technological self-reliance. However, in view of the strong contextuality of startup entrepreneurship, it is important to always carefully assess the fit of particular policy measures with the local conditions—and to adapt them to these conditions, if necessary. In contrast, an uncontextualised "copy and paste" transfer of policies across ecosystems and countries is bound to fail.

11.7 Concluding Remarks

As we finish writing this book at the end of September 2025, it is important for us to reflect a little on some of the profound and unprecedent changes that have happened to startup ecosystems around the world and, in particular, across East Asia, over the past year or so. Described by Startup Genome as "tectonic shifts", the world has witnessed increased geopolitical tensions and supply chain volatilities (not least as a consequence of US tariff policies) that have dampened investor sentiment and impacted cross-border capital flows. Stagnant national economic growth rates, declining consumer spending, a growing dissatisfaction with globalisation and other headwinds have also combined to impact negatively on the growth prospects of new ventures. As a consequence, ecosystem valuations globally declined significantly in 2024 and 2025, driven by smaller and fewer exits of startup firms.[20]

At the same time, technological revolutions, and most particularly in artificial intelligence (AI), have dramatically reshaped the startup landscape over the past two years, and in all likelihood will continue to do so for many years to come. The disruptive effects of AI on established business models are undoubted, with numerous commentators arguing that AI will displace and eliminate millions of jobs. However, AI will also create countless jobs in established firms as well as in technology-intensive and AI-focused startups. Indeed, according to Startup Genome, AI is currently eclipsing all other growth sectors for startups and their funding sources. As we enter the "AI-era"—the next stage in the digitisation process described in Chap. 2—those startup ecosystems and the policymakers who administer them that are able to effectively support the transition of their startups towards the full exploitation of this technology and its associated applications will surely "steal a march" on those ecosystems that remain reliant on startup policies, communities, and infrastructure built for the web era.

Whilst the "AI-era" has only just begun, we as authors can already see ample evidence that East Asian startups and their ecosystems are well-positioned to take full advantage of the AI-related technological revolution that is currently underway. For example, we know that East Asian entrepreneurs are good at jumping on new trends very quickly and that East Asian consumers are very open to the adoption of new technology tools, especially those delivered via smartphones and computers.

AI-focused East Asian startups like DeepSeek, Zhipu AI, and Manus in China; Upstage and LG AI Research in Korea, and LayerX and CADDi in Japan (to name but a few), have recently brought highly effective large language models (LLMs), AI agents, AI-powered business automation, and enterprise AI solutions to the market. These East Asian startups are not only increasingly challenging the long-held dominance of Silicon Valley-based behemoths such as Alphabet and Apple, as well as other USA technology giants such as Meta and Microsoft, but they are also now competing effectively against US AI developers like OpenAI (ChatGPT), Anthropic (Claude AI), and Perplexity, each of whom are headquartered in San Francisco, USA (i.e., Silicon Valley).

In response to these developments, Startup Genome has started from 2025 to report on "AI-Native" startup ecosystems. The assumption is that, even in an "AI-era", being geographically close to foundational technologies, leading higher education providers, research laboratories and institutions, high-calibre talent pools, venture capitalists, and other ecosystem stakeholders will continue to be important for startup success, notwithstanding the advent of cloud computing and online platforms that lower entry barriers to practically zero for any entrepreneur irrespective of their location. According to Startup Genome (2025), while Guangzhou, Tokyo, Seoul, and Shanghai are positioned towards the bottom of the list of the Top 40 Global Startup Ecosystems on the AI-Native criterion, Hangzhou and henzhen are listed in the middle and Beijing at the very top, alongside Silicon Valley, the highest ranked ecosystem in the world.

Such developments will likely necessitate a reconfiguration of how startup ecosystems are conceptualised and how their performance is measured, by scholars and policymakers alike. Nevertheless, we are confident that geographically-defined startup ecosystems in general, and East Asian startup ecosystems in particular, will continue to maintain their relevance and importance within national and global innovation frameworks. We look forward to observing and reporting on how East Asian startups respond to these developments, and how they engage with the new fundamental realities that AI brings. Success will surely belong to those East Asian founders, investors, and policymakers who can adeptly navigate the complex landscape of volatility, geopolitical uncertainties, and—perhaps most importantly—the technological shifts engendered by AI, and who can further unleash the innovation potential of East Asian startup ecosystems.

Notes

1. See Global Startup Ecosystem Reports by Startup Genome (2024, 2025) and StartupBlink (2021–2024).
2. See Gresov and Drazin (1997). The concept resonates with the ideas of system complementarity introduced by Milgrom and Roberts (1992).
3. See, for example, Spigel (2017), Isenberg (2010), Stam (2015), Vedula and Kim (2019). The elements and their typologies were explored in more detail in Chap. 3 of this book.
4. See, for example, Alves et al. (2019), Kapturkiewicz (2022), and Spigel (2017).
5. The case of the Japanese Internet entrepreneur Takafumi Horie discussed in Chap. 8 offers one example of such perceived cultural transgressions that can potentially end the careers of startup entrepreneurs in East Asian countries.
6. OECD (2023).
7. Hofstede et al. (2010).
8. De Sordi et al. (2021), 65.
9. Hemmert and Kim (2021), 82, 136.
10. Hemmert et al. (2019) and Kapturkiewicz (2022).
11. OECD (2025b).
12. Angel investors need to invest only KRW 100mn (around US$100,000) and then can secure public investment of 5–10 times this amount to fund a startup. Thereby, angel investors can strongly limit the amount they need to invest themselves.
13. Gompers and Chan (2024), 67.
14. Hemmert and Kim (2021), 91–92, 130–131.
15. Hemmert and Kim (2021), 60.
16. Sbampato et al. (2025).
17. Katz and Allen (1982).
18. OECD (2023).
19. Hemmert (2025).
20. Startup Genome (2025).

References

Abo, T. (1994). *Hybrid factory: The Japanese production system in the United States*. Oxford University Press.

Acs, Z. J., Lafuente, E., & Szerb, L. (2023). Introduction: Entrepreneurial ecosystems. In Z. J. Acs, E. Lafuente, & L. Szerb (Eds.), *The entrepreneurial ecosystem: A global perspective* (pp. 1–28). Palgrave Macmillan.

Acs, Z. J., Stam, E., Audretsch, D. B., & O'Connor, A. (2017). The lineages of the entrepreneurial ecosystem approach. *Small Business Economics, 49*, 1–10.

Akamatsu, K. (1962). A historical pattern of economic growth in developing countries. *The Developing Economies, 1*(1), 3–25.

Alvedalen, J., & Boschma, R. (2017). A critical review of entrepreneurial ecosystems research: Towards a future research agenda. *European Planning Studies, 25*(6), 887–903.

Alves, A. C., Fischer, B., Vonortas, N. S., & Queiroz, S. R. R. D. (2019). Configurations of knowledge-intensive entrepreneurial ecosystems. *Revista de Administração de Empresas, 59*(4), 242–257.

Amsden, A. H. (1989). *Asia's next giant: South Korea and late industrialization*. Oxford University Press.

Anchordoguy, T. (2005). *Reprogramming Japan: The high-tech crisis under communitarian capitalism*. Cornell University Press.

Angeles, L. (2017). The great divergence and the economics of printing. *The Economic History Review, 70*(1), 30–51.

Aoki, M., & Dore, R. (Eds.). (1994). *The Japanese firm: The sources of competitive strength*. Oxford University Press.

Aoki, M., & Patrick, H. T. (1994). *The Japanese main bank system: Its relevance for developing and transforming economies*. Oxford University Press.

Aoyama, Y., & Izushi, H. (2003). Hardware gimmick or cultural innovation? Technological, cultural, and social foundations of the Japanese video game industry. *Research Policy, 32*(3), 423–444.

Bailey, D., Harte, G., & Sugden, R. (1994). *Making transnationals accountable: A significant step for Britain*. Routledge.

Baumol, W. J. (1993). In W. J. Baumol (Ed.), *Entrepreneurship, management, and the structure of payoffs by*. MIT Press.

Boot, W.J. (2013). The adoption and adaptation of neo-Confucianism in Japan: The role of Fujiwara Seika and Hayashi Razan.

Born2global Center (2022). 2021 Korea Startup Index. Seongnam: Born2global Center (in Korean).

Bosch (2024). *Bosch smart manufacturing initiatives (2024)*. Retrieved 17, June, 2024 from. https://www.bosch.com/stories/automation-in-manufacturing/

Y. Cheng et al., *Unleashing Innovation the East Asian Way*,
https://doi.org/10.1007/978-981-95-6513-9

Bresnahan, T., Gambardella, A., & Saxenian, A. (2001). Old economy inputs for new economy outcomes: Cluster formation in the new silicon valleys. *Industrial and Corporate Change, 10*(4), 835–860.

Brown, R., & Mason, C. (2017). Looking inside the spiky bits: A critical review and conceptualisation of entrepreneurial ecosystems. *Small Business Economics, 49*(1), 11–30.

Brown, R., & Mawson, S. (2019). Entrepreneurial ecosystems and public policy in action: A critique of the latest industrial policy blockbuster. *Cambridge Journal of Regions, Economy and Society, 12*(3), 347–368.

Buckley, P. J., Clegg, L. J., Cross, A. R., Liu, X., Voss, H., & Zheng, P. (2007). The determinants of Chinese outward foreign direct investment. *Journal of International Business Studies, 38*(4), 499–518.

Callon, S. (1995). *Divided sun: MITI and the breakdown of Japanese high-tech industrial policy, 1975–1993*. Stanford University Press.

Cao, C. (2004). Zhongguancun and China's high-tech parks in transition: Growing pains or premature senility? *Asian Survey, 44*(5), 647–668.

Cao, C. (2008). Chinas brain drain at the high end: Why government policies have failed to attract first-rate academics to return. *Asian Population Studies, 4*(3), 331–345.

Cao, Z., & Shi, X. (2020). A systematic literature review of entrepreneurial ecosystems in advanced and emerging economies. *Small Business Economics, 57* (1), 75–110.

CB Insights (2025). *Global unicorn club: Private companies valued at $1B+* (Retrieved July 3rd, 2025 from). https://www.cbinsights.com/research-unicorn-companies

Chang, S.-J. (2003). *Financial crisis and transformation of Korean business groups: The rise and fall of chaebols*. Cambridge University Press.

Chen, C.-C., & Lee, Y.-T. (2008). Introduction: The diversity and dynamism of Chinese philosophies on leadership. In C.-C. Chen & Y.-T. Lee (Eds.), *Leadership and management in China: Philosophies, theories, and practices* (pp. 1–27). Cambridge University Press.

Chen, G., & Li, J. (2022). *Seeing the unseen: Decoding Chinese tech giants*. John Wiley & Sons.

Chen, H. (2012). *Jiu er pai: Business ethics and ideals of the new scholar-entrepreneurs*. CITIC Press.

China Youth Daily (2019). *Survey on University Students' Entrepreneurial Interest*. (in Chinese).

Chongqing Investment Promotion Association (2024). *Building the new western land-sea corridor, Chongqing gains momentum*. Retrieved 14, August, 2025 from. https://cqipa.com/index.php?c=content&a=show&id=2638. (in Chinese).

Chongqing Municipal Bureau of Statistics (2024). Chongqing Statistical Bulletin on National Economic and Social Development 2023.

Chongqing Municipal Government (2022) Notice on Issuing Several Policy Recommendations to Support High-Quality Development of the Manufacturing Industry. (in Chinese).

Choung, J. Y., Hwang, H. R., & Song, W. (2014). Transitions of innovation activities in latecomer countries: An exploratory case study of South Korea. *World Development, 54*, 156–167.

Chu, Y. W. (2004). Taiwan's economic growth and democratization. In E. M. Kim (Ed.), *The four Asian tigers: Economic development and the global political economy* (pp. 140–167). Academic.

CKGSB Knowledge. (2022). *China's tech-based unicorn companies are popular for investment*. Retrieved 19, June, 2024 from. https://english.ckgsb.edu.cn/knowledge/article/chinas-tech-based-unicorn-companies-are-popular-for-investment/

Clifford, M. L. (1998). *Troubled tiger: Businessmen, bureaucrats, and generals in South Korea* (2nd ed.). Sharpe.

Cooke, P., Uranga, M. G., & Etxebarria, G. (1997). Regional innovation systems: Institutional and organisational dimensions. *Research Policy, 26*(4-5), 475–491.

CVINFO. (2023). *Report on the Government Guidance Fund*. Retrieved 25, September 2025 from. https://pic.chinaventure.com.cn/reportFiles/7137700947689472.pdf. (in Chinese).

Dang, G. (2009). *China's 30-Year political system reform: Retrospect and prospect*. Retrieved 26, May, 2025 from. http://www.reformdata.org/2009/1021/9198.shtml

De Sordi, J. O., Azevedo, M. C., Bianchi, E. M. P. G., & Carandina, T. (2021). Defining the term knowledge worker: Toward improved ontology and operationalization. *Knowledge and Process Management, 28*(1), 56–70.

Dennett, D. C. (2017). *From bacteria to Bach and back: The evolution of minds*. W.W. Norton & Company.

Dore, R. (2000). *Stock market capitalism: Welfare capitalism: Japan and Germany versus the Anglo-Saxons*. Oxford University Press.

Dunning, J. H. (1988). The eclectic paradigm of international production: A restatement and some possible extensions. *Journal of International Business Studies, 19*(1), 1–31.

Encarnation, D. J. (1992). *Rivals beyond trade: America versus Japan in global competition*. Cornell University Press.

Erez, M., & Gati, E. (2004). A dynamic, multi-level model of culture: From the micro level of the individual to the macro level of a global culture. *Applied Psychology, 53*(4), 583–598.

Fan, P. (2006). Catching up through developing innovation capability: Evidence from China's telecom-equipment industry. *Technovation, 26*(3), 359–368.

Farh, J.-L., & Pi, X. (2018). Huawei the Ren Zhengfei way: The tough guy and his corporate philosophy. Harvard Business School Case CB0099-PDF-ENG. Revised 15th October 2020.

Feld, B. (2012). *Startup communities: Building an entrepreneurial ecosystem in your city*. John Wiley & Sons.

Feldman, M., Fleming, L., Heaton, S., Desai, S., & Teece, D. (2022). Uncommon methods and metrics for local entrepreneurial ecosystems. *Research Policy, 51*(9), 104583.

Ferrary, M., & Granovetter, M. S. (2009). The role of venture capital firms in Silicon Valleys complex innovation network. *Economy and Society, 38*(2), 326–359.

Filatotchev, I., Liu, X., Lu, J., & Wright, M. (2011). Knowledge spillovers through human mobility across national borders: Evidence from Zhongguancun Science Park in China. *Research Policy, 40*(3), 453–462.

Flath, D. (2022). *The Japanese economy* (4th ed.). Oxford University Press.

Forbes (2009). *Villain Or Hero?*, Forbes.

Frenkenberger, B. R. (2023). Ties of possibility: Selecting future founders in Tokyos start-up ecosystem. *Social Science Japan Journal, 26*(1), 93–112.

Fukuoka Growth Next (2024). *About Fukuoka growth next*. https://growth-next.com/en/about2024

Gala, K., Schwab, A., & Mueller, B. A. (2024). Star entrepreneurs on digital platforms: Heavy-tailed performance distributions and their generative mechanisms. *Journal of Business Venturing, 39*, 106347.

Gassmann, O., & Han, Z. (2004). Motivations and barriers of foreign R&D activities in China. *R&D Management, 34*(4), 423–437.

Ghalayini, M. (2023). *Exploring the rise of technology startups in China: From centralized control to government guided entrepreneurship? McGill Business Review*. Retrieved 17th June, 2024 from. https://mcgillbusinessreview.com/articles/exploring-the-rise-of-technology-startups-in-china-from-centralized-control-to-government-guided-entrepreneurship

Global Entrepreneurship Monitor (GEM). 2019 *China national entrepreneurial activity report*. London: GEM.

Global Entrepreneurship Monitor (GEM) (2024). *Global entrepreneurship monitor 2023/2024 global report: 25 years and growing*, London: GEM.

Globis Capital Partners (2024). *Japan startup ecosystem report 2023*. Tokyo: Globis Capital Partners Co., Ltd. 14th March, 2024.

Gompers, P.A. & Chan, B. (2024). Korea Venture Investment Corporation. Harvard Business School Case 9–224-022. Revised: July 18th, 2024.

Google for Startups Campus (2025). Welcome to Campus Seoul, Google for Startups stats. Retrieved on September 24, 2025 from. https://www.campus.co/seoul/about/

Goswami, K., & Ivey, R. (2018). Accelerator expertise: Understanding the intermediary role of accelerators in the development of the Bangalore entrepreneurial ecosystem. *Strategic Entrepreneurship Journal, 12*(1), 117–150.

Gradillas, M., & Thomas, L. D. W. (2023). Distinguishing digitization and digitalization: A systematic review and conceptual framework. *Journal of Product Innovation Management, 42*(1), 112–143.

Gresov, C., & Drazin, R. (1997). Equifinality: Functional equivalence in organization design. *The Academy of Management Review, 22*(2), 403–428.

Griswold, W. (2012). *Cultures and societies in a changing world* (4th ed.). Sage.

Gupta, V., & Hanges, P. J. (2004). Regional and climate clustering of societal cultures. In R. J. House, P. J. Hanges, M. Javidan, P. W. Dorfman, & V. Gupta (Eds.), *Culture, leadership, and organizations: The GLOBE study of 62 societies* (pp. 178–218). Sage.

Haigh, T., & Ceruzzi, P. E. (2021). *A new history of modern computing.* MIT Press.

Hall, P. A., & Soskice, D. W. (Eds.). (2001). *Varieties of capitalism: The institutional foundations of comparative advantage.* Oxford University Press.

Hanada, J., & Tomita, S. (2025). Trajectory of water, land and community development in the country of abundant rice fields and its future. *Community chapter*. https://www.aric.or.jp/kiseki/en/sato/index.html

Hannigan, T. R., Briggs, A. R., Valadao, R., Seidel, M.-D. L., & Jennings, P. D. (2022). A new tool for policymakers: Mapping cultural possibilities in an emerging AI entrepreneurial ecosystem. *Research Policy, 51*(9), 104315.

Hao, X., Yan, K., Guo, S., & Wang, M. (2017). Chinese returnees motivation, post-return status and impact of return: A systematic review. *Asian and Pacific Migration Journal, 26*(1), 143–157.

Haughton, C. (2024). *The history of information.* Penguin Books.

Hayakawa, M., & Whittaker, D. (2009). Takeovers and corporate governance: Three years of tensions. In D. Whittaker & S. Deakin (Eds.), *Corporate governance and managerial reform in Japan* (pp. 70–92). Oxford University Press.

Hayek, F. A. (1964). Kinds of order in society. *New Individualist Review, 3*(2), 3–12.

Hayton, J.C. & Cacciotti, G. (2013). Is there an entrepreneurial culture? A review of empirical research. *Entrepreneurship & Regional Development, 25*(9–10), 708–731.

Heath, F. G. (1972). Origins of the binary code. *Scientific American., 227*(2), 76–83.

Helper, S., & Sako, M. (1995). Supplier relations in Japan and the United States: Are they converging? *Sloan Management Review, 36*(3), 77–84.

Hemmert, M. (2018). *The evolution of tiger management: Korean companies in global competition.* Routledge.

Hemmert, M. (2025). Unpacking the role of context in east Asian innovation and entrepreneurship: Insights and research implications. *Asian Business & Management, 24*(2), 167–186.

Hemmert, M., Cross, A. R., Cheng, Y., Kim, J.-J., Kohlbacher, F., Kotosaka, M., Waldenberger, F., & Zheng, L. J. (2019). The distinctiveness and diversity of entrepreneurial ecosystems in China, Japan, and South Korea: An exploratory analysis. *Asian Business & Management, 18*(3), 211–247.

Hemmert, M., Cross, A. R., Cheng, Y., Kim, J.-J., Kotosaka, M., Waldenberger, F., & Zheng, L. J. (2022). New venture entrepreneurship and context in East Asia: A systematic literature review. *Asian Business & Management, 21*(5), 831–865.

Hemmert, M., Cross, A. R., Cheng, Y., Kim, J.-J., Kotosaka, M., Waldenberger, F., & Zheng, L. J. (2023). Environmental uncertainty and the entrepreneurial orientation-performance relationship among east Asian new technology-based firms: An institutional perspective. *Asian Business & Management, 22*(4), 1683–1711.

Hemmert, M., Cross, A. R., Cheng, Y., Kim, J.-J., Kotosaka, M., Waldenberger, F., & Zheng, L. J. (2024). The influence of founders human capital on the performance of new technology-based firms in China, South Korea and Japan: An exploratory study. *Asia Pacific Business Review., 30*(4), 808–832.

Hemmert, M., & Kim, J.-J. (2021). *Entrepreneurship in Korea: From chaebols to start-ups.* Routledge.

Henning, C. R. (1994). *Currencies and politics in the United States, Germany, and Japan.* Peterson Institute for International Economics.

Hirschmeier, J. (1970). The Japanese spirit of enterprise, 1867–1970. *Business History Review, 44*(1), 13–38.
Hitachi-UTokyo Laboratory (Ed.) (2020). *Society 5.0: A people-centric super-smart society.* Springer Nature.
Hoang, H., & Antoncic, B. (2003). Network-based research in entrepreneurship: A critical review. *Journal of Business Venturing, 18*(2), 165–187.
Hofstede, G. (1991). *Cultures and organizations: Software of the mind*. McGraw-Hill.
Hofstede, G., Hofstede, G. J., & Minkov, M. (2010). *Cultures and organizations: Software of the mind* (3rd ed.). McGraw-Hill.
House, R. J., Hanges, P. J., Javidan, M., Dorfman, P. W., & Gupta, V. (Eds.). (2004). *Culture, leadership, and organizations: The GLOBE study of 62 societies.* Sage.
Hsueh, R. (2011). *Chinas regulatory state: A new strategy for globalization.* Cornell University Press.
Huang, Y. (2008). *Capitalism with Chinese characteristics: Entrepreneurship and the state.* Cambridge University Press.
Huawei. (2024). *Huawei Cloud: Empowering developers, winning together in the ecosystem.* Retrieved June, 18, 2025 from. https://www.huaweicloud.com/news/2024/20240921104641076.html
Hundt, D. (2009). *Koreas developmental alliance: State, capital and the politics of rapid development.* Routledge.
Hwang, D., Y.C. Cheong & Chung, S. (2018). The evolution of innovation cluster: focusing on the Daedeok Innopolis, *Korea Technology Innovation Society Journal, 21*(4), 1207–1236 (in Korean).
IBM (2024). *IBM innovation and incubation programs.* Retrieved 17, June, 2024 from. https://research.ibm.com/collaborate/open-source-incubator
Inagami, T., & Whittaker, D. H. (2005). *The new community firm: Employment, governance and management reform in Japan.* Cambridge University Press.
Inkpen, A. C., & Pien, W. (2006). An examination of collaboration and knowledge transfer: China–Singapore Suzhou Industrial Park. *Journal of Management Studies, 43*(4), 779–811.
Isenberg, D. J. (2010). How to start an entrepreneurial revolution. *Harvard Business Review, 88*(6), 40–50.
Ito, T. (2015). The plaza accord and Japans monetary policy in the 1980s and 1990s. *Asian Economic Policy Review, 10*(2), 180–199.
Japan Investment Corporation. (2024). *Global and Japan venture capital market update 2023.* Japan Investment Corporation.
Japan Open Innovation Council (JOIC) (2018). *Open innovation white paper* (2nd Ed.). Japan Open Innovation Council (in Japanese).
Johnson, C. A. (1982). *MITI and the Japanese miracle: The growth of industrial policy, 1925–1975.* Stanford University Press.
Joongang Daily. (2017). Ideas, people and money all tightly aligned: Gangnam is now startup style.14 May 2017 (in Korean).
Kantis, H. D., & Federico, J. S. (2012). Entrepreneurial ecosystems in Latin America: The role of policies. In *International research and policy roundtable (Kauffman foundation)* (pp. 11–12). Liverpool.
Kapturkiewicz, A. (2016). *IT startup communities in Tokyo, Japan (MPhil dissertation).* University of Oxford.
Kapturkiewicz, A. (2022). Varieties of entrepreneurial ecosystems: A comparative study of Tokyo and Bangalore. *Research Policy, 51*(9), 104377.
Kapturkiewicz, A. (2025). Understanding the role of place in emerging organisational fields: A comparative analysis of nascent ICT entrepreneurial ecosystems in Japan. *Small Business Economics, 65*(3), 1385–1406.

Kapturkiewicz, A., & Kotosaka, M. (2019). Field transformations: Cross-field and intra-field institutional work in entrepreneurial ecosystems. *Academy of Management Proceedings, 2019*(1), 15796.

Katz, R. (2023). *The contest for Japan's economic future: Entrepreneurs vs. corporate giants.* Oxford University Press.

Katz, R., & Allen, T.J. (1982). Investigating the not invented here (NIH) syndrome: A look at the performance, tenure, and communication patterns of 50 R&D project groups. *R&D Management, 12*(1), 7–19.

Kaur, M., Ahmad, W., Hari, K. S., & Kattumuri, R. (2024). FinTech entrepreneurial ecosystem in India: Role of incubators and accelerators. *Global Finance Journal, 60*, 100933.

Kazuo, K. (2005). *The economics of work in Japan* (3rd ed.). LTCB International Library Foundation.

Keane, M., & Zhao, E. J. (2012). Renegades on the frontier of innovation: The shanzhai grassroots communities of Shenzhen in Chinas creative economy. *Eurasian Geography and Economics, 53*(2), 216–230.

Kenney, M., & Florida, R. (1993). *Beyond mass production: The Japanese system and its transfer to the U.S.* Oxford University Press.

Kenney, M., & von Burg, U. (1999). Technology, entrepreneurship and path dependence: Industrial clustering in Silicon Valley and route 128. *Industrial and Corporate Change, 8*(1), 67–103.

Kim, L. (1997). *Imitation to innovation: The dynamics of Koreas technological learning.* Harvard Business School Press.

Kim, L., & Nelson, R. R. (2000). *Technology, learning, and innovation: Experiences of newly industrializing economies.* Cambridge University Press.

Kim, S., & Kim, Y. (2023). *Innovative startup and entrepreneurship monitoring, Vol. 1: Analysis of local entrepreneurial ecosystems*, STEPI Policy Report 2023-16-01, Sejong City: Science and Technology Policy Institute (STEPI) (in Korean).

Kim, S. H. (2021). Hyundais innovation strategy and global expansion. *Asian Business & Management, 20*(3), 345–367.

Kim, Y. M., & Kim, D. H. (2009). Innovation in the Korean national innovation system: Introduction of new public management in Korea. *Journal of Technology Transfer, 34*(4), 431–449.

Kitchin, R. & McArdle, G. (2016). What makes big data, big data? Exploring the ontological characteristics of 26 datasets. *Big Data & Society, 3*(1), 1–10.

Klingler-Vidra, R., & Pardo, R. P. (2025). *Startup capitalism: New approaches to innovation strategies in East Asia.* Cornell University Press.

Ko, H,. & Shin, H. Y. (1999). Venture capital in Korea? Special law to promote venture capital companies. *American University International Law Review, 15*(2), 457–480.

Koike, K. (1988). *Understanding industrial relations in modern Japan.* St. Martin's Press.

Koike, R. (2019). Interpolation of Japan's household consumption during World War II. *IMES Discussion Paper Series.* Tokyo: Institute for Monetary and Economic Studies (IMES), Bank of Japan.

Kojima, K. (2000). The flying geese model of Asian economic development: Origin, theoretical extensions, and regional policy implications. *Journal of Asian Economics, 11*(4), 375–401.

Korea Times. (2020). Tada forced to end van-hailing service in April. March 11th 2020.

Korea Venture Capital Association (KVCA) (2025). *VC Data: VC Statistics.* Retrieved on September 24, 2025 from. http://www.kvca.or.kr/en/Program/vc_firm/list.html?a_gb=eng&a_cd=2&a_item=0&sm=4_1

Korea Venture Investment Corp. (2025). Korea fund-of-funds statistics. Retrieved September 24, 2025 from. https://k-vic.co.kr/

Korea Venture Investment Corporation (KVIC) (2025). *KVIC is the government-backed venture investment arm, the general partner of Korea fund-of-funds.* Retrieved September 24, 2025 from. https://www.kvic.or.kr/en/index

Kotosaka, M. (2017). The gradual accumulation of professionals has started to accelerate the growth of Japanese startups. In *VEC yearbook 2016: Annual report on Japanese startup businesses* (pp. 84–87). Venture Enterprise Center (VEC).

Kotosaka, M. (2018). Transfigurations of venture management personnel: An outline from the perspective of board composition at the time of company listing on the TSE mothers index. In *VEC yearbook 2017: Annual report on Japanese startup businesses* (pp. 51–58). Venture Enterprise Center (VEC).

Kotosaka, M. (2019). Large firms and ICT startups in Japan—The new forms of the relationship. In *VEC yearbook 2018: Annual report on Japanese startup businesses* (pp. 51–57). Venture Enterprise Center (VEC).

Kotosaka, M., & Sako, M. (2017). The evolution of the ICT start-up eco-system in Japan: From corporate logic to venture logic? In T. Nakano (Ed.), *Japanese management in evolution: New directions, breaks, and emerging practices* (pp. 237–261). Routledge Frontiers of Business Management, Vol. 12). Routledge.

K-Startup. (2025). K-Startup offers support services for early entrepreneurs (in Korean). (Retrieved June 24, 2025 from). https://www.k-startup.go.kr/

Kurzweil, R. (2024). *The singularity is nearer: When we merge with AI*. Penguin Publishing Group.

Kushida, K. E. (2018). *Abenomics and Japan's entrepreneurship and innovation: Is the third arrow pointed in the right direction for global competition in the digital era of Silicon Valley?* SVNJ Working Paper 2018–1, Stanford University.

Leavitt, H. J. & Whisler, T.L. (1958). Management in the 1980s. Harvard Business Review, (November–December), 41–48.

Lechevalier, S. (2014). *The great transformation of Japanese capitalism*. Routledge.

Lee, J., & Kim, S. (2020). Global startup strategies from emerging markets: The case of South Korea. *Technology in Society, 63*, 101428.

Lee, J., & Lim, H. (2001). Samsung electronics and the struggle for leadership in the mobile phone industry. *Asian Case Research Journal, 5*(2), 239–259.

Lee, K. (2013). *Schumpeterian analysis of economic catch-up: Knowledge, path-creation, and the middle-income trap*. Cambridge University Press.

Levi-Faur, D. (1997). Friedrich list and the political economy of the nation-state. *Review of International Political Economy, 4*(1), 154–178.

Li, D., Wei, L. Q., Cao, Q., & Chen, D. Q. (2022). Informal institutions, entrepreneurs' political participation, and venture internationalization. *Journal of International Business Studies, 53*(6), 1062–1090.

Li, X., Chen, Y., Huang, H., & Liu, T. (2023). Digital transformation path of manufacturing enterprises in the digital industry: A case study of Hengtong group. *Journal of Management Science in China, 26*(11), 22–38.

Li Y., Hernandez E., & Gwon S. (2019). When do ethnic communities affect foreign location choice? Dual entry strategies of Korean banks in China. *Academy of Management Journal, 62*(1), 172–95.

Lin, Z., & Zhang, Y. (2009). The internationalisation of Chinese multinationals: A multi-dimensional analysis. *Asia Pacific Journal of Management, 26*(2), 187–217.

Liu, H., & Buck, T. (2007). Innovation performance and channels for international technology spillovers: Evidence from Chinese high-tech industries. *Research Policy, 36*(3), 355–366.

Liu, W., & Dicken, P. (2006). Transnational corporations and 'obligated embeddedness': Foreign direct investment in China's automobile industry. *Environment and Planning A, 38*(7), 1229–1247.

Liu, Y. J. (2024). *Start-up wolf: The Shenzhen model of high-tech entrepreneurship*. Routledge.

Lundvall, B.-Å. (Ed.). (1992). *National systems of innovation: Towards a theory of innovation and interactive learning*. Pinter Publishers.

Luo, Y., & Tung, R. L. (2007). International expansion of emerging market enterprises: A springboard perspective. *Journal of International Business Studies, 38*(4), 481–498.

Mair, A., Florida, R., & Kenney, M. (1988). The new geography of automobile production: Japanese transplants in North America. *Economic Geography, 64*(4), 352–373.

Marinova, S. (Ed.). (2015). *Institutional impacts on firm internationalisation.* Palgrave Macmillan.

Marlow, S., & Patton, D. (2005). All credit to men? Entrepreneurship, finance, and gender. *Entrepreneurship Theory and Practice, 29*(6), 717–735.

Marshall, A. (1920). *Principles of economics.* Macmillan.

Mathews, J. A. (2002). *Dragon multinational: A new model for global growth.* Oxford University Press.

Mazzucato, M. (2013). *The entrepreneurial state: Debunking public vs. private sector myths.* Anthem Press.

McSweeney, B. (2015). Hall, Hofstede, Huntington, Trompenaars, GLOBE: Common foundations, common flaws. In Y. Sánchez & C. F. Brühwiler (Eds.), *Transculturalism and business in the BRIC states: A handbook* (pp. 13–58). Gower.

Meo, S. A., Bukhari, I. A., Akkram, J., Meo, A. S., & Klonoff, D. C. (2021). COVID-19 vaccines: Comparison of biological, pharmacological characteristics and adverse effects of Pfizer/BioNTech and Moderna vaccines. *European Review for Medical and Pharmacological Sciences, 25*, 1663–1669.

Milgrom, P., & Roberts, J. (1992). *Economics, organization and management.* Prentice-Hall.

Ministry of Economy, Trade and Industry (METI). (2024). *Report compiled on results of FY2023 survey on university-developed venture businesses (preliminary report).* 15th May, 2024. Tokyo: Ministry of Economy, Trade and Industry. https://www.meti.go.jp/english/press/2024/0515_001.html.

Ministry of Education (2024). Statistics & documents: Schools, students, teachers and classes & departments by metropolitan area and province. 2024. Retrieved June 4, 2024 from. http://english.moe.go.kr/sub/info.do?m=050101&page=050101&num=1&s=english

Ministry of SMEs and Startups (2024). KRW 3.712 billion central and local government support for entrepreneurship in 2024. Ministry of SMEs and Startups. Press release, January 3, 2024 (in Korean).

Moon, H., & Yim, S. (2018). Creative economy and innovation policy in South Korea. *AI & SOCIETY, 33*(3), 343–357.

Moore, J. F. (1993). Predators and prey: A new ecology of competition. *Harvard Business Review, 71*(3), 75–86.

Morita, A. (1986). *Made in Japan: Akio Morita and Sony.* Penguin.

Nakamura, T. (2017). *The Japanese economy: Its development and structure* (3rd ed.). University of Tokyo Press.

Nambisan, S., Zahra, S. A., & Luo, Y. (2019). Global platforms and ecosystems: Implications for international business theories. *Journal of International Business Studies, 50*(9), 1464–1486.

Nathan, J. (1999). *Sony: The private life.* Houghton Mifflin Harcourt.

Naughton, B. (2007). *The Chinese economy: Transitions and growth.* MIT Press.

Nurse, P. (2020). *What is life?: Understand biology in five steps*, W.W. Norton & Company.

O'Connor, A., Stam, E., Sussan, F., & Audretsch, D. B. (2018). Entrepreneurial ecosystems: The foundations of place-based renewal. In A. O'Connor, E. Stam, F. Sussan, & D. B. Audretsch (Eds.), *Entrepreneurial ecosystems. Place-based transformations and transitions* (Vol. 38, pp. 1–21). Springer International Publishing.

Okamoto, S. (2000). *Net companies! Let those idiots work on it.* Bungei Shunshu (in Japanese).

Okimoto, D. I. (1989). *Between MITI and the market: Japanese industrial policy for high technology.* Stanford University Press.

Organisation for Economic Co-operation and Development (OECD) (2023). *OECD reviews of innovation policy: Korea 2023.* OECD Publishing. https://doi.org/10.1787/bdcf9685-en

Organisation for Economic Co-operation and Development (OECD) (2024). *OECD Data Explorer: Venture capital investments.*

Organisation for Economic Co-operation and Development (OECD) (2025a). Recommendation of the council on digital technologies and the environment. OECD/LEGAL/0380 https://legalinstruments.oecd.org/en/instruments/OECD-LEGAL-0380.

Organisation for Economic Co-operation and Development (OECD) (2025b). What are the key trends in international student mobility (= Education Indicators in Focus #88, March 2025). https://www.oecd.org/en/publications/what-are-the-key-trends-in-international-student-mobility_2a423a76-en.html

Osaka Business Development Agency (2024). *Discover Osaka: Upcoming startups hotspot in Asia.* https://www.innovation-osaka.jp/2024

Ou, T. (2000). *The home of entrepreneurship: China's high-tech business incubator*. Beijing University of Posts and Telecommunications Press. (in Chinese).

Oviatt, B. M., & McDougall, P. P. (1994). Toward a theory of international new ventures. *Journal of International Business Studies, 25*(1), 45–64.

Ozawa, T. (2005). *Institutions, industrial upgrading, and economic performance in Japan.* Edward Elgar Publishing.

Park, J., & Song, H. (2022). Korean startup ecosystem globalization through venture capital networks. *Asian Journal of Technology Innovation, 30*(1), 45–68.

Parker, G. G., Van Alstyne, M. W., & Choudary, S. P. (2016). *Platform revolution: How networked markets are transforming the economy and how to make them work for you.* W. W. Norton & Company.

Peng, M. W., Li, Y., Xie, E., & Su, Z. (2018). CEO duality, institutional transitions, and firm performance in China. *Journal of Management & Organization, 24*(1), 1–20.

Plehn-Dujowich, J. M. (2010). A theory of serial entrepreneurship. *Small Business Economics, 35*(4), 377–398.

Porter, M. E. (1998). Clusters and the new economics of competition. *Harvard Business Review, 76*(6), 77–90.

Porter, M. E., & Kramer, M. R. (2011). Creating shared value. *Harvard Business Review, 89*(1/2), 62–77.

Porter, M. E., Takeuchi, H., & Sakakibara, M. (2000). *Can Japan compete?* Macmillan.

Ramirez, C. (2024). Revisiting developmental state theory in East Asia and Latin America. *Journal of International Studies, 9*(1), 25–41.

Root, H. L. (2023). The ecology of innovation: The evolution of a research paradigm. In Z. J. Acs, E. Lafuente, & L. Szerb (Eds.), *The entrepreneurial ecosystem: A global perspective* (pp. 363–376). Palgrave Macmillan.

Rowley, C., & Bae, J. (2002). Globalization and transformation of human resource management in South Korea. *The International Journal of Human Resource Management, 13*(3), 522–549.

Sako, M., & Kotosaka, M. (2011). Institutional change and organizational diversity in Japan. In C. Lane & G. W. Routledge (Eds.), *Capitalist diversity and diversity within capitalism* (pp. 69–96). Routledge.

Sako, M., & Kotosaka, M. (2012). Continuity and change in the Japanese economy: Evidence of institutional interactions in financial and labor markets. In A. Walter & X. Zhang (Eds.), *East Asian capitalism: Diversity, continuity, and change* (pp. 132–158). Oxford University Press.

Sauvant, K. P., Mendoza, K., & Ince, I. (Eds.) (2010). *The rise of transnational corporations from emerging markets: Threat or opportunity?* Edward Elgar Publishing.

Saxenian, A. (1994). *Regional advantage: Culture and competition in Silicon Valley and route 128.* Harvard University Press.

Sbampato, K., Proença, A. & Silva, E.R. (2025). What do we know about corporate-startup engagement? A systematic review of the main modes of collaboration between corporations and startups. *Innovation & Management Review, 22*(2), 82–99.

Schumpeter, J. A. (1934). *Theorie der wirtschaftlichen Entwicklung.* Dunker & Humblot, Leipzig, 1912. English translation: *The theory of economic development.* Harvard University Press.

Schumpeter, J. A. (1939). *Business cycles. A theoretical, historical and statistical analysis of the capitalist process.* McGraw-Hill.

Schumpeter, J. A. (1942). *Capitalism, socialism and democracy.* Harper & Brothers, 1942, e-book edition by Routledge (2003).

Schwartz, S. H. (1999). A theory of cultural values and some implications for work. *Applied Psychology: An International Review, 48*(1), 23–47.

Seoul Open Data Square (2024). Statistics. Retrieved March 15, 2024 from. https://data.seoul.go.kr/dataList/91/S/2/datasetView.do

Shapiro, C., & Varian, H. R. (1998). *Information rules: A strategic guide to the network economy.* Harvard Business School Press.

Sheff, D. (1993). *Game over: How Nintendo conquered the world*. Game Press.

Smith, P. B. (2006). When elephants fight, the grass gets trampled: The GLOBE and Hofstede projects. *Journal of International Business Studies, 37*(6), 915–921.

Song, J. (2018). Samsung next and the evolution of Korean corporate venture capital. *Korean Journal of Policy Studies, 33*(2), 89–115.

Song, K., & Lee, Y. (2019). The K-startup grand challenge and internationalisation of Korean entrepreneurship. *Entrepreneurship & Regional Development, 31*(5–6), 456–478.

Song, Z. (2024). 10 apocalypses of Shenzhen innovation, *China Entrepreneur Magazine*, June 5, 2024. Retrieved 16 June, 2024 from. https://baijiahao.baidu.com/s?id=180107570249945 5392&wfr=spider&for=pc. (in Chinese).

Sorenson, O., Dahl, M. S., Canales, R., & Burton, M. D. (2021). Do startup employees earn more in the long run? *Organization Science, 32*(3), 587–604.

Spennemann, D. H. R. (2025). The origins and veracity of references cited by generative artificial intelligence applications: Implications for the quality of responses. *Publications, 13*(1), 1–23.

Spigel, B. (2017). The relational organization of entrepreneurial ecosystems. *Entrepreneurship Theory and Practice, 41*(1), 49–72.

Spigel, B., & Harrison, R. T. (2018). Towards a process theory of entrepreneurial ecosystems. *Strategic Entrepreneurship Journal, 12*(1), 151–168.

Stam, E. (2015). Entrepreneurial ecosystems and regional policy: A sympathetic critique. *European Planning Studies, 23*(9), 1759–1769.

Stam, E., & Spigel, B. (2016). Entrepreneurial ecosystems. *USE Discussion Paper Series* 16(13). UU USE Tjalling C. Koopmans Research Institute.

Stam, E., & van de Ven, A. (2021). Entrepreneurial ecosystem elements. *Small Business Economics, 56*(2), 809–832.

Startup Genome (2024). Global startup ecosystem report GSER 2024. Retrieved June 11, 2024 from. https://startupgenome.com/report/gser2024

Startup Genome (2025). Global startup ecosystem report 2025. https://startupgenome.com/report/gser2025/introduction (and earlier editions).

Statista (2022). Number of unicorn companies in China in selected quarters from 4th quarter 2017 to 4th quarter 2022. Retrieved 16, June, 2024 from. https://www.statista.com/statistics/1011894/china-number-of-unicorn-companies-quarterly/

Statista, Number of unicorn companies in South Korea from. 2017 to 2023. Retrieved June 4, 2024 from. https://www.statista.com/statistics/1313099/south-korea-number-of-unicorns/

Stephens, B., Butler, J. S., Garg, R., & Gibson, D. V. (2019). Austin, Boston, Silicon Valley, and New York: Case studies in the location choices of entrepreneurs in maintaining the technopolis. *Technological Forecasting and Social Change, 146*, 267–280.

STEPI (Science and Technology Policy Institute) (2024). *Korean startup ecosystem dashboard* (3rd quarter, 2023). Retrieved September 24, 2025 from. https://stepi.re.kr/site/stepiko/report/View.do;jsessionid=15070BF698B80D296A32F3B23A0F7D30?cbIdx=1292&reIdx=78&cateCont=A0204

Sutmeier, R. P. (2003). China's innovation challenge and the remaking of the Chinese academy of sciences. *Innovations, 8*(3), 78–97.

Suzhou Industrial Park Administration Commission (2020). Suzhou Industrial Park Annual Report 2020–2022 (in Chinese).

Takahashi, F. (2023). Tokyo-overconcentration. https://journal.startup-db.com/articles/tokyo-overconcentration2024

Talke, K., Salomo, S., & Kock, A. (2011). Top management team diversity and strategic innovation orientation: The relationship and consequences for innovativeness and performance. *Journal of Product Innovation Management, 28*(6), 819–832.

Teece, D. J. (2007). Explicating dynamic capabilities: The nature and microfoundations of (sustainable) enterprise performance. *Strategic Management Journal, 28*(13), 1319–1350.

The Nikkei (2014). 2. The flag-bearers of IPO–Different from Horiemon. 6th January 2014 morning edition. Nihon Keizai Shimbun (in Japanese).

The Nikkei (2018). *The new form of alliance between startups and large companies*. Morning Edition.

Theodoraki, C., Dana, L., & Caputo, A. (2022). Building sustainable entrepreneurial ecosystems: A holistic approach. *Journal of Business Research, 140*, 346–360.

Theodoraki, C., Messeghem, K., & Rice, M. P. (2018). A social capital approach to the development of sustainable entrepreneurial ecosystems: An explorative study. *Small Business Economics, 51*(1), 153–170.

Thompson, T. A., Purdy, J. M., & Ventresca, M. J. (2018). How entrepreneurial ecosystems take form: Evidence from social impact initiatives in Seattle. *Strategic Entrepreneurship Journal, 12*, 96–116.

Tipton, E. (2016). *Modern Japan: A social and political history* (3rd ed.). Routledge.

Tokyo Metropolitan Government (2024). *Tokyo's urban strength*. https://www.investtokyo.metro.tokyo.lg.jp/2024

Torch High Technology Industry Development Center, Ministry of Science and Technology (2022). *China business incubation development report 2022*. Science and Technology Literature Publishing House.

Trompenaars, F., & Hampden-Turner, C. (2020). *Riding the waves of culture: Understanding diversity in global business* (4th ed.). McGraw-Hill.

Tschang, F. T., & Almirall, E. (2021). Artificial intelligence learning through trial and error: China, entrepreneurship, and global competition. *Industrial and Corporate Change, 30*(4), 1034–1052.

Ueno, H., Murakoso, T., & Hirai, T. (2006). Supplier system and innovation policy in Japan. In C. Storz (Ed.), *Small firms and innovation policy in Japan* (pp. 137–150). Routledge.

Vedula, S., & Kim, P. H. (2019). Gimme shelter or fade away: The impact of regional entrepreneurial ecosystem quality on venture survival. *Industrial and Corporate Change, 28*(4), 827–854.

Velt, H., Torkkeli, L., & Laine, I. (2020). Entrepreneurial ecosystem research: Bibliometric mapping of the domain. *Journal of Business Ecosystems, 1*(2), 1–31.

von Hippel, E. (2005). *Democratizing innovation*. MIT Press.

Voss, H., Buckley, P. J., & Cross, A. R. (2008). The impact of home country institutional effects on the internationalisation strategy of Chinese firms. *Multinational Business Review, 16*(3), 25–50.

Wade, R. (1990). *Governing the market: Economic theory and the role of government in east Asian industrialization*. Princeton University Press.

Waldenberger, F. (2016). In-house careers: A core institution of the Japanese firm in need of reform. *Journal of Strategic Management Studies, 8*(1), 23–32.

Wang, H. (2002). The political economy of China's outward foreign direct investment. *Asian Survey, 42*(3), 502–518.

Wang, J., & Liu, X. (2018). Returnee entrepreneurs and innovation in China: Evidence from Zhongguancun. *Research Policy, 47*(4), 722–734.

Welter F. (2012). All you need is trust? A critical review of the trust and entrepreneurship literature. *International Small Business Journal, 30*(3), 193–212.

Westney, D. E. (1987). *Imitation and innovation: The transfer of western organizational patterns to Meiji Japan*. Harvard University Press.

Wheeler, T. (2024). *From Gutenberg to Google and on to AI: The history of our future*. Brookings Institution Press.

Whittaker, D. H. (1997a). *Small firms in the Japanese economy*. Cambridge University Press.

Whittaker, D.H. (1997b). Where will the new jobs come from?. *Japan Forum (Oxford, England), 9*(2), 165–171.

Whittaker, D. H., Byosiere, P., Momose, S., Morishita, T., Quince, T., & Higuchi, J. (2009). *Comparative entrepreneurship: The UK, Japan, and the shadow of Silicon Valley.* Oxford University Press.

Whittaker, D. H., Zhu, T., Sturgeon, T., Tsai, M. H., & Okita, T. (2020). *Compressed development in China: Comparing local and global impacts.* MIT Press.

Wurth, B., Stam, E., & Spigel, B. (2022). Toward an entrepreneurial ecosystem research program. *Entrepreneurship Theory and Practice, 46*(3), 729–777.

Xiaobo, W. (2017). *Tencent: The extraordinary story of a Chinese internet enterprise (1998–2016).* Zhengjiang University Press. (in Chinese).

Xie, Z., Wang, X., Xie, L., & Duan, K. (2021). Entrepreneurial ecosystem and the quality and quantity of regional entrepreneurship: A configurational approach. *Journal of Business Research, 128*, 499–509.

Yang, K. M. (2007). *Entrepreneurship in China.* Routledge.

Yang, X.-H., Peng, Y.-Q., & Lee, Y. T. (2008). The Confucian and Mencian philosophy of benevolent leadership. In C.-C. Chen & Y.-T. Lee (Eds.), *Leadership and management in China: Philosophies, theories, and practices* (pp. 31–50). Cambridge University Press.

Yoo, S., & Kim, N. (2015). The creative economy policy framework and innovation ecosystem development in South Korea. *Science and Public Policy, 42*(6), 852–864.

Yoon, S. (2021). K-pop and hardware symbiosis: Cultural content driving technology innovation in South Korea. *Popular Music and Society, 44*(3), 298–317.

Young, M. (2004). Revolution at Sony. *Fortune, 150*(6), 64–70.

Yusuf, S., Nabeshima, K., & Perkins, D. H. (2014). *Under new ownership: Privatizing China's state-owned enterprises.* Stanford University Press.

Zhang, L. H. (2017). *HUAWEI research and development* (3rd ed.). China Machine Press.

Zhang, Y. (2025). Research and judgment on the development status and trends of China's technology business incubator industry in 2025: Diversification of investment entities and diversification of development types are the directions. Beijing: Zhiyan Consulting. Retrieved 7th February, 2025 from. https://www.chyxx.com/industry/1211625.html (in Chinese).

Zhang Y., & Qian W. (2019) *Huaqiangbei: The epitome of industry development and transformation in Shenzhen.* Retrieved 19, June, 2024 from. https://repository.ceibs.edu/zh/publications/huaqiangbei-the-epitome-of-industry-development-and-transformation

Zhongguancun (2020). Take on the challenge! Zhongguancun has launched the Chain Strengthening Project" and released the first batch of technology demand lists to the whole society. 2020(12), 40–41. (in Chinese).

Zucchella, A., & Magnani, G. (2016). Theoretical foundations of international entrepreneurship: International business studies. In *International entrepreneurship: Theoretical foundations and practices* (2nd ed., pp. 37–76). Palgrave Macmillan.

Zweig, D. (2006). Competing for talent: Chinas strategies to reverse the brain drain. *International Labour Review, 145*(1–2), 65–89.

Zweig D., Changgui C., & Rosen S. (2004). Globalization and transnational human capital: Overseas and returnee scholars to China. *The China Quarterly, 179*, 735–57.

Index

Y. Cheng et al., *Unleashing Innovation the East Asian Way*,
https://doi.org/10.1007/978-981-95-6513-9

D

K

L

M

MIX
Papier aus verantwortungsvollen Quellen
Paper from responsible sources
FSC® C105338

If you have any concerns about our products,
you can contact us on
ProductSafety@springernature.com

In case Publisher is established outside the EU,
the EU authorized representative is:
Springer Nature Customer Service Center GmbH
Europaplatz 3, 69115 Heidelberg, Germany

Printed by Libri Plureos GmbH
in Hamburg, Germany